**Fighting the rising
Stalinist bureaucracy**

Bookmarks
London, Chicago and Melbourne

Trotsky:
Fighting the rising
Stalinist bureaucracy
1923-1927

Tony Cliff

Trotsky: Fighting the rising Stalinist bureaucracy 1923-1927 /
Tony Cliff
First published July 1991.
Bookmarks, 265 Seven Sisters Road, London N4 2DE, England
Bookmarks, PO Box 16085, Chicago, Il. 60616, USA
Bookmarks, GPO Box 1473N, Melbourne 3001, Australia
Copyright © Bookmarks and Tony Cliff

ISBN 0 906224 65 9

Printed by Cox and Wyman Limited, Reading, England
Cover design by Roger Huddle

Bookmarks is linked to an international grouping of socialist organisations:
Australia: *International Socialists*, GPO Box 1473N, Melbourne 3001
Belgium: *Socialisme International,* rue Lovinfosse 60, 4030 Grivegnée
Britain: *Socialist Workers Party,* PO Box 82, London E3 3LH
Canada: *International Socialists,* PO Box 339, Station E, Toronto,
            Ontario M6H 4E3
Denmark: *Internationale Socialister,* Ryesgade 8, 3, 8000 Århus C
France: *Socialisme International*, BP 189, 75926 Paris Cedex 19
Germany:*Sozialistische Arbeitergruppe,* Wolfsgangstrasse 81, 6000
            Frankfurt 1
Greece: *Organosi Sosialistiki Epanastasi*, PO Box 8161, 10010 Omonia,
            Athens.
Holland: *Groep Internationale Socialisten*, PO Box 9720, 3506 GR Utrecht
Ireland: *Socialist Workers Movement,* PO Box 1648, Dublin 8
Norway: *Internasjonale Sosialister,* Postboks 5370, Majorstua, 0304 Oslo 3
Poland: *Solidarnosc Socjalistyczna,* PO Box 12, 01-900 Warszawa 118
United States: *International Socialist Organization,* PO Box 16085,
            Chicago, IL 60616

Contents

Acknowledgements

Several people have helped in the writing of this book. Many thanks are due to Chris Bambery, Alex Callinicos, Donny Gluckstein, Chris Harman and John Rees for their advice and suggestions. I owe a debt to Ahmed Shawki for help in locating material. Chanie Rosenberg deserves special thanks for writing Chapter Five, 'Trotsky on culture', for participating in the editing of the manuscript and for typing it. Thanks are due to John Molyneux for expert critical comments and most valuable stylistic suggestions, and Duncan Blackie for editing.

Tony Cliff, 25 April 1991

Tony Cliff is a member of the Socialist Workers Party in Britain and has written many previous books. The first two volumes of this biography, **Trotsky: Towards October 1879-1917** and **Trotsky: The sword of the Revolution 1917-1923**, were published by Bookmarks in July 1989 and July 1990 respectively. His other books include the classic **State Capitalism in Russia** (1974) and two previous political biographies: **Rosa Luxemburg** (1959) and **Lenin** (in three volumes 1975-79).

Preface

THE PRESENT volume deals with the interval separating two decisive periods of Trotsky's life.

In the years of the revolution and civil war Trotsky was leading millions. Together with Lenin he was *the* leader of the Bolshevik Party, the government and the Communist International. At the end of 1927 Trotsky was expelled from the Party, exiled first to Alma Ata in the far east of the USSR, then banished from the country. From 1927 until his assassination in 1940 he was isolated and led only tiny groups of supporters throughout the world. The intervening years 1923-7 saw him moving into opposition against the rising Stalinist bureaucracy.

During the revolution and civil war Trotsky was in his element. His voice articulated the aspirations of the fighting revolutionary workers. From 1927 onward hardly any workers listened to him.

The fate of his main antagonist—Stalin—was the exact opposite.

During 1917 Stalin played a minor role. Dull as a writer and poor as an orator, without the spark of imagination needed to fire the masses (whom anyway he did not trust), Stalin lived a shadowy existence at the time of the great revolutionary events. As Sukhanov, the perspicacious chronicler of the revolution writes: 'Stalin... doing his modest activity in the Executive Committee [of the Soviets] produced—and not only on me—the impression of a grey blur, looming up now and then dimly and not leaving any trace. There is really nothing more to be said about him.'[1]

John Reed, throughout his brilliant **Ten Days that Shook the World**, did not record one speech or action of Stalin.

Many writers have explained Stalin's victory over Trotsky in terms of his superior organisational abilities. This is a ridiculous proposition given Trotsky's known role in organising the October revolution and in building and leading the many-millioned Red Army.

It was changes in the objective conditions, namely the retreat of the revolution, that explains the rise of Stalin. Marxism recognises the important role of the individual in history. But it sees him or her as a link in a chain of objective conditions. In **The Eighteenth Brumaire of Louis Bonaparte** Marx showed how 'the class struggle created the circumstances and the conditions that permitted a mediocre and vulgar personage to play the role of a hero.' Elsewhere Marx wrote: 'Every social epoch needs its great men, and when it does not find them it invents them...'[2] Stalin perfectly fitted the period of reaction. Had he not existed, someone similar to him would have emerged to play this role.

A period of reaction will always find a figurehead because reaction relies on all the old habits of thought, the deference and lack of confidence of the workers, their submission to routine, the natural conservatism of the state bureaucracy and so on. But, as Trotsky noted of Lenin's role in October, a period of advance and especially of revolution cannot simply wait on history to invent its great men.

The bureaucratic degeneration of the Russian revolution and the rise of Stalin were rooted in Russia's economic and social backwardness and its isolation. The civil war brought about the disintegration of the Russian proletariat as a class. Its regroupment was further weakened by the defeat of the international proletariat—in the German revolutions of 1918 and 1923, the British general strike in 1926 and the Chinese revolution of 1925-27. The workers were exhausted and depressed. This was the background for the rise of the bureaucracy with Stalin at its head.

It was the workers' weariness that led them to accept Stalin's doctrine of 'socialism in one country', which fitted the popular craving for stability, safety and peace. The same weariness made them indifferent to Trotsky's theory of permanent revolution, which looked like a call for risky experiments.

The support of a minority of the working class was not enough for Trotsky to win; he needed the active and conscious following of the majority. For Stalin minority support was enough to win so long as the majority were passive and acquiescent.

Trotsky, who during the revolution and civil war motivated millions, now found himself out in the cold, unable to rouse the workers. While many thousands of workers were ready to give their lives at his call during the civil war, now they were hardly ready even to listen to him.

'Men make their own history, though not in circumstances of their own choosing'. For Trotsky the objective circumstances were not only the material, economic and social conditions at the time, but also the the level of consciousness of the working class. This gravely circumscribed his ability to resist Stalinist reaction.

The workers' retreat was accompanied by the danger of capitalist restoration. In the years of the New Economic Policy, NEP, with the increasing strength of the kulaks and NEPmen, this threat was by no means a figment of Trotsky's imagination and, combined with the weariness of the mass of workers, restricted Trotsky's ability to act. His fear of splitting the party and encouraging counter-revolution was very real.[3]

In the years 1923-27 Trotsky's genius co-existed with a serious weakness. His Achilles heel can be summed up by one word: conciliationism.

His genius is illuminated in the wealth of his writings. He reacted to every event at home and abroad. His strategic and tactical mastery is exceptional. From this period we inherit a body of writings that is unsurpassed as a rich source of applied Marxism. He also made the first powerful attempt at an historical materialist analysis of Stalinism. (All subsequent serious analyses, even if deviating from his, have taken his as a point of departure.) At the same time his sure touch, sharpness and iron will co-existed with zigzags and compromises with his partners in the United Opposition, Zinoviev and Kamenev. Conciliating these two meant indirectly conciliating the leading group in the party and state.

This intransigence and strict adherence to revolutionary principles alongside volatility and a fudging of the issues is reminiscent of the earlier period between 1903 and his joining the Bolsheviks in July 1917, when Trotsky combined brilliant revolutionary politics and theory—above all the theory of permanent revolution—with conciliation with the Mensheviks.

Trotsky's attempt to conciliate the Mensheviks derived from his belief that they would move towards revolutionary politics when the objective situation became revolutionary. As he wrote many years later: 'My conciliationism flowed from a sort of social-revolutionary fatalism.'[4]

Now—in the years 1923-27—his conciliationism was the product of a belief that the Russian Communist Party and the Communist International were not lost to the revolution, that they were still the instruments of the future proletarian revolution.

On 12 July 1928, in a declaration to the Sixth Congress of the Comintern, Trotsky wrote:

> We base all our calculations on the fact that there exist within the AUCP, the Comintern, and the USSR enormous internal revolutionary forces, which now are suppressed by the false leadership and the onerous regime, but which, with experience, criticism, and the advance of the class struggle throughout the world, are perfectly capable of correcting the line of the leadership and assuring a correct proletarian course.[5]

Until 1933, when the Comintern's disastrous policy led to the catastrophe of the Nazi victory, Trotsky continued to argue that the Soviet regime, the party and the Comintern, were still susceptible to reform. He wrote:

> The recognition of the present Soviet state as a workers' state not only signifies that the bourgeoisie can conquer power only by means of an armed uprising but also that the proletariat of the USSR has not forfeited the possibility of subordinating the bureaucracy to it, of reviving the party again, and of regenerating the regime of the dictatorship—without a new revolution, with the methods and on the road of *reform*.[6]

Only in 1933 did Trotsky change his mind and abandon the belief that the Russian party and Comintern could be reformed. On 1 October 1933 he wrote:

> After the experiences of the last few years, it would be

childish to suppose that the Stalinist bureaucracy can be removed by means of a party or soviet congress. In reality, the last congress of the Bolshevik Party took place at the beginning of 1923, the Twelfth Party Congress. All subsequent congresses were bureaucratic parades. Today, even such congresses have been discarded. No normal 'constitutional' ways remain to remove the ruling clique. The bureaucracy can be compelled to yield power into the hands of the proletarian vanguard only by *force*.[7]

If the Stalinist bureaucracy could not be removed except by force in 1933, it was no more removable a number of years earlier. When in 1927 Stalin said to the Opposition: 'These cadres can be removed only by civil war',[8] he was stating a fact.

However, if it is easy to see with hindsight that the Stalinist bureaucracy could 'be removed only by civil war', this was not so obvious at the time. The situation was extremely complicated and confusing, and Trotsky had no historical experience on which to fall back. The degeneration of a workers' state was a new and unprecedented phenomenon—the only previous workers' state, the Paris Commune, existed only in one city and was crushed after 74 days.

As a consequence, Trotsky seriously underestimated the threat posed by both Stalin as an individual and the Stalinist bureaucratic faction. He was acutely aware of the danger of capitalist restoration posed by the rise of the NEPmen and the kulaks, but failed to conceive of the possibility of capitalist restoration, on the basis of state property, by the bureaucracy itself: he lacked a conception of state capitalism.*

This, in turn, meant that Trotsky failed to understand the character of the bureaucracy as a ruling class bent on pursuing its own independent interests in fundamental opposition to both the working class and the peasantry. Thus when Trotsky wrote about the bureaucracy his terms of reference were the bureaucracy of the trade unions and Social Democratic parties. This labour

---

*For a full analysis of state capitalism as it developed in Russia after 1928, see T. Cliff, **State Capitalism in Russia**. This matter will also be discussed further in the next volume of this biography.

movement bureaucracy balances between the two main classes in capitalist society—the employers and the workers. Its behaviour is characterised above all by vacillation; moving, now to the left under pressure from the working class, now to the right under pressure from the capitalists. Similarly Trotsky characterised the Stalinist bureaucracy as 'centrist', vacillating between the pressure of the Russian working class and the aspirant bourgeoisie of NEPmen and kulaks. His expectation and fear was that Stalin would capitulate to the right. His hope, and all his efforts, were directed to this end; that pressure from the working class and the left could prevent this capitulation. In the event neither Trotsky's fear nor his hope materialised. Instead the Stalinist bureaucracy moved against both the left (Trotsky, the 'United Opposition' etc.) and the right (Bukharin, Rykov, Tomsky, etc.) in quick succession. In the space of a couple of years the bureaucracy completely crushed the workers, the kulaks and the peasantry as a whole, and emerged as the sole political power in Russia with Stalin at its head as personal dictator.

The Stalin faction was able to do this because it was fundamentally different from the trade union bureaucracy under capitalism. In a society where the state is already the principle repository of the means of production and the bourgeoisie has been decisively smashed and expropriated (as the Russian bourgeoisie was in 1917-18) a state bureaucracy which frees itself completely from control by the working class (as the Stalinist bureaucracy did in the years 1923-28) becomes the *de facto* owner and controller of those means of production and the employer of the workers. In short it becomes a new exploiting class.

The political intransigence of revolutionary Marxists in the struggle against capitalism is founded on the knowledge that the class antagonism between the bourgeoisie and the proletariat is fundamentally irreconcilable. Trotsky, in general, was not lacking in this intransigence. But at this point in time, when the Stalinist bureaucracy was just taking shape, his failure to see it as a class enemy disorientated him strategically and blunted his political edge. In particular it hindered him from seeing that the Russian Communist Party, and hence the Comintern, were dead for the purposes of revolution.

It led him also to continue to argue for the one-party state. Thus in 1923 he wrote: 'We are the only party in the country, and in the period of the dictatorship *it could not be otherwise.*'[My emphasis][9]

Trotsky restated this idea in September 1927 in the Platform of the Opposition: 'We will fight with all our power against the idea of two parties, because the dictatorship of the proletariat demands as its very core a single proletarian party.'[10]

A corollary of the acceptance of the one-party state was an acceptance of the banning of factions in the party.

This attitude plus the belief that the party, even if under the control of the Stalinist bureaucracy, could still be peacefully reformed, created impossible barriers to any consistent policy of opposition: it forced Trotsky to retreat again and again whenever the leadership decided to ban his activities, which happened throughout the years 1923-27.

He was caught on the horns of a dilemma—how to fight the bureaucracy while avoiding factionalism. In these circumstances he repeatedly succumbed to the pressure of the Zinovievites and of the Stalin-Bukharin group.

Trotsky's conciliationism in 1923-27 was demonstrated repeatedly in his going into battle against the ruling group in party and state, then stopping, retreating, keeping quiet, then starting again. This volume will describe these zigzags.

At the Twelfth Party Congress (April 1923) Trotsky failed to carry out Lenin's wish to attack Stalin's policy on the national question, his role in Rabkrin, (the Workers' and Peasants' Inspectorate) his 'rude and disloyal' behaviour as General Secretary. He made no effort to prevent Stalin's reappointment as General Secretary at the Central Committee meeting following the Congress. He hid his differences with the Troika—Stalin, Zinoviev and Kamenev—from the party.

Against the protests of Krupskaya the Central Committee voted by an overwhelming majority for the suppression of Lenin's Testament; Trotsky did not come to Krupskaya's aid but kept silent. He praised the indiscriminate mass recruitment to the party involved in the 'Lenin Levy', which he was later to describe as 'a death blow to the party of Lenin'.[11]

After the flare-up of the inner-party struggle around **The New Course** and **The Lessons of October**—from the end of 1924 until the middle of 1926—Trotsky avoided controversy, going to the extraordinary length of denouncing Max Eastman's account of Lenin's Testament in his book **Since Lenin Died**.

It took a great effort in mid-1926 to reassemble the 1923 Opposition and its strength was very much smaller than originally. The Zinoviev group which joined with Trotsky's in the United Opposition was a broken reed. The ease with which Stalin overwhelmed the Zinovievite Leningraders demonstrated the actual feebleness of Zinoviev's influence; outside Leningrad no support was forthcoming for Zinoviev at all.

The adherence of Zinoviev and Kamenev to the United Opposition was double edged. It was an added force, but it was also a source of weakness. Zinoviev and Kamenev had always been compromisers. Even when they joined Trotsky in the United Opposition they continued to look over their shoulders to avoid sharpening their differences with Stalin and Bukharin. They insisted that they had not 'capitulated' to Trotskyism.

To keep his alliance with Zinoviev and Kamenev intact Trotsky went so far as to publicly reject the theory of permanent revolution, to accept the slogan of the 'democratic dictatorship of the proletariat and peasantry', and to give up his demands for the break-up of the Anglo-Russian Committee and the withdrawal of the Chinese Communist Party from the Kuomintang.

With regard to the last point: Zinoviev, as President of the Comintern until May 1926, was in fact largely responsible for the policy of the Comintern in China. Although since 1923 Trotsky opposed the Chinese Communist Party's adherence to the Kuomintang, he made no public statement to this effect. Not only was the general public and the rank and file of the party unaware of his position, but even the Central Committee and the Executive Committee of the Comintern were not informed. The first time he argued openly in writing for the Chinese Communist Party to leave the Kuomintang was on 10 May 1927, ie *after* Chiang Kai-shek, leader of the Kuomintang, had carried out a massacre of workers and Communists in Shanghai. The fact that the United Opposition dealt with the Chinese events so late and with so many reservations, weakened its impact considerably.

It was the pressure of Zinoviev and Kamenev that got Trotsky to agree to ask the Politburo for a truce on 4 October 1926, to admit to being guilty of factionalism, to accept the break-up of the faction and to denounce co-thinkers of the Opposition in other Comintern sections. The surrender was to no avail. Stalin only pressed home his attack.

In the winter of 1926-7 the Opposition was torn by internal discord. Trotsky did his best to prevent the partnership from falling apart, repeatedly making concessions to the Zinovievists and thus indirectly to Stalin, for which the United Opposition paid with indecision and vacillation.

A number of writers sympathetic to Trotsky have either overlooked the concessions he made or saw them as accidental aberrations. Harold Isaacs, in his outstanding book, **The Tragedy of the Chinese Revolution**, does not mention any of Trotsky's statements in support of the Chinese Communist Party being inside the Kuomintang, or his denial of the theory of permanent revolution. Isaac Deutscher points to single concessions Trotsky made, but as he takes them as separate, isolated items, he does not see a pattern in them nor look for any *general explanation*. Trotsky, however, was too great a man to need any falsehood, cover-up or downplaying of mistakes he may have committed.

The zigzags in the fight against Stalin could not but weaken Trotsky's own supporters. Cadres cannot be kept if they have to abstain from action. Trotsky could keep up his own spirit however tough the going; throughout the years 1923-27 he did not stop criticising official policies and the regime, even if he had to use hints and allusions obscure to many. Rank and file oppositionists cannot survive politically without a fight in the here and now.

The problem of how to keep the cadres together without involving them in a struggle going beyond the party ranks, which meant appealing to the workers en masse; how to carry on the inner-party struggle without breaking the ban on factionalism, posed a real dilemma for Trotsky.

He was clear about the need for a revolutionary not to reflect the reactionary mood of tired workers. He knew he must be ready to remain isolated and to pursue the struggle, whether in the end he lived to see his cause triumph, like Lenin, or served his cause through martyrdom like Liebknecht.

But his conciliationism undermined this understanding. Adolf Ioffe recognised this weakness when he wrote Trotsky a letter a few hours before he committed suicide, criticising him because he 'lacked Lenin's *unbending will*, his unwillingness to yield, his readiness to remain alone on the path that he thought right in anticipation of a future majority, of a future recognition by everyone of the rightness of his path... you have *abandoned your rightness* for the sake of an overvalued agreement or compromise.'[12]

Nevertheless, even when all the compromises and vacillations have been taken into account, the fact remains that Trotsky fought the Stalinist reaction and continued to fight it when so many others capitulated or fell by the wayside. Moreover he did so when the physical and psychological pressures to give in were immense. This was an enormous historical achievement.

By 1927 Trotsky grasped the enormity of Stalin's crimes and called him 'the gravedigger of the revolution' when the bloc with Zinoviev and Kamenev fell apart. From then on he became completely uncompromising.

Even if the gap between the grand aims and the puny means were as wide as ever, even if the consciousness of the masses lagged far behind the objective needs for the liberation of the proletariat, Trotsky never again failed to draw the political conclusion. His clarity of vision in the years following 1927 do not lessen the tragedy of his life, where ends and means were as far apart as ever; but then it was grand tragedy. This will be dealt with in the next volume of this biography.

Chapter one

The New Course Controversy

THE TROIKA of Stalin, Zinoviev and Kamenev was formed with the prime aim of fighting Trotsky, who had missed the opportunity at the Twelfth Party Congress (April 1923) to carry out Lenin's wish to fight Stalin's bureaucratism.

Lenin and Trotsky had agreed to unite against Stalin and against the bureaucracy, concentrating their attack on two main issues: Georgia, whose national rights Stalin was denying, and Rabkrin, the Workers' and Peasants' Inspectorate which was supposed to check bureaucratic tendencies, but was being manipulated by Stalin to reinforce them. Trotsky reported a remark by Lenin's secretary, Fotieva: 'Vladimir Ilyich is preparing a bomb for Stalin at the congress'. The word 'bomb' was Lenin's, not hers. 'Vladimir Ilyich asks you to take the Georgian case in your hands. He will then feel confident.'[1]

However, at the Congress Trotsky avoided any controversy. Stalin's resolution on the nationalities question was adopted unanimously. Lenin's denunciation of Rabkrin and of the party Central Control Commission was easily defied by Stalin, and the Congress passed a resolution 'On the Central Committee Report'—again delivered by Stalin—which was complacent about the organisational state of the party, Rabkrin, and the Central Control Commission. Trotsky remained silent, not even hinting at disagreement with Stalin. In fact he even reprimanded people who spoke up in his defence against the Troika.[2]

He actually strengthened the Troika by declaring his 'unshaken' solidarity with the Politburo and Central Committee and calling on the rank and file 'at this critical juncture' to exercise the strictest self-restraint and utmost vigilance. Speaking on a motion appealing for unity and discipline in Lenin's absence, he stated: 'I shall not be the last in our midst to defend [this motion], to put it into effect, and to fight ruthlessly against all who may try to infringe it... If in the present mood the party warns you emphatically about things which seem dangerous to it, the party is right, even if it exaggerates, because what might not be dangerous in other circumstances must appear doubly and trebly suspect at present.'[3]

Unrest among industrial workers

NEP brought with it a relative worsening of the economic and social position of the proletariat.

First of all they suffered unemployment. *Khozrashchet* (the principle of 'cost accountancy' or 'economic accountancy') which Lenin described as a 'transition to commercial principles' and an inescapable element of NEP, immediately resulted in sackings.

The process of dismissing superfluous staffs proceeded at a cumulative rate. The number of railway workers was reduced from 1,240,000 in the summer of 1921 to 720,000 in the summer of 1922; the number of workers and employees per 1000 spindles in a leading textile factory was reduced from 30 in 1920-21 to 14 a year later.[4]

The number of unemployed workers rose very steeply:

January 1922	175,000
January 1923	625,000
January 1924	1,240,000[5]

Another whip lashing the industrial workers was the red managers. NEP massively increased their powers. More and more managers came from traditional managerial families and were progressively integrated into the party hierarchy. They acted in an increasingly high-handed fashion towards the workers. In August 1922 the trade union paper **Trud** launched a strong attack on the new 'united front' of managers, which it accused of aiming at 'a diminution in the role of the unions', especially in the engagement and dismissal of workers, and of wanting ' "free trade" in matters of hiring and firing'. The article ended with the rhetorical question, 'Have our managers so far entered into the role of the "masters" that they prefer to unorganise workers and disciplined members of trade unions'?[6]

What about the workers' wages? The real earnings of workers in 1922-3 were still only half those of 1913. In 1923 the managers went on the offensive to cut workers' wages. A leading article in **Trud** on 11 March 1923, under the title 'Wages are, However, Falling', reported a general decline since December, referred to 'the campaign of the industrialists for a gradual reduction in wages', and complained of the passivity of 'some' trade unions. In a resolution of 14 April 1923, on the eve of the Twelfth Party Congress, the central council of trade unions admitted that wages were 'falling in real terms', and called for action to arrest the decline.[7]

One ploy which was resorted to by management was postponing the payment of wages so as to benefit from the depreciation of the rouble. As early as the winter of 1921-2, complaints had been heard of wage payments falling into arrears, especially in regions remote from the centre. With the currency frequently depreciating by as much as 30 per cent in a month, the loss to the workers was heavy. For the last three months of 1922 the workers in the Don were reported to have lost 34, 23 and 32 per cent respectively of their real wages through currency depreciation. In January 1923 the trade union newspaper alleged that 'cases of failure to pay in full for two or three months are more and more becoming a daily occurrence'.[8] E. H. Carr estimates that real wages were cut in 1923 by as much as 40 per cent.[9] He sums up the situation of the workers in general in the following words:

> While the standard of living of the industrial worker in 1923 was higher than in the harsh years of War Communism, there had been no time since the revolution when discrimination was so overtly practised against him, or when he had so many legitimate causes of bitterness against a regime which claimed to govern in his name.[10]

At the same time the NEPmen and kulaks were thriving, enormously widening the gap between them and the workers. Wealth and luxury became legitimate, eliminating any need to conceal opulence. *Parvenus,* with little culture and fat wallets, showed no restraint at all. In the atmosphere of feverish speculation, when it was not clear how long they would be free to make money, the NEPmen and kulaks were guided by one slogan: 'Seize the time'. They hurried to make money and to squander it. Wealth and luxury ostentatiously paraded everywhere.

Soviet novels of the time frequently dealt with the disillusion of revolutionaries with NEP as privileges proliferated. Evidence of the social corruption of the time can be found in the reminiscences of an American journalist whose grasp of politics was poor but whose reportage of life in Russia in the early 1920s was unsurpassed. He described the life of the privileged in Moscow during NEP as *la dolce vita*. Champagne and vintage wines from France and Germany, fifty-year old cognac, fragrant coffee, sugar, meat and chicken, fresh caviare were available. People gorged themselves with the sweets of pleasure, trying to tear from life the joys they had been denied for so long.

> It was a strange sight, this *Praga* in the centre of the world's first Proletarian Republic. Most of the men looked like the low-class jackals and hangers-on of any boom... but there were also former nobles in faded broadcloth and Red Army soldiers in uniform... eager for Moscow's fleshpots and the flutter at the tables. A smattering, too, of foreigners, fixers, agents and the commercial vanguard of a dozen big firms attracted by Lenin's new policy of concessions, hurrying to see if it was true that Russia might again become a honey-pot for alien wasps. And women of all sorts... mostly daughters of joy, whom NEP had hatched in flocks, noisy...as sparrows. Later, in increasing numbers, the wives and families of NEPmen, the new profiteers, with jewels on their stumpy fingers.[11]

Prostitution, the complete degradation of women in the interests of men with money, not only appeared in brothels and bars, but was admitted as a commonplace in contemporary Soviet literature. For instance, Isaac Babel wrote a number of stories dealing with prostitutes, such as **My First Fee** (1922), **The Chinaman** (1923) and **Through the Fanlight** (1923).

Society was sinking into a cesspool.

The fall in real wages led to increasing conflicts in state

industry during the winter of 1922-3, and these spread on a significant scale a few months later. In July and August 1923 Moscow and Petrograd were shaken by industrial unrest. Workers felt they were made to carry far too great a burden. Their wages were a pittance, and often they did not even receive them. The trade unions, reluctant to disturb the peace, refused to press workers' claims. Unofficial strikes broke out in many places, and were accompanied by violent explosions of anger. The trade union leaders, as well as the party leaders, were caught by surprise.

In November 1923 rumours of a general strike circulated throughout Moscow, and the movement seemed on the point of turning into a political revolt. Not since the Kronstadt rising of 1921 had there been so much tension in the working class and so much alarm in ruling circles.[12]

The strike wave gave a new lease of life to the Mensheviks, who were blamed for instigating a large number of them. Mensheviks and SRs were accused of causing a major strike at the textile plant Trekhgornaia Manufaktura in 1923. One report linked unspecified 'opponents' to a strike of railroad workers in Sokolnicheskii *raion*(district). And at a May non-party conference in Krasno-Presnenskii *raion* speakers with a 'Menshevik odour' criticised wage iniquities and the poor conditions affecting workers.

On 4 June 1923 the Central Committee issued a circular 'On Measures of Struggle with Mensheviks', in which they were accused of consciously supporting counter-revolution. Simultaneously the GPU carried out a massive round-up of Mensheviks, and as many as 1,000 were arrested in Moscow alone.[13]

A more serious challenge to the Soviet government came from two dissident groups within the party: 'Workers' Truth' and the Workers' Group.

The Workers' Truth group was composed largely of students, disciples of Bogdanov, the old Bolshevik who broke from Lenin in 1907. It consisted of no more than 20 members. Outside of discussion circle activity the organisational work of the group consisted of publishing two numbers of its journal.

Far more influential was the Workers' Group, composed mainly of workers led by Miasnikov, Kuznetsov and Moiseev, who had been expelled from the party in 1922. The group was formed in the spring of 1923. Immediately after the Twelfth Party Congress it issued a manifesto denouncing the 'New Exploitation of the Proletariat', and urging workers to fight for Soviet democracy. In May Miasnikov was arrested, but his group continued its propaganda. When the strikes of July-August broke out they wondered whether they should go to the factories with a call for a general strike. They were still arguing about this when in September the GPU arrested a number of them, about twenty people in all. The group apparently had about 200 members in Moscow.[14] It was estimated that about 200 Communists were expelled from the party at the end of 1923 for their involvement with Workers' Truth and the Workers' Group.[15]

However small the Workers' Group, its influence was quite widespread. Rank and file party members listened sympathetically to their appeals. In the presence of mass discontent when the trade unions did not voice the workers' grievances, and the party paid little attention to them, a small group could have a far wider impact than its size warranted. After all, the instigators of the Kronstadt revolt had not been more numerous or influential.

The party leaders sought to stamp out the sparks. Dzerzhinsky, head of the GPU, was charged with the business of suppression. When he found that many party members were sympathetic to the two groups, he turned to the Politburo and asked it to declare that it was the duty of all party members to denounce to the GPU party members who cooperated with these subversive groups: in effect this meant their acting as policemen. Dzerzhinsky's stance could be explained only by the bureaucratic nature of the party and the massive alienation of the rank and file from it.

Trotsky's reaction to workers' unrest

Dzerzhinsky's statement led Trotsky to speak out. He did not condone the existence of Workers' Truth or the Workers' Group and did not condemn their persecution. He did not protest at the arrest of their supporters. He did not support their incitement of workers to industrial action. He did not see how the government could meet workers' demand when industrial output was still negligible. He saw the way to assuage workers' demands by a long-term industrialisation policy. Nor was Trotsky ready to support the demand for workers' democracy in the extreme form in which the Workers' Group and Workers' Truth raised it. But he found that Dzerzhinsky had gone too far, and on 8 October 1923 he wrote a letter to the Central Committee and the Central Control Commission complaining about Dzerzhinsky's stance.

Trotsky admitted that he himself had at first been sceptical about the arguments of the illegal groupings about democracy. Referring to the Twelfth Party Congress he stated:

> Many of the speeches of that time made in defence of *workers' democracy* seemed to me exaggerated, and to a considerable extent demagogic, in view of the *incompatibility of a fully developed workers' democracy with the regime of a dictatorship...*

However, things went from bad to worse:

> the regime which had essentially taken shape even before the Twelfth Congress and which, after it, was fully consolidated and given finished form, is much further removed from workers' democracy than was the regime during the fiercest period of war communism. The *bureaucratisation of the party apparatus* has reached unheard-of proportions through the application of the methods of secretarial selection. Even in the cruellest hours of the civil war we argued in the party organisations and in the press as well... while now there is not a trace of such an open exchange of opinions on questions that are really troubling the party...

As a result,

> *Within the basic stratum of the party there is an extraordinary degree of discontent...* This discontent is not being alleviated through an open exchange of opinions in party meetings or by mass influence on the party organisations (in the election of party committees, secretaries, etc.), but rather it continues to build up in secret, and, in time, leads to *internal abscesses.* [16]

Trotsky also renewed his attack on the Troika's economic policy. The ferment within the party was intensified, he argued, by the industrial unrest. And this was brought about by a lack of economic planning. He found out that the concession the Troika had made to him at the Twelfth Congress was spurious. The congress had adopted his resolution on industrial policy, but this had remained a dead letter.

Trotsky ends his letter with a statement that although hitherto he had declined to make his views public, now he would have to spread his ideas—not to the public as a whole, not even to all party members, but to those 'mature' enough.

> I have deliberately avoided submitting the struggle within the Central Committee to the judgment of even a very narrow circle of comrades: specifically to those who, given any party course that was at all reasonable, would surely occupy a prominent place in the Central Committee and the Central Control Commission. I am compelled to state that my efforts over the past year and a half have yielded no result.
>
> I think it is not only my right but my duty to make the true state of affairs known to every party member whom I consider to be sufficiently prepared, mature, self-restrained, and consequently capable of helping the party find a way out of this impasse without factional convulsions and upheavals.[17]

Trotsky's letter was kept secret from the party rank and file.

On 15 October another letter was written, this time by a group of forty-six prominent party members. They issued a statement directed against the official leadership, criticising it in terms practically identical to those Trotsky had used. They declared that the country was threatened with economic ruin, because the 'majority of the Politburo' did not see the need for planning in industry. The Forty Six also protested against the rule of the hierarchy of secretaries and the stifling of discussion:

> Members of the party who are dissatisfied with this or that decision of the central committee or even of a provincial committee, who have this or that doubt on their minds, who privately note this or that error, irregularity or disorder, are afraid to speak about it at party meetings, and are even afraid to talk about it in conversation... Nowadays it is not the party, not its broad masses, who promote and choose members of the provincial committees and of the central committee of the RKP. On the contrary the secretarial hierarchy of the party to an ever greater extent recruits the membership of

conferences and congresses which are becoming to an ever greater extent the executive assemblies of this hierarchy...

The position which has been created is explained by the fact that the regime is the dictatorship of a fraction within the party...

The fractional regime must be abolished, and this must be done in the first instance by those who have created it; it must be replaced by a regime of comradely unity and internal party democracy.[18]

The Forty Six went beyond Trotsky's letter of 8 October. They demanded that the ban on inner party groupings should be abolished. They finally asked the Central Committee to call an emergency conference to review the situation.

Among the Forty Six were Trotsky's closest political friends: Evgenii Preobrazhensky, the brilliant economist; Iuri Piatakov, the most able of the industrial administrators; Lev Sosnovsky, **Pravda**'s gifted contributor; Ivan Smirnov, the victor over Kolchak; Antonov-Ovseenko, hero of the October insurrection, now chief political commissar of the Red Army; N. Muralov, commander of the Moscow garrison. Radek expressed solidarity with the Forty Six in a separate declaration. They formed the core of the so-called 1923 Opposition, and represented the Trotskyist element in it.

Besides them there were former adherents of the Workers' Opposition and Decemists (Democratic Centralists), like V. Smirnov, T. Sapronov, V. Kossior, A. Bubnov and V. Ossinsky, whose views differed from that of the Trotskyists. Many of the signatories appended strong reservations on special points to the common statement or expressed plain dissent. The Forty Six did not represent a solid faction, but a loose coalition of groups and individuals united only in a general protest against the lack of democracy in the party.

The fact that Trotsky did not sign the document of the Forty Six was symptomatic of his irresolute attitude and his unwillingness, so long as Lenin's recovery was still possible, to openly challenge the Troika. He thus also avoided the accusation of 'factionalism'.

The declaration of the Forty Six lost some of its sting by its admission that 'the present leaders would not in any conditions fail to be appointed by the party to the outstanding posts in the workers' dictatorship'—thus accepting that there was no alternative leadership available. The declaration was also weakened by the fact that the only concrete recommendation was the summoning of a conference of the Central Committee and active party workers to consider what should be done.

On 24 October Trotsky wrote another letter to the Central Committee criticising the inner-party regime, and referring especially to Lenin's sharp criticism of Rabkrin.

The Troika reacts

The Central Committee and the Central Control Commission, together with delegates of ten leading party organisations, met for a plenary session from 25 to 27 October. The Troika used this session for counter measures against Trotsky and the Forty Six. Trotsky was kept away from the meeting by the onset of the mysterious illness which affected him most of that winter. In the latter part of October he had caught a severe chill while on a duck-hunting expedition, an occasion narrated at some length in his autobiography and accompanied by philosophical reflections on the role of accidents in history.[19] The sequel was what he later called 'a dogged, mysterious infection, the nature of which still remains a mystery to my physicians'.[20] The intermittent fever lasted well into January when Trotsky left Moscow for the Caucasus.

At the party conference, which followed this plenum on 16-18 January 1924, Preobrazhensky was the main Opposition spokesman, and he continued to carry this major task throughout the ensuing few months of what has become known as the New Course controversy. He offered to the Central Committee and the Plenum of the Central Control Commission a resolution embodying the principle of workers' democracy, including free expression and discussion, real control and election by the membership and an end to the dominance of the secretariat.[21]

Preobrazhensky's proposal was rejected out of hand by the Troika. Instead they counter-attacked, accusing Trotsky and the Forty Six of factionalism.

The Troika justified the Central Committee's decision not to distribute the Declaration of the Forty Six on the grounds that it would violate the banning of factional activities pronounced by the Tenth Party Congress. At the same time, the Central Committee declared its acceptance of the principle of workers' democracy.[22]

The resolution embodying both these elements was carried overwhelmingly at the party conference: by 102 votes to 2, with 10 abstentions. This was the springboard for the campaign against the Opposition which was shortly to begin.

News about the Opposition spread, and interest in their ideas was widespread. So the Troika was not satisfied merely with the refusal to publish Trotsky's letters of 8 and 15 October and the Declaration of the Forty Six, plus the threat of persecution of the Opposition. They decided to take the wind out of the Opposition's sails by adopting its principles as their own. In an article in **Pravda** on 7 November, entitled 'New Tasks of the Party', Zinoviev proclaimed:

> It is necessary that inner-party democracy, of which we have spoken so much, begins to a greater degree to take on flesh and blood... Our chief trouble consists in the fact that almost all very important questions are pre-decided from above downwards.

A note appended to the article announced that the columns of the paper would be thrown open for a discussion in which party members, trade unionists and non-party people were invited to participate. The response was massive and the debate carried on in the columns of **Pravda** throughout the greater part of November. The Politburo appointed a sub-committee consisting of Stalin, Kamenev and Trotsky, to elaborate a resolution on party democracy. The Troika was ready to make verbal concessions to Trotsky, doing everything necessary to maintain the appearance of unity. They asked Trotsky to put his signature next to theirs under the text they had plagiarised from him. Since Trotsky himself had never come out openly in opposition to the Troika, this manoeuvre worked.

In terms of a description of the problems facing the country, the government and the party, the resolution proposed by Stalin, Kamenev and Trotsky was quite close to Trotsky's thinking. It was vague when prescribing for inner-party democracy, but did demand 'a serious change of the party course in the direction of a real and systematic application of the principles of workers' democracy'. But on the crucial issue of the control exercised by the centre over the appointment of local party secretaries it remained equivocal. It recalled that the party statute required the confirmation of such appointments by the highest party authority, but thought that the time had come, 'in the light of the experience which we now have, especially of the lower organisations', to 'verify the usefulness' of this and other similar restrictions on the autonomy of local branches. 'In any case', concluded this section of the resolution, 'the right to confirm secretaries cannot be allowed to be converted into their virtual nomination.'

Whilst paying lip service to inner-party democracy, the resolution was adamant in condemning any factional grouping in the party.

> Workers democracy means the liberty of frank discussion of the most important questions of party life by all members, and the election of all leading party functionaries and commissions by those bodies immediately under them. It does not, however, imply the freedom to form factional groupings, which are extremely dangerous for the ruling party, since they always threaten to split or fragment the government and the state apparatus as a whole.[23]

While accepting inner-party democracy, the resolution condemned the Workers' Group and Workers' Truth, and by implication the Declaration of the Forty Six. It cited and endorsed the earlier resolution of the Central Committee of 25 October approving the 'course set by the Politburo for inner-party democracy', sharply condemned the Forty Six and criticised Trotsky's letter of 8 October. This resolution was unanimously approved at the joint session of the Politburo and the Presidium of the Central Control Commission on 5 December. The members of the Troika could heave a sigh of relief: the danger of an open split in which Trotsky would lead the rank and file of the party against them had once again been averted.

Trotsky attached the utmost importance to this resolution which he treated as a vindication of his own point of view. In the heat of subsequent controversy he described it as initiating a fourth period in party history, the previous periods being 'pre-October', 'October', and 'post-October'.[24] In May 1924, at the Thirteenth Party Congress, he declared that the resolution gave him the essentials of what he wanted.[25]

In words, the 5 December resolution was perhaps a victory for Trotsky. But the actual power to nominate the secretaries of provincial and local party committees, who played a crucial role in deciding the election of delegates to party congresses and conferences, remained with the Central Committee. The implementation of workers' democracy was to remain in the hands of the bureaucracy, and since the bureaucracy was determined to hold on to its power, the resolution settled nothing.

Trotsky's elaboration on the New Course

Although he put his name to the Politburo resolution, Trotsky still feared it could become a paper concession by the Troika, who tried to use it to escape censure, as with the concessions they made to the resolutions at the Twelfth Party Congress. To prevent its becoming a dead letter, he decided to appeal to the rank and file of the party to put pressure on the leadership.

In a series of brief articles written for **Pravda** in December 1923 Trotsky elaborated on the theme of bureaucratic abuse and the lack of rank and file initiative and independence. In January 1924 this collection, together with another couple of hitherto unpublished articles, was issued as a pamphlet with the title **The New Course**. These articles contained in a nutshell most of the ideas which became the hallmark of 'Trotskyism'.

On 8 December Trotsky wrote an Open Letter to party members in which he made clear his position. He described the New Course as a historical turning point, but warned the rank and file that some of the leaders were already having second thoughts and trying to sabotage the New Course.

> The excessive centralisation of the apparatus at the expense of initiative engendered a feeling of *uneasiness,* an uneasiness which, at the extremities of the party, assumed an exceedingly morbid form and was translated, among other ways, in the appearance of illegal groupings directed by elements undeniably hostile to communism. At the same time, the whole of the party disapproved more and more of apparatus methods of solving questions. The idea, or at the very least the feeling, that bureaucratism threatened to get

the party into a blind alley, had become quite general. Voices were raised to point out the danger. The resolution on the 'new course' is the first official expression of the change that has taken place in the party. It will be realised to the degree that the party, that is, its 400,000 members, want to realise it and succeed in doing so.[26]

Trotsky then went on to appeal to the youth to assert themselves and not regard the Old Guard's authority as,

> absolute. *It is only by constant active collaboration with the new generation, within the framework of democracy, that the Old Guard will preserve itself as a revolutionary factor.* Of course, it may ossify and become unwittingly the most consummate expression of bureaucratism.

This was the first time Trotsky charged the Old Guard with the danger of 'bureaucratic degeneration'. He supported the charge by referring to the historical experience of the Second International.

> History offers us more than one case of degeneration of the 'Old Guard'. Let us take the most recent and striking example: that of the leaders of the parties of the Second International. We know that Wilhelm Liebknecht, Bebel, Singer, Viktor Adler, Kautsky, Bernstein, Lafargue, Guesde, and many others were the direct pupils of Marx and Engels. Yet we know that in the atmosphere of parliamentarism and under the influence of the automatic development of the party and the trade union apparatus, all these leaders turned, in whole or in part, to opportunism.
>
> ...we, the 'elders', ought to say to ourselves plainly that our generation, which naturally enjoys the leading role in the party, is not *absolutely* guaranteed against the gradual and imperceptible weakening of the revolutionary and proletarian spirit in its ranks if the party were to tolerate the further growth and stabilisation of bureaucratic methods...[27]

Thus, after a delay of some nine months, Trotsky at last threw the bombshell Lenin expected him to throw at the Twelfth Party Congress. Now that Trotsky put himself publicly at the head of the Opposition, open political combat between the factions became inevitable.

Trotsky for the first time developed a critique of the Soviet bureaucracy in a sustained way. He rejected the view that the bureaucracy was an accidental phenomenon, insisting that it was rooted in the objective difficulties confronting the revolution.

It is unworthy of a Marxist to consider that bureaucratism is only the aggregate of the bad habits of office holders. Bureaucratism is a social phenomenon in that it is a definite system of administration of people and things. Its profound causes lie in the heterogeneity of society, the difference between the daily and the fundamental interests of various groups of the population. Bureaucratism is complicated by the lack of culture among the broad masses. With us, the essential source of bureaucratism resides in the necessity of creating and sustaining a state apparatus that unites the interests of the proletariat and those of the peasantry in perfect economic harmony from which we are still far removed. The necessity of maintaining a permanent army is likewise another important source of bureaucratism.[28]

To fight the stranglehold of the party and state bureaucracy one had to confront the economic and social conditions of Russia's backwardness and its isolation in the world capitalist system.

The weaker state industry was relative to the kulak and NEPman, the further was the rise of the bureaucracy in state and party.

...the growing discord between the state and peasant economy, the growth of the kulaks in the countryside, their alliance with private commercial-industrial capital: these would be—given the low cultural level of the toiling masses of the countryside and in part of the towns—the causes of the eventual counter-revolutionary dangers.[29]

The struggle against the rising bureaucracy was therefore a struggle on many fronts: a struggle for inner-party democracy plus a struggle to overcome the economic backwardness of the country and the low cultural level of the masses plus a struggle to spread the revolution internationally.

The struggle against the bureaucratism of the state apparatus is an exceptionally important but prolonged task, one that runs more or less parallel to our other fundamental tasks—economic reconstruction and the elevation of the cultural level of the masses.[30]

In the last analysis, the question will be resolved by two great factors of international importance: the course of the revolution in Europe and the rapidity of our economic development.[31]

In arguing for the need to accelerate industrial development in Russia, **The New Course** elaborated the guiding lines that epitomised Trotskyism from then on.

To maintain and strengthen the *smychka* (alliance) between the proletariat and the peasantry, a correct relationship between industry and agriculture was needed. The economic planning of the former must aid and shape the latter.

State industry must adapt,

itself to the peasant market and to the individual peasant as a taxpayer. But this adaptation has as its fundamental aim to raise, consolidate, and develop state *industry as the keystone of the dictatorship of the proletariat and the basis of socialism.*[32]

Trotsky then goes on to explain that the industrial plan must not be made at the cost of the peasantry, but must aid it.

The workers' state must come to the aid of the peasants (to the degree that its means will permit!) by the institution of agricultural credits and agronomical assistance, so as to lighten the task of exporting their products (grain, meat, butter, etc.) on the world market... it is mainly through industry that we can act directly, if not indirectly, upon agriculture. It must furnish the countryside with agricultural implements and machines at accessible prices. It must give it artificial fertilizers and cheap domestic articles. In order to organise and develop agricultural credits, the state needs a substantial revolving fund. In order to procure it, its industry must yield profits, which is impossible unless its constituent parts are rationally harmonised among themselves. That is the genuinely practical way of working toward the realisation of the *smychka* between the working class and the peasantry.[33]

How different this plan is from the Stalinist command economy from 1928 onwards, and from the caricature Stalinists and others made of Trotsky's arguments for economic planning.

Weaknesses in Trotsky's New Course

The New Course, brilliant though it was, had some significant defects.

First of all it was weak on specific proposals and demands. It is true that Trotsky confronted the Old Guard with the charge, still strongly qualified, of bureaucratic degeneration. But he did not call for its overthrow.

He also heavily qualified his warning about the dangers of the degeneration of the leaders of the party and the state:

> ...*in actuality*, is the danger of such degeneration really great? The fact that the Party has understood or felt this danger and has reacted to it energetically—which was the specific cause of the resolution of the Central Committee—bears witness to its profound vitality and by that very fact reveals the potent sources of antidote which it has at its disposal against bureaucratic poison. There lies the principal guarantee of its preservation as a revolutionary party.[34]

Further, the bureaucracy was not beyond redemption. The apparatus was not,

> composed exclusively of bureaucratised elements, or even less of confirmed and incorrigible bureaucrats. Not at all! The present critical period, whose meaning they will assimilate, will teach a good deal to the majority of the apparatus workers and will get them to abandon most of their errors. The ideological and organic regrouping that will come out of the present crisis will, in the long run, have healthful consequences for the rank and file of the communists as well as for the apparatus.[35]

The most damaging weakness of **The New Course** was that

it represented the Opposition as the best defenders of party unity and the strongest opponents of inner party factions. Trotsky proposed not the allowing of factions, but a style of leadership that would render them unnecessary.

> We are the only party in the country, and in the period of the dictatorship it could not be otherwise... the Communist Party is obliged to monopolise the direction of political life.[36]

> It is incontestable that factions are a scourge in the present situation, and that groupings, even if temporary, may be transformed into factions... The party does not want factions and will not tolerate them.[37]

On the one hand the party was strangled by the bureaucracy, but on the other Trotsky was unwilling to call on social forces outside the party to combat the bureaucracy.

The very fact of the Opposition arguing against factionalism could not but play into the hands of the Troika who repeatedly accused the Opposition of being a faction.

The New Course calls on the party to guard its monopoly of power as the sole guarantee of the survival of the revolution. At the same time, within the party, it objects to the monopoly of power of the Old Guard. It was quite easy for the Troika and its adherents to argue that the latter was the necessary consequence of the former. If one had to substitute the 400,000 party members for the millions of the proletariat, should not the latter be substituted by the 'more reliable' veterans—especially as 97 per cent of the party members in 1923 joined the party only after the October revolution?

There was a further weakness in **The New Course**. It urged the party to preserve its proletarian outlook, while at the same time it pointed out that only a sixth of the party members currently held manual occupations (by 1923 nearly two-thirds of all party members held administrative posts of one kind or another.)[38] With such a composition, inner-party democracy must mean insignificant proletarian, and predominant bureaucratic influence. The author's **Trotsky** (Vol. 2) states:

> Lenin and Trotsky could not turn to the proletarian element in the party because this was now only a small minority. They

could not rely on inner-party democracy—even if by a miracle it had been restored—because the party was made up largely of factory managers, government officials, army officers and party officials. Such a democracy would have reflected the aspirations of the bureaucracy. Lenin and Trotsky could not call on the 'Old Guard', first because these were a tiny minority of the party—a mere 2 per cent—and secondly because many of them made up an important part of the bureaucratic caste.[39]

Finally, the stand for democracy in **The New Course** seemed of questionable validity when compared with Trotsky's (and Lenin's) position on the same issue at the Tenth Party Congress in March 1921. This is what Trotsky said then:

> The Workers' Opposition has come out with dangerous slogans, fetishising the principles of democracy. They seem to have placed the workers' voting rights above the Party, as though the Party did not have the right to defend its dictatorship even if that dictatorship were to collide for a time with the transitory mood of the workers' democracy... What is indispensible is the consciousness, so to speak, of the revolutionary historical birthright of the Party, which is obliged to maintain its dictatorship in spite of the temporary vacillations in the elemental stirrings of the masses, in spite of the temporary vacillations even in the workers' milieu. That consciousness is for us the indispensible cement. It is not on the formal principle of workers' democracy that the dictatorship is based at any given moment, though the workers' democracy is, of course, the only method by whose help the masses are increasingly drawn into political life.[40]

Furthermore, **The New Course** was couched in terms so general and elusive that very few grasped its meaning.

When sketching the defects of **The New Course** one glaring omission must not be overlooked: the wages issue, which was so convulsing the workers at the time, is missing. The failure of the Opposition to make common cause with the industrial workers and reflect their discontent, was one of its greatest weaknesses. As a matter of fact, the industrial unrest paralysed Trotsky. He was afraid of splitting the party and encouraging counter-revolution.[41] So we find Trotsky in the grip of a contradiction. The industrial unrest of 1923 was a spur to **The New Course**, but also a shackle on it.

Significantly Shliapnikov, the former leader of the Workers' Opposition, could argue that 'there is no reason to separate Comrade Trotsky in question of policy from the other members of the Central Committee', and that Trotsky, who merely wanted greater concentration of industry and more power in the hands of Gosplan, was indifferent to 'the fate of the working class'.[42]

Above all, the New Course controversy demonstrated the tragic problem of a proletariat which made up a small minority of the population, weakened by civil war, in the midst of a mass of peasantry in a backward rural country surrounded by world capitalism. In 1904 Trotsky wrote: 'It is only too clear that a proletariat capable of exercising its dictatorship over society will not tolerate any dictatorship over itself'.[43] But what if the proletariat, due to conditions, ceases to be 'capable of exercising its dictatorship over society'?

Chapter two

The campaign against Trotsky

The Troika's reaction to Trotsky's New Course

THE REACTION of the Troika to Trotsky's **New Course** was vehement. It began on 15 December 1923 with an article by Stalin in **Pravda** and a speech by Zinoviev in Petrograd (published in **Pravda** on 20 and 21 December). They both charged Trotsky with violating the unanimity of the Politburo by making a public statement in opposition to the unanimously adopted resolution of 5 December. From mid-December until the Thirteenth Party Conference—of 16-18 January 1924—violent controversy raged in the key party organisations.

The Troika fired a barrage of criticism against Trotsky. He was accused of disloyalty to the Politburo, of criminally inciting the young against the Old Bolsheviks, who were the bearers of the revolutionary tradition. It was said to be wicked to turn the rank and file of the party against the apparatus: every good Bolshevik was aware of the crucial role of the apparatus in preserving and leading the party. Trotsky was equivocal over the ban on factions: he did not dare to challenge the decision of the Tenth Congress on the ban, but sought surreptitiously to undermine this decision. The Troika said he pretended to speak for the workers, but played up to the students and the intelligentsia. His hatred of the party apparatus, his slander of the Old Guard, his disrespect for the Bolshevik traditions and his underestimation of the peasantry; all these clearly demonstrated that he was alien to the party, to Lenin—that he was still a semi-Menshevik.

Stalin's article of 15 December lashed out. It stated:

I must dispel a possible misunderstanding. As is evident from his letter, Trotsky includes himself among the Bolshevik old guard, thereby showing readiness to take upon himself the charges that may be held at the old guard if it does indeed take the path of degeneration. It must be admitted that this readiness for self-sacrifice is undoubtedly a noble trait. But I must protect Trotsky from Trotsky, because, for obvious reasons, he cannot, and should not, bear responsibility for the possible degeneration of the principal cadres of the Bolshevik old guard. Sacrifice is a good thing, of course, but do the old Bolsheviks need it? I think that they do not.

...it is impossible to understand how opportunists and Mensheviks like Bernstein, Adler, Kautsky, Guesde, and the others, can be put on a par with the Bolshevik old guard, which has always fought, and I hope will continue to fight, with honour, against opportunism, the Mensheviks and the Second International...[1]

Stalin's article opened the floodgates for the anti-Trotsky campaign. It aimed to divert the party's attention from the New Course discussion. The editor of **Pravda**, Nikolai Bukharin, made it clear that he supported the Troika by publishing an article entitled 'Down with Factionalism', which was described as 'The Reply of the Central Organ' to the critics, and continued through five issues of **Pravda** (28, 29, 30 December 1923, and 1 and 4 January 1924). Bukharin wrote:

After October our Party lived through three strong crises: Brest, the trade unions and the present.
In all these stages of party development Comrade Trotsky was *wrong*...
The Brest Peace. In what consisted the mistakes of Comrade Trotsky (and the Left Communists)? It consisted in being carried away by the revolutionary phrase, blueprint, *pretty plan*. The opponents of the Brest Peace had such blueprints, but they did not see the damned *reality* that Lenin's genius so brilliantly saw. Above all, they did not see the *peasantry*, which did not want and were not able to wage the war.

At present, Bukharin said, Trotsky was exhibiting the same one-sidedness and utopian predilection in his call for planning, for the 'dictatorship of industry'.

Bukharin was ferocious in bashing Trotsky. He conveniently forgot that during the Brest-Litovsk controversy he, Bukharin, was associated with the Left Communists, and took a position far more extreme in opposition to Lenin than Trotsky. He was a great enthusiast for the militarisation of labour (in 1919-20), and supported to the hilt Trotsky's position in the trade union controversy (December 1920-March 1921).

Scores of articles attacking the Opposition appeared in **Pravda** and only a tiny number of articles defending it. Certain **Pravda** staff members who favoured reporting both sides of the argument impartially were summarily sacked by order of the Central Control Commission.[2] Trotsky's pamphlet **The New Course** was hardly to be found in any bookshop, as Max Eastman recorded.[3] Everything possible was done to propagate the argument that Trotsky had always been hostile to Bolshevism, and that Trotskyism had always been a trend hostile to Lenin.

Isaac Deutscher is correct when he writes:

> In the long history of inner-party oppositions none had been weighed down by so heavy a load of accusations and none had been ground down so remorselessly by the party machine as was the 1923 Opposition. By comparison the Workers' Opposition had been treated fairly, almost generously; and the oppositions which had been active before 1921 had as a rule enjoyed unrestricted freedom of expression and organisation.[4]

The party crisis of November-December 1923 was the last occasion on which **Pravda** provided a forum for conflicting groups within the party. Thereafter it spoke exclusively as the official voice of the Politburo.

The Thirteenth Party Conference

The preparations for the Thirteenth Party Conference, held in January 1924, were in the hands of the secretaries. The election of delegates was indirect and proceeded through several stages. At every stage the secretaries did their best to eliminate supporters of the Opposition. Bukharin himself admitted the steamroller tactics the supporters of the Troika used in party meetings.

Our cell secretaries...are usually appointed by the district committees... As a rule, the voting takes place according to a definite pattern. They come into the meeting and ask: 'Is anyone opposed?' and since everyone is more or less afraid to voice dissent, the individual who was appointed becomes secretary of the cell bureau. If we were to conduct a survey and ask how often the voting takes place with the chairman asking 'All in favour?' and 'All opposed?' we would easily discover that in the majority of cases the elections in our party organisations have in fact been transformed into a mockery of elections, because the voting takes place not only without preliminary discussion, but, again, according to the formula, 'Is anyone opposed?' And since it is considered bad form for anyone to speak against the 'leadership', the matter is automatically settled. This is what elections are like in the local cells...[5]

The fear of reprisal was especially great because of the threat of the sack, with unemployment so massive and the power of the 'Red Manager' so great.

How much support did the opposition get? It is difficult to guage this since the press tended to give prominence only to results favourable to the official line. But there is a record of a large party meeting in Moscow in which Kamenev, appearing as spokesman for the Central Committee, could muster only 6 votes against an overwhelming majority of Opposition supporters.[6] Rykov admitted that both Piatakov and other Opposition speakers 'frequently' obtained majorities at party meetings.[7] Again Iaroslavsky admitted that a majority of party cells in higher education institutions had voted for the Opposition.[8]

The lower down the party structure the stronger was the Opposition. At the district conferences of Moscow Province the Opposition had far greater weight than in the regional conference. In different districts of Moscow the Opposition fared not badly. At the Baumanskii party district conference, it received 178 votes against 234 for the Central Committee. At the Zamostvoretskii party district conference it won 205 votes against the Central Committee vote of 327. In the Ragozhko-Simonovskii party district conference it won 90 votes while the Central Committee gained 121. In Khamobvnicheskii party district conference it won

157 votes against the Central Committee's 178 (with four abstentions). At the Krasno-Presnenskii party district conference it received 188 votes against 605 for the Central Committee (with three abstentions).

In the *uezd* (local) party organisations, the Opposition won a majority in four, the Central Committee in nine, while one remained neutral.[9]

Of all the delegates to the conferences of the district party organisations in the Moscow Province which were held on 23 December, 36 per cent were supporters of the Opposition. At the higher level conference, that of the Province of Moscow, held on 10-11 January 1924, only 18 per cent of the delegates belonged to the Opposition. Sapronov, pointing out these facts at the Thirteenth Party Conference, asks:

> If the Opposition lost 18 per cent between the district conferences and the provincial conferences, then I pose the question: of how many votes was the Opposition deprived in the workers' cells by the pressure of the apparatus, when these votes went to the district conferences?

And Sapronov drew the conclusion that the Opposition had been defrauded of an actual majority in the Moscow Province.[10]

The Opposition was far weaker in Petrograd. **Pravda** reported that a mass meeting of party members addressed by Zinoviev adopted a resolution condemning the Opposition by 3,000 votes to 5 (with five abstentions).[11] Altogether, in meetings held in December, of the 21,167 party members who took part, 1,132 voted for the Opposition, and 280 abstained.[12]

The Opposition captured the party organisations in Riazan, Penza, Kaluga, Khabarovsk, Kiev, Odessa, Viatka, Simbirsk and Chelyabinsk.[13]

As the majority of the Central Committee of the Komsomol were not reliable supporters of the Troika, the general secretariat of the party, violating the statutes of the Komsomol, replaced it with its own nominated Central Committee.[14]

Students sympathetic to the Opposition were expelled from the universities in large numbers.[15]

Opposition sympathisers were quite strong in the Red Army, so the oppositionist Antonov-Ovseenko was removed from the crucial post of head of the Political Administration of the Army.

(Antonov-Ovseenko was replaced by A. Bubnov, a former Democratic Centralist and one of the signatories of the Declaration of the Forty Six, who now switched to the side of the Troika and became a supporter of Stalin until he was purged in the 1930s.)

The main cause of the Opposition's defeat, however, was to be found not in the machinations of the bureaucracy, but in the lack of fighting spirit in the proletariat. As Trotsky wrote many years later:

> At the time of the party discussion in the autumn of 1923, the Moscow organisation was divided approximately in half, with a certain preponderance in favour of the Opposition in the beginning. However, the two halves were not of equal strength in their social [potential]. On the side of the Opposition was the youth and a considerable portion of the rank and file; but on the side of Stalin and the Central Committee were first of all the specially trained and disciplined politicians who were most closely connected with the political machine of the general secretary. My illness and my consequent non-participation in the struggle was, I grant, a factor of some consequence; however, its importance should not be exaggerated. In the final reckoning it was a mere episode. [All-important was the fact that] the workers were tired. Those who supported the Opposition were not spurred on by a hope for great and serious changes. On the other hand, the bureaucracy fought with extraordinary ferocity.[16]

The party apparatus demonstrated its decisive power. The Opposition got only three delegates to the Thirteenth Party Conference out of 128 delegates with deciding votes (and 222 with consultative votes.)

Trotsky was not present at the conference. As we have already mentioned, in early January he left Moscow to recuperate at the Black Sea resort of Sukhum. The leadership of the Opposition at the conference fell to Preobrazhensky, Piatakov, Osinsky and Sapronov, none of whom had the authority of Trotsky.

The conference turned into an orgy of ferocity against the Opposition led by Stalin and supported by Zinoviev and Kamenev. Stalin's vitriolic attacks on Trotsky, in which he called him a

Menshevik, 'patriarch of bureaucrats', and so on, culminated in a quote from the resolution of the Tenth Party Congress on the banning of factions in which the following hitherto undisclosed clause was revealed, requiring the Central Committee

> ...in case (cases) of breach of discipline or of a revival or toleration of factionalism, to apply all-party penalties up to and including expulsion from the party and... A condition for the application of such an extreme measure (to members and candidate members of the CC and members of the Control Commission) must be the convocation of a plenum of the Central Committee to which all candidate members of the Central Committee and all members of the Control Commission shall be invited. If such a general assembly of the most responsible leaders of the Party by a two-thirds majority, considers it necessary to reduce a member of the Central Committee to the status of a candidate member, or to expel him from the Party, this measure shall be put into effect immediately.[17]

The conference adopted a resolution denouncing the Opposition—Trotsky and the Forty Six—as guilty of 'petty-bourgeois deviation from Leninism' and going on to state categorically:

> The Party will politically annihilate anyone who makes an attempt on the unity of the Party ranks. Party unity is more assured now than ever before...
> Decisive measures, up to expulsion from the Party, must be adopted against the spreading of unverified rumours and prohibited documents...
> The Conference orders the Central Committee to publish the previously unpublished seventh paragraph of the resolution 'On Party Unity' adopted at Comrade Lenin's proposal by the Tenth Congress, which entitles a joint meeting of the Central Committee and the Central Control Commission by two-thirds majority to demote from member to candidate member, or even to expel from the Party, any Central Committee member who has violated Party discipline or has 'tolerated factionalism'.[18]

The resolution was passed with three votes against.

The death of Lenin

On 21 January 1924, after nine months of total disability, Lenin suffered another severe stroke and died. Trotsky, as we have mentioned, was away from Moscow. On the day of Lenin's death his train was halted at Tiflis. There he received a coded message from Stalin informing him of Lenin's death. Trotsky wondered whether he should return to Moscow. In his autobiography he writes:

> I got the Kremlin on the direct wire. In answer to my inquiry I was told: 'The funeral will be on Saturday, you can't get back in time, and so we advise you to continue your treatment'. Accordingly, I had no choice.

Stalin had cheated.

> As a matter of fact the funeral did not take place till Sunday, and I could easily have reached Moscow by then. Incredible as it may appear, I was even deceived about the date of the funeral. The conspirators surmised correctly that I would never think of verifying it and later on they could always find an explanation.[19]

Thus Trotsky was kept away from the elaborate funeral ceremonies in the course of which the triumvirate presented themselves to the world as Lenin's successors.

Trotsky's wife Natalia wrote in her diary:

> Considerably delayed by the snow, the newspapers began to bring us the memorial speeches, obituaries and articles. Our friends were expecting LD to come to Moscow, and thought that he would cut short his trip in order to return, since no one imagined that Stalin's telegram had cut off his return. I remember my son's letter, received at Sukhum. He was terribly shocked by Lenin's death, and though suffering from a cold, with a temperture of 104, went in his not very warm coat to the Hall of Columns to pay his last respects, and waited, waited, and waited with impatience for our arrival. One could feel in his letter his bitter bewilderment and diffident reproach.[20]

Trotsky's absence from Lenin's funeral must have left a very damaging impression on the minds of millions.

The opportunity which Trotsky missed was seized upon by Stalin, who assumed the lead in the funeral proceedings. The elaborate ceremony was altogether out of gear with Lenin's simple style that detested all pomp.

Its aim was to build the new Lenin cult.

At a session of the Second All-Union Congress of Soviets held on the evening of 26 January, the day before the funeral, Stalin made his famous oration pledging the party to execute Lenin's will, a speech peppered with liturgical refrains.

Comrades, we Communists are people of a special mould. We are made of a special stuff. We are those who form the army of the great proletarian strategist, the army of Comrade Lenin. There is nothing higher than the honour of belonging to this army. There is nothing higher than the title of member of the Party whose founder and leader was Comrade Lenin. It is not given to everyone to be a member of such a party... DEPARTING FROM US, COMRADE LENIN ENJOINED US TO HOLD HIGH AND GUARD THE PURITY OF THE GREAT TITLE OF MEMBER OF THE PARTY. WE VOW TO YOU, COMRADE LENIN, THAT WE SHALL FULFIL YOUR BEHEST WITH HONOUR!

There followed much repetition of the same kind of bombast, after which the same liturgical refrain repeats.

DEPARTING FROM US, COMRADE LENIN ENJOINED US TO GUARD THE UNITY OF OUR PARTY AS THE APPLE OF OUR EYE. WE VOW TO YOU, COMRADE LENIN, THAT THIS BEHEST, TOO, WE SHALL FULFIL WITH HONOUR!... DEPARTING FROM US, COMRADE LENIN ENJOINED US TO GUARD AND STRENGTHEN THE DICTATORSHIP OF THE PROLETARIAT. WE VOW TO YOU, COMRADE LENIN, THAT WE SHALL SPARE NO EFFORT TO FULFIL THIS BEHEST, TOO, WITH HONOUR!... DEPARTING FROM US, COMRADE LENIN ENJOINED US TO STRENGTHEN WITH ALL OUR MIGHT THE ALLIANCE OF THE WORKERS AND PEASANTS. WE VOW TO YOU,

COMRADE LENIN, THAT THIS BEHEST TOO, WE SHALL FULFIL WITH HONOUR!...

DEPARTING FROM US, COMRADE LENIN ENJOINED US TO STRENGTHEN AND EXTEND THE UNION OF REPUBLICS. WE VOW TO YOU, COMRADE LENIN, THAT THIS BEHEST, TOO, WE SHALL FULFIL WITH HONOUR!...

DEPARTING FROM US, COMRADE LENIN ENJOINED US TO REMAIN FAITHFUL TO THE PRINCIPLES OF THE COMMUNIST INTERNATIONAL. WE VOW TO YOU, COMRADE LENIN, THAT WE SHALL NOT SPARE OUR LIVES TO STRENGTHEN AND EXTEND THE UNION OF THE WORKING PEOPLE OF THE WHOLE WORLD—THE COMMUNIST INTERNATIONAL![21]

Stalin's funeral oration was a combination of Marxist terminology with the language of the Orthodox Prayer Book. The vow to Lenin was sheer hypocrisy in view of what had recently happened to the relations between Lenin and Stalin: Lenin's assault on Stalin's Great Russian chauvinism, Stalin's bureaucratic high-handedness in Rabkrin and his rudeness to Krupskaya that led Lenin finally to break off all personal relations.

No sooner had Lenin died than the bureaucracy initiated a Lenin cult that would have revolted the great revolutionary and would never have been tolerated while he was alive. Petrograd, the city of the revolution, was renamed Leningrad, and Lenin's body, despite the indignant protests of Krupskaya, was embalmed and put on display in a Mausoleum in Red Square.* Trotsky commented: 'The attitude towards Lenin as a revolutionary leader gave way to an attitude like that towards the head of an ecclesiastical hierarchy'.[22]

Krupskaya was disgusted with the new Lenin cult. In a letter in **Pravda** of thanks for condolences received she wrote:

I have a great request to you: do not allow your mourning for Ilyich to take the form of external reverence for his person.

---

*In June 1924 Iuzovka, an iron and steel town in the Ukraine, was renamed Stalinsk, the neighbouring railway station known as Iuzovo became Stalino. In September 1924 Elizavetgrad, also in the Ukraine, was named Zinoviesk. In April 1925 Tsaritsin was renamed Stalingrad.

Do not raise memorials to him, palaces named after him, solemn festivals in commemoration of him, etc. To all this he attached so little importance in his life, all this was so burdensome to him. Remember how much poverty and neglect there still is in our country. If you wish to honour the name of Vladimir Ilyich, build creches, kindergartens, houses, schools, libraries, medical centres, hospitals, homes for the disabled, etc., and, most of all, let us put his precepts into practice.[23]

The creation of the Lenin cult was a springboard for further attacks on Lenin's comrade in arms, Trotsky. Here is Trotsky's description of what happened shortly after Lenin's death:

At a signal from **Pravda** a campaign against Trotskyism burst forth simultaneously on all platforms, in all pages and columns, in every crack and corner. It was a majestic spectacle of its kind. The slander was like a volcanic eruption. It was a great shock to the large mass of the party. I lay in bed with a temperature, and remained silent. Press and orators did nothing but expose Trotskyism, although no one knew exactly what it meant. Day after day they served up incidents from the past, polemical excerpts from Lenin's articles of twenty years' standing, confusing, falsifying and mutilating them, and in general presenting them as if everything had happened just the day before. No one could understand anything of all this. If it had really been true, then Lenin must have been aware of it. But was there not the October revolution after all that? Was there not the civil war after the revolution? Had not Trotsky worked together with Lenin in creating the Communist International? Were not Trotsky's portraits hanging everywhere next to those of Lenin? But slander poured forth in a cold lava stream. It pressed down automatically on the consciousness, and was even more devastating to the will.[24]

Natalia's diary around this time is poignant. Not only did it show Trotsky ill, but also his impotence in the face of the deluge.

The second attack of LD's illness coincided with a monstrous campaign of persecution against him, which we felt as keenly as if we had been suffering from the most malignant disease.

The pages of **Pravda** seemed endless, and every line of the paper, even every word, a lie. LD kept silent. But what it cost him to maintain that silence! Friends called to see him during the day and often at night. I remember that someone asked him if he had read that day's paper. He replied that he no longer read the newspapers. And it is true that he only took them up in his hands, ran his eyes over them and then threw them aside. It seemed as if it were enough for him merely to look at them to know all that they contained. He knew only too well the cooks who had made the dish, and the same dish every day, to boot. To read the papers at that time was exactly, he would say, like pushing a funnel brush into one's own throat. It might have been possible for him to force himself to read them if LD had decided to reply. But he remained silent. His cold lingered on, thanks to his critical nervous condition. He looked pale and thin. In the family we avoided talking about the persecution, and yet we could talk of nothing else. I remember how I felt when I went to my work every day at the Commissariat of Education; it was like running a gauntlet.[25]

The Lenin Levy

After Lenin's death the Central Committee decreed a three months' recruiting campaign into the party called the 'Lenin Levy'. Rules governing admission were relaxed. In the months February, March and April, the 'Lenin Levy' brought in 240,000, increasing the total membership of the party by more than 50 per cent.

This mass recruitment made a mockery of Trotsky's demand to increase the number of manual workers in the party, as it simply meant its dilution. When unemployment was so widespread, belonging to the party was attractive, as its members were the last to be discharged. The new raw recruits were used by the Troika to fight 'Trotskyism'.

Trotsky found it impossible to oppose the 'Lenin Levy'. As a matter of fact he even praised it. In a speech on 11 April 1924 he said:

The most important fact of recent weeks and months has been the influx of workers from the plant floors into the ranks of our party. This is the best way for the fundamental revolutionary class in our country to show its will: by raising its hand and saying, we vote our confidence in the RKP... This vote is a reliable, sure, and unerring verification by comparison with which parliamentary votes seem phantom like, superficial, and, most of all, simply charlatanistic.[26]

Twelve years later, in his book **The Revolution Betrayed**, he gave a much more incisive judgment of the 'Lenin Levy':

> The political aim of this manoeuvre was to dissolve the revolutionary vanguard in raw human material without experience, without independence, and yet with the old habit of submitting to the authorities. The scheme was successful. By freeing the bureaucracy from the control of the proletarian vanguard, the 'Leninist levy' dealt a death blow to the party of Lenin.[27]

The Thirteenth Party Congress

The Central Committee met on 22 May 1924, on the eve of the Thirteenth Party Congress. The question of what to do with Lenin's Testament was the decisive issue on the agenda. Krupskaya, who must have known Lenin's wishes, desired that it should be read at the forthcoming Congress which then would take action upon it. The idea was received with consternation by Stalin. After all, a postscript to the Testament recommended his removal from the post of General Secretary of the party. Zinoviev and Kamenev were reminded in the Testament that their failure at the crucial moment of the 1917 revolution was 'not accidental'. None of the leaders except Trotsky had anything to gain from the publication of the Testament; Stalin had most to lose.

At the meeting of the Central Committee the Testament was read by Kamenev who presided over the proceedings. Then Zinoviev spoke in terms which were recorded from memory by one of those present:

> Comrades, the last wish of Ilyich, every word of Ilyich, is without doubt law in our eyes. More than once we have vowed to fulfil everything which the dying Ilyich recommended us to do. You know well that we shall keep that promise... But we are happy to say that on one point

Lenin's fears have not proved well founded. I mean the point about our general secretary. You have all been witnesses of our work together in the last few months; and, like myself, you have been happy to confirm that Ilyich's fears have not been realised.

Kamenev followed in support of the plea not to carry out the injunction to depose Stalin. Nobody seems to have taken up the indictment against him even though many of those present may have shared Lenin's doubts. Trotsky remained silent throughout the proceedings. If, however, Stalin (and with him the present leadership) were to remain, nothing but harm could be done by divulging Lenin's reflections and apprehensions to the world. By a majority of 30 votes to 10, and against the opposition of Krupskaya, it was decided not to read the Testament to the Congress, but to communicate it confidentially to the heads of the delegations attending the Congress.[28]

Stalin sought a vote of confidence from the CC by offering to resign as general secretary. Zinoviev and Kamenev called for a vote by a show of hands, but nobody voted for his removal. Trotsky, who was present, remained silent. The result was a unanimous endorsement. Stalin could later boast at the joint plenum of the Central Committee and the Central Control Commission in October 1927 that everybody 'including Trotsky, Kamenev and Zinoviev, obliged Stalin to remain at his post.'[29]

How depressed and paralysed must Trotsky have been! In payment for his support for Stalin at this difficult time Zinoviev earned the right to be the main speaker at the coming Congress by delivering the political report of the Central Committee. This turned out to be an almost hysterical call for unity of the party: 'In this hall there is not one man who would not be ready to give up everything for our party to be united, for this is the single serious prerequisite of all further successes of the revolution and all further successes of the Comintern.'

In his extreme propagation of the idea of monolithic unity Zinoviev accused Trotsky of responsibility for the formation of factions and groupings. He taunted Trotsky for his charge of lack of inner-party democracy and the dominance of the bureaucracy in the party, argued that the party must become 'a thousand times more monolithic than hitherto', and concluded by issuing a challenge to Trotsky to get up before the Congress and recant his errors.

> The most sensible step, and most worthy of a Bolshevik, which the opposition could take, is what a Bolshevik does when he happens to make some mistake or other—to come before the party on the tribune of the party congress and say: 'I made a mistake, and the party was right.'...
> There is one way really to liquidate the controversy and end it once for all—to come forward on this tribune and say: 'The party was right, and those were wrong who said that we were on the brink of ruin'.[30]

This was the first time that dissidents in the party were called upon to disavow their ideas in order to escape censure. The demand for contrition would later be made of Zinoviev as well as all those who joined him in his demand for Trotsky to recant.

Trotsky was very isolated at the Congress. The Congress was attended by 748 delegates with a deciding vote and 416 with a consultative vote. The Opposition was represented by two with a consultative vote, Trotsky and Preobrazhensky. The party apparatus had done its job ruthlessly. Only four months before, on the eve of the Thirteenth Party Conference, thousands of party members had supported the Opposition.

Trotsky made a much shorter speech than he usually did at party congresses. He said very little about the economic issues, although he reiterated his demand for more planning and repeated his accusation that 'the party, in the form of its leading apparatus, did not approach the tasks of planned guidance of the economy with the necessary energy'.[31] He spoke with extreme moderation, reasserting his opposition to factionalism and his loyal submission to the discipline of the party. He went on to praise the 'Lenin Levy' as a demonstration of the 'increased confidence of the working masses in the party... Undoubtedly the Lenin levy brought our party closer to being an elected party.' This is a demonstration of proletarian democracy:

> ...the working class at a certain stage of its development has shown in a particularly impressive way how it views the balance sheet of the party's work over many years and has raised on its shoulders two or three hundred thousand

workers and presented them to the party.[32]*

Trotsky went on to reiterate the danger of bureaucratisation in the party, supporting his case with a quotation from Bukharin (quoted above) about party meetings that start with 'Who is for?' and 'Who is against?' and end with unanimous support for appointed officials and official resolutions.

He went on to vehemently deny the allegation that he supported the right of factions or groupings to exist in the party.

> ...party democracy in no way implies freedom for factional groupings, which are extremely dangerous for the ruling party, since they always threaten to split or divide the government and the state apparatus as a whole. I believe this is undisputed and indisputable....
> The report that I was in favour of allowing groupings is not true. It was impermissible to draw distinctions between factions and groupings... under the present historical conditions groupings are merely another name for factions.[34]

In the final part of his speech Trotsky could not but express his real anger at Zinoviev's call on him to recant:

> Comrades, an invitation was extended here for all who have committed errors to stand up and confess them. Nothing could be simpler or easier, morally and politically, than to admit before your own party that you have made this or that mistake. For that, I believe, no great moral heroism is required.

> But the resolution of 5 December 1923 constituted an admission by the Central Committee that it had made mistakes and that a new course should be set. Those whose warnings had prompted that resolution could not now declare themselves to have been wrong.

> Comrades, none of us wants to be or can be right against the party. In the last analysis, the party is always right, because

---

*A few weeks after the Congress Stalin said the 'Lenin Levy' was 'evidence of the Party's profound democracy... It actually is the elected organ of the working class.'[33]

the party is the sole historical instrument that the working class possesses for the solution of its fundamental tasks. I have already said that nothing would be simpler than to say before the party that all these criticisms, all these declarations, warnings, and protests—all were mistaken from beginning to end. I cannot say so, however, comrades, because I do not think it. I know that no one can be right against the party. It is only possible to be right with the party and through it since history has not created any other way to determine the correct position.

The English have a proverb: My country right or wrong. We can say with much greater historical justification: whether it is right or wrong in any particular, specific question at any particular moment, this is my party.[35]

Trotsky went on to say he could not vote for the resolution of the Thirteenth Party Conference which had condemned him.

Not only an individual party member but even the party itself can make occasional mistakes; such mistakes, for instance, were represented by individual decisions of the last conference, certain parts of which I believe were incorrect and unjustified. But the party could not make any decision, no matter how incorrect and unjustified, that could shake by even one iota our total devotion to the cause of the party, and the readiness of every one of us to shoulder the responsibility of party discipline under all circumstances. And if the party passes a resolution that one or another of us considers unjust, that comrade will say: Right or wrong, this is my party, and I will take responsibility for its decision to the end.[36]

Trotsky refused to recant his ideas—party discipline required only that once outvoted he agreed to abide by the majority in action.

Trotsky's restrained speech did not save him from torrents of abuse. One delegate after another attacked him. All the leaders of the European communist parties present, except the French, rose to add their voices to the shower of abuse rained upon him. Hypocritically seizing on the ambiguity in Trotsky's statement that 'none of us wants to be or can be right against the party',

Stalin and Zinoviev twisted the knife in the wound. Said Stalin:

> ...the Party, Trotsky says, makes no mistakes. That is wrong. The Party not infrequently makes mistakes. Ilyich taught us to teach the Party, on the basis of its own mistakes, how to exercise correct leadership. If the Party made no mistakes there would be nothing from which to teach it... It seems to me that this statement of Trotsky's is a kind of compliment accompanied by an attempt—an unsuccessful one it is true—to jeer at the Party.[37]

And Zinoviev, following in Stalin's footsteps, declared:

> Comrade Stalin said, and I, of course, am in full accord with him, that the party can make mistakes. It is useless to hand us these sour-sweet compliments. The party has no need of that. Can you imagine Vladimir Ilyich ever coming out on the platform and saying that the party can not make a mistake?[38]

The main resolution of the Congress confirmed the verdict of the Thirteenth Party Conference on the 'petty bourgeois deviation' of the Opposition, and praised the Central Committee for its 'firmness and Bolshevik intransigence... in defending the foundations of Leninism against petty bourgeois deviations.' 'The slightest factionalism must be prosecuted most severely. The firm and monolithic quality of the RKP, based on the firm principles of Leninism, are the most important prerequisite for the further successes of the revolution.'[39]

The Thirteenth Congress closed the discussion in the party, and prohibited Trotsky from speaking in public about the disputed questions.

Trotsky, isolated and depressed, had been routed in his absence at the Thirteenth Party Conference in January; now in May, at the Party Congress, the complete collapse of his influence and authority was further confirmed.

In the elections to the Central Committee at the Thirteenth Congress Trotsky came very low indeed, No. 51 out of 52.

After the Congress the Central Committee elected Bukharin to full membership of the Politburo to fill Lenin's place and added Dzerzhinsky. Frunze and Sokolnikov became candidates. Bukharin, Dzerzhinsky and Frunze were supporters of Stalin at the time; Sokolnikov was a supporter of Zinoviev.

Trotsky's situation was very depressing indeed. He was completely isolated in both the Politburo and the Central Committee. As he was ill, the Politburo held lengthy sessions in his apartment so that he could participate in drawing up resolutions that were bound to boomerang on him. Trotsky has left no record of these sessions except a description which he quoted from Natalia's unpublished memoirs.

> These were hard days, days of tense fighting for Lev Davidovich at the Politburo against the rest of the members. He was alone and ill, and had to fight them all. Owing to his illness, the meetings were held in our apartment. I sat in the adjoining bedroom and heard his speeches. He spoke with his whole being. It seemed as if with every such speech he lost some of his strength—he spoke with so much 'blood'. And in reply I heard cold, indifferent answers. Everything, of course, had been decided in advance, so what was the need of getting excited? After each of these meetings LD's temperature mounted. He came out of his study soaked through and undressed and went to bed. His linen and clothes had to be dried as if he had been drenched in a rain storm. At that time, the meetings were frequent and were held in LD's room, whose faded, old carpet appeared in my dream every night in the shape of a live panther. The meetings during the day became nightmares.[40]

The real tragedy of Trotsky was that while he opposed the Troika that dominated the party, he still was not ready to go to the mass of the workers outside of the party or even the rank and file of the party as this would violate the ban on factionalism that Lenin, with his support, had imposed on the party at the Tenth Congress. Above all Trotsky was afraid to mobilise non-party people, many of whom were influenced by Mensheviks, SRs and others, who, together with the new bourgeoisie of the NEP, raised their heads in opposition to Bolshevism. He still considered the Communist Party to be the *revolutionary party* and thought that his place was inside it whatever happened. When many years later Trotsky wrote in an obituary of Krupskaya that 'her revolutionary instinct came into conflict with her spirit of discipline'[41] he was laying bare his own plight.

Chapter three
The German revolution of 1923

The German Revolution and stirrings in Russia

THE 1923 Opposition was not only the child of internal developments in Russia—the increasing estrangement of workers from the state and party leadership—but also of a very significant international event: the German revolution of autumn 1923.

Renewed hope of revolution rose in Germany. A victory for the German working class would have ended the isolation of the Russian working class and radically changed the whole international situation.

Excitement about the German revolution gripped people throughout Russia. Ruth Fischer described Moscow in September 1923.

> It was plastered with slogans welcoming the German revolution. Banners and streamers were posted in the centre of the city with such slogans as 'Russian Youth, Learn German—the German October is approaching'. Pictures of Clara Zetkin, Rosa Luxemburg and Karl Liebknecht were to be seen in every shop window. In all factories meetings were called to discuss 'How can we help the German revolution?'[1]

Such discussions were not mere formalities. The Russian workers were expected by the government to make genuine sacrifices for the German revolution. According to the records of the Communist International, 'the Russian working class agreed to suspend the increase of their wages and to submit to reductions if it were necessary in the interests of the German revolution'. The workers were told that a defeat for the German proletariat would constitute a defeat for the Russian workers as well. Women were asked at public meetings to donate their wedding rings and other valuables for the German cause. The Trade Commissariat distributed circulars which stated that 'the advance of the German revolution confronted the Trade Commissariat with new problems; the present routine of trading must be replaced by the establishment of two German reserves: gold and corn, for the benefit of the victorious German proletariat; and the agencies of this Commissariat in the individual Soviet republics were ordered to send a total of 60 million pud of grain towards Russia's western frontiers. The Russian Communist Party, by order of its Politburo, drew up lists of members who spoke German in order to create a communist-trained reserve corps which could, at the appropriate moment, be transferred to Germany where it would assist the revolution. Special attention was paid to the mobilisation of the Komsomol organisations, whose members were told that they might have to risk their lives on behalf of the German proletariat and the cause of revolution. In October revolutionary slogans became current: 'Workers' Germany and our Workers' and Peasants' Union are the bulwark of peace and labour'. 'German Steam Hammers and Soviet Bread will Conquer the World'. Soviet newspapers wrote that if the German workers were successful the new German government would join with Soviet Russia and thereby 'unite in Europe the tremendous power of 200 million people, against which no war in Europe will be possible... because no one will be able to face such a force.'[2]

A Short Sketch of the German Revolution

In 1923 a fierce class struggle broke out in Germany as a result of a serious crisis. The immediate cause was the occupation of the Ruhr by France on 11 January 1923 in retaliation for Germany falling behind with its reparations payments. Two days later the German government, led by the conservative Cuno, issued an appeal to the population of the Ruhr for 'passive resistance' and non-cooperation with the occupying authorities. The immediate result was an increase in German resistance, ranging from strikes to acts of sabotage. A crucial by-product of the French occupation and German resistance was an acceleration of the rate of inflation to astronomic proportions. The changes in the mark's exchange rate with the dollar tell the story:

January	17,920
February	20,000
May	48,000
June	110,000
July	349,000
August	4,600,000
September	98,860,000
October	25,260,208,000
November	4,200,000,000,000 [3]

The result was the absolute pauperisation of the whole of the working population, ruin for the petty bourgeoisie, the rapid enrichment of the owners of capital, massive speculation and corruption; the closing of all safety valves. Never had a highly industrial society been in such deep economic, social and political turmoil.

The traditional reformist working class organisations were impotent in this situation. One writer, Evelyn Anderson, stated:

> In those days...the influence of the Social Democrats and the trade unions was waning. Although membership of the unions was larger than ever before, the inflation had robbed them of all funds with which to support their members, to finance strikes, or even to pay their officials. Moreover, normal Trade Union activity had become quite impossible in a situation in which nominal wages and salaries had lost all meaning.[4]

Pierre Broué, in his monumental history of the German revolution, **Révolution en Allemagne (1917-1923)**, writes:

> The traditional trade union practice of Social Democracy was empty of all meaning, trade unionism was impotent, collective agreements derided. The workers left the trade unions and often directed their anger against them, blaming them for their passivity, sometimes for their complicity. The collapse of the trade union apparatus and Social Democracy was paralleled by that of the state. What became of notions of property, order and legality? How in such an abyss can one justify an attachment to parliamentary institutions, to the right to vote, to universal suffrage? Neither the police nor the army were free of sickness. A world was dying.[5]

From May onwards massive spontaneous strikes took place throughout the country. They were denounced by trade union leaders and opposed by the Social Democrats. The authority of the factory committees leading the struggle increased dramatically. Their national action committee began to represent an alternative workers' leadership, a serious counter-balance to the trade union leaders.

On 16 June, in the name of the factory councils, its president, Grothe, addressed a solemn appeal to the workers, employees and intellectuals. Describing the catastrophe that was threatening German society, he reaffirmed that the working class could prevent it by getting rid of the capitalist system:

> Only the struggle of all, only the class struggle, can bring you what you need, simply in order to assure your survival. The whole working people is in motion. In this flood that the trade unions today try to dam and sabotage, important tasks and initiatives fall to the factory councils.

He invited the factory councils to form local and regional organisations to give the working masses 'objectives and leadership' in the coming struggles. Committees for the control of prices and proletarian defence organisations—Proletarian Hundreds—were needed: with factory councils they would form the base for a workers' government, which alone could produce a positive outcome to the crisis.

Strikes and demonstrations followed. Workers demonstrated at Bautzen on 2 June, at Dresden and at Leipzig on 7 June. On this date more than 100,000 miners and engineers were on strike in Upper Silesia under the leadership of an elected strike committee which included six communists out of a total of 26 members. On 11 June there broke out a historically unique strike of 100,000 agricultural workers in Silesia, soon followed by 10,000 Brandenburg day workers. On 11 June a merchant marine strike also began at Emden, Bremen and Lübeck, on the initiative of the Federation of Seamen, which belonged to the Communist-led Profintern, the red international of trade unions.

In Berlin it was the engineering workers who took action. 153,000 of the total of 250,000 engineers were organised in trade unions. Workers' pressure achieved a referendum in the union on strike action, the result of which was massive support. The union then organised a second referendum open to non-trade unionists. The majority in favour was even greater. Finally, workers at 60 enterprises called for the strike. Immediately the employers began to negotiate. On 10 July 150,000 engineers struck and the trade union leadership was overthrown in many factories. On the same day the management agreed to a rise in wages, from 9,800 marks for the second week of June to 12,000 for the first week of July. One clause of the agreement proposed to set up a parity commission to establish a price index that would serve as the basis for indemnity against inflation. At the demand of the employers this remained secret, to prevent the idea spreading. The results, however, were visible. The wages of the engineers after 10 June were 38 per cent higher than the figure demanded by the unions and rejected on 3 June. It was soon the turn of the building workers to strike, and then the woodworkers in the capital. Everywhere the communists were in the forefront in launching the strikes and also in the return to work, not only in trade union meetings where they were often in the majority, but in the 'workers' assemblies' which they had forced the trade union leaders to call, and which were open to all.[6]

For the first time (and, as history was to show, the last) the Communist Party of Germany had the majority of the proletariat under its influence. According to one historian, 'In the summer of 1923 the KPD undoubtedly had the majority of the German proletariat behind it.'[7]

'Bread riots became commonplace: in Berlin, Dresden, Frankfurt am Main, Mannheim, Cologne.' The bourgeois state machine was under tremendous strain.

The disruption of economic life endangered the legal structure of the Weimar Republic. Civil servants lost their ties to the state; their salaries had no relation to their daily needs. They felt themselves in a boat without a rudder. Police and troops, in sympathy with the rioting populace, lost their combative spirit against the hunger demonstrations and closed their eyes to the sabotage groups and clandestine military formations mushrooming throughout the Reich. Hamburg was so tense that the police did not dare interfere with looting of foodstuffs by the hungry masses. In August large demonstrations of dockworkers in the Hamburg harbour led to rioting. 'Parts of the police', [a leading Hamburg communist] wrote, 'are regarded as unreliable; they sympathise with the working class'.[8]

On 8 August things came to a head. Chancellor Cuno justified his policies to the Reichstag in a lengthy speech. The debate went on until the next day. The Reichstag was then besieged by workers' delegations which it refused to receive. The debate ended on 10 August with a vote of confidence for the government, the Social Democrats abstaining and the Communists voting against. The Communist Wilhelm Könen addressed the workers from parliament, calling for 'the mass movement of the workers to go over the head of parliament and form a workers' revolutionary government'. The strike movement gained momentum. The tram workers in Berlin went on strike. A short while later it was the turn of the printers, who followed the call of the communist cell, and whose strike included the 8,000 workers at the national mint. The production of notes stopped. In a few hours the government would not even have money at its disposal. The workers in big enterprises followed the movement, led by those in Siemens and Borsig. Workers from eleven striking Berlin enterprises took up communist demands for the resignation of Cuno and for the formation of a workers' government. Urban transport was at a complete standstill, gas and electricity cut off. In Hamburg all building work ground to a halt, and there were workers' demonstrations at Krefeld and Aachen: the police intervened and there were some deaths. The midday editions of the newspapers announced that the Reichsbank was going to close due to lack of notes.[9]

On 11 August a hastily summoned conference of the Berlin factory councils proclaimed a general strike in the city, and urged the working class throughout the country to join the strike. The proclamation was carried by a special edition of the communist paper **Die Rote Fahne**, but the entire issue was promptly confiscated by the authorities, who invoked a one-day-old government decree 'for the protection of public order.'

Despite this, the Communists succeeded in eliciting a strong response from several groups of workers in the city. Moreover, sporadic wildcat strikes erupted on this and subsequent days in various parts of the country.

Evelyn Anderson, in her book, **Hammer or Anvil**, described the situation.

> The Cuno strike was entirely spontaneous and as such it was a unique action in the history of the German labour movement. Shop stewards and local workers' representatives took the initiative and led the movement. The parties began to realise what was happening only after this movement of the masses had created an accomplished fact. All this had important consequences. The movement exhausted and spent itself once it had achieved the maximum that spontaneous and unguided action of this kind could possibly achieve, ie., the resignation of the government. To exploit this success for more positive and constructive would have been the task of the political working-class parties.

Regrettably, however, 'None of the existing parties was up to this task.'[10]

The policy of the KPD

All the objective conditions for the revolution were in place: a general crisis of society, loss of confidence among the ruling class that they could go on in the old way, a rebellion of the proletariat against the old conditions. As regards the subjective factors: the Communist Party was a mass party and its influence over the working class was overwhelming. To understand the outcome of events, we need to look at its policies.

During the first seven months of 1923, between the start of the occupation of the Ruhr by French troops and the collapse of the Cuno government, the policy of the KPD lacked cohesion and clear direction and the leaders were deeply pessimistic. Thus on 17 March, at an international conference in Frankfurt, Brandler, Chairman of the KPD, said:

> While we experienced then [in 1918] a rising revolutionary tide on account of the Russian revolution, we face today a receding tide because of the seizure of power by the bourgeoisie, and now our primary task is to rally the proletariat.[11]

Throughout 1923 the KPD leadership lacked independence and was totally subservient to the orders of the Comintern in

Moscow. This was the catastrophic result of the Märzaktion in 1921 (an ultra-left adventure that failed), since when Brandler, Thalheimer, Walcher and Ernest Meyer, had become, in Broué's description,

> 'rightists', systematically, obstinately, prudent, armed with precautions against any tendency towards putschism and even the simple leftist reflex. Convinced by the leaders of the International of the grave fault they had committed, they lost confidence in their capacity to think and often surrendered their own point of view entirely in order to agree with the Bolsheviks who, at least, had known how to win.[12]

In contrast with Brandler's pessimism regarding the immediate prospect of revolution, the bourgeois press was convinced that the revolution was imminent! On 26 July **Kreuz-Zeitung** declared: 'We are now without doubt, who can fail to see this after what we have seen before our very eyes, on the eve of a new revolution.' **Germania** the next day reported: 'Trust in the Reich government is seriously shaken... Discontent has reached a dangerous degree. The fury is general. The air is charged with electricity. Any spark and it would explode... We have the state of mind of 9 November',[13] ie, the day the Kaiser was deposed.

Every paper in Germany was using the expression *'Novemberstimmung'* (the mood of November) with the exception of the Communist press.

Still the rising wave of industrial strikes, plus the rise of the extreme right, including the Nazis in Bavaria, stirred the KPD leadership into action. Early in July it decided to organise an Anti-Fascist Day with three demonstrations in the large cities on Sunday 29 July. This should have been the beginning of a general offensive against the Right.

But then on 23 July the Prussian government prohibited all demonstrations on the day fixed. Brandler telegraphed Moscow for advice. The leadership of the Russian party, with the exception of Radek, was away from Moscow on holiday. Radek telegraphed the most distant parts of Russia for the individual opinion of the leaders who in fact had very little knowledge of the situation in Germany. Zinoviev and Bukharin were for offensive tactics, but Radek knew that they had taken the same position during the

Märzaktion and had burned their fingers. Trotsky was honest enough to admit that he did not have a clear idea of the situation on the ground in Germany and therefore was not ready to express an opinion. Stalin—this was one of the first times anyone had bothered to ask his advice about international questions—expressed strong disbelief in the chances of a German revolution.

On 26 July a telegram was sent from the Presidium of the Comintern to the Zentrale of the KPD: 'The presidium of the Comintern advises the abandonment of street demonstrations on 29 July... We fear a trap'.[14]

The KPD called off the demonstrations, except for Saxony, Thuringia and Wurtenburg where the demonstrations had not been banned. Thus the vacillation of the KPD leadership and the Comintern was laid bare.

On 23 August an extraordinary meeting of the Politburo was summoned, attended also by Radek, Piatakov, Shmidt and Tsiuriupa. Radek, who throughout the year had been in Berlin as the representative of the Executive Committee of the Comintern, reported on the situation. Trotsky argued that the revolution was maturing very quickly and in weeks the decisive battles would take place. Zinoviev rejected such optimism, and thought it safer to reckon in months rather than weeks. Stalin was more cautious still. He saw no revolution in Germany now or in the autumn: it might come in the spring, but even that was dubious. In a letter to Zinoviev and Bukharin, Stalin explained his views:

> Should the Communists at the present stage try to seize power without the Social Democrats? Are they sufficiently ripe for that? That, in my opinion, is the question. When we seized power, we had in Russia such resources in reserve as (a) the promise of peace; (b) the slogan—the land to the peasants; (c) the support of the great majority of the working class; and (d) the sympathy of the peasantry. At the moment the German Communists have nothing of the kind. They have of course a Soviet country as neighbour, which we did not have; but what can we offer them? ...Should the government in Germany topple over now, in a manner of speaking, and the Communists were to seize hold of it, they would end up in a crash. That, in the 'best' case. While at worst, they would be smashed to smithereens and thrown away back. The

whole point is not that Brandler wants to 'educate the masses' but that the bourgeoisie plus the Right Wing Social Democrats is bound to turn such lessons—the demonstration—into a general battle (at present all the odds are on their side) and exterminate them [the German Communists]. Of course the Fascists are not asleep; but it is to our advantage to let them attack first: that will rally the entire working class around the Communists.[15]*

Whatever the differences between the Russian leaders, they did not deny the possibility of a revolution in Germany, however unclear they were about the timing. Brandler, however, had grave doubts about the insurrectionary perspectives.

Many years later he told Isaac Deutscher:

I did not oppose the preparations for the uprising of 1923. I simply did not view the situation as acutely revolutionary yet, reckoning rather with a further sharpening. But in this affair I considered Trotsky, Zinoviev and other Russians to be more competent.[16]

In a meeting between the German leaders and the Politburo of the Russian party, Trotsky argued that the situation was so ripe for revolution that a date had to be fixed for the insurrection—as had been done in Russia on the eve of the October revolution. Elaborating on his views in an article published in **Pravda** on 23 September (and reprinted as a special issue of the central journal of the Comintern **Internationale Press-Korrespondenz**), entitled 'Is it Possible to Fix a Definite Schedule for a Counter-revolution or a Revolution?' Trotsky wrote:

Obviously, it is not possible to create artificially a political situation favourable for a...coup, much less to bring it off at a fixed date. But when the basic elements of such a situation are at hand, then the leading party does...choose beforehand a favourable moment, and synchronises accordingly its political, organisational and technical forces, and—if it has not miscalculated—deals the victorious blow.

---

*This letter is not included in Stalin's **Works**. The last sentence of the letter is a portent of the future Stalinist tactics regarding the Nazis on the eve of Hitler's victory.

...let us take our own October revolution as an example... From the moment when the Bolsheviks were in the majority of the Petrograd, and afterwards in the Moscow Soviet, our party was faced with the question—not of the struggle for power in general, but of preparing for the seizure of power according to a definite plan, and at a fixed date. The chosen day, as is well known, was the day upon which the All-Russian Congress of the Soviets was to convene.[17]

Brandler objected to the idea of a fixed date for the insurrection. (Trotsky had suggested the anniversary of the Russian revolution, 7 November), but he was sufficiently persuaded by Trotsky's appeal to suggest that Trotsky be sent to Germany to prepare the uprising. The idea enthused Trotsky, but the Troika would have none of it. The thought that Trotsky could go to Germany and return triumphant, thus dwarfing them as the acknowledged leader of both the Russian and German revolutions, terrified them, so they vetoed it.

It is interesting to speculate what the impact would have been on the history of Germany and the history of the world if Trotsky had gone to Germany!

The Collapse of the German Revolution

One issue raised during 1923 was that of German Communists joining coalition governments with Social Democrats in Saxony and Thuringia. It was presented in terms of using this action as the springboard for the revolution. Among other advantages it was hoped that the participation of Communists in the state governments would allow them to lay hands on stocks of arms. On 1 October a telegram signed by Zinoviev on behalf the Executive Committee of the Communist International was despatched to the Zentrale of the KPD:

Since we estimate the situation to be such that the decisive moment will arrive not later than in four-five-six weeks, we think it necessary to occupy at once every position which can be of immediate use [for our purposes]. On the basis of the [present] situation we must approach the question of our entry into the Saxon government in practical terms. We must enter [the Saxon goverment] on the condition that the Zeigner people are actually willing to defend Saxony against

Bavaria and the Fascists. 50,000 to 60,000 workers have to be immediately armed; ignore General Müller.* The same in Thuringia.

According to Brandler, he opposed the sending of Communists into the governments of Saxony and Thuringia, but to no avail.

I strongly objected to the attempt to hasten the revolutionary crisis by including communists in the Saxon and Thuringian governments—allegedly in order to procure weapons. I knew, and I said so in Moscow, that the police in Saxony and Thuringia did not have any stores of weapons. Even single sub-machine guns had to be ordered from the Reichswehr's arsenal near Berlin. The workers had already seized the local arsenals twice, once during the Kapp putsch, and again in part in 1921. I declared further that the entry of the communists into the government would not breathe new life into the mass actions but rather weaken them: for now the masses would expect the government to do what they could only do for themselves.

In answer to that Zinoviev thundered, banged his fist on the table and so on.

Outvoted, Brandler declared that he would submit to the decisions of the Comintern. This is how he explains his motives:

I told myself that these people had made three revolutions. To me their decisions seemed nonsensical. However, not I but they were considered seasoned revolutionaries who had achieved victory. They had made three revolutions and I was just about to try to make one. Well, I had to follow their instructions. During my return journey from Moscow to Berlin I bought a newspaper at the railway station in Warsaw. From this newspaper I learnt that I had become a Minister in the Saxon government. What a situation! Things were being done behind my back and I knew nothing. All this meant to put me before a *fait accompli*.[18]

On 10 October the Communists entered the government of

*General Müller was the newly appointed commander of the Reichswehr for Saxony.

Saxony and on the 11th, the government of Thuringia. Trotsky was as strong as any in advocating that the KPD join the coalition governments in Saxony and Thuringia. In a speech on 20 October on the events in Germany he said:

> ...The Social Democratic Party in Saxony, under the pressure of this proletariat, is the most left-wing section of the German Social Democratic Party as a whole. We put forward the slogan of the united front, and the Social Democratic workers, especially in Saxony, demanded it be realised. Under their pressure, their leaders, those Left-wing Social Democrats most of whom are articles of very dubious quality, found themselves obliged, nevertheless, to enter into a united front, a bloc, for the purpose of forming coalition governments in Saxony and Thuringia. We joined these governments as a minority: our people have two ministries (one of them is in charge of the affairs of the Council of Ministers), and the others are the majority. But the very fact of the formation of a coalition government in Saxony meant a mortal blow for German Social Democracy.[19]

The entry of Communists into a coalition government dominated by Social Democrats did not help the German revolution. Calling for common action, a united front with Social Democrats is one thing. Entering into a coalition with them where they dominate, is a different matter. Remember Lenin's stand during the Kornilov coup of 27-30 August 1917. Although Lenin called for common action with the Kerensky government against Kornilov he was very much against supporting the Kerensky government. In a letter to the Central Committee of the Bolsheviks of 30 August 1917 he stated:

> *Even now* we must not support the Kerensky government. This is unprincipled. We may be asked: aren't we going to fight against Kornilov? Of course we must! But this is not the same thing; there is a dividing line here.
>
> We shall fight, we are fighting against Kornilov, *just as* Kerensky's *troops* do, but we do not support Kerensky. *On the contrary*, we expose his weakness. There is the difference. It is rather a subtle difference, but it is highly essential and must not be forgotten.[20]

The Communists who entered the coalition governments in Saxony and Thuringia found themselves trapped by the Social Democrats, taking responsibility without power over the capitalist state machine. Instead of the governments arming the workers, they disarmed them ideologically and politically confused them.

The German government reacted strongly to the entry of Communists into the state governments of Saxony and Thuringia. On 20 October it sent an ultimatum to dissolve the 'Proletarian Hundreds'—the armed workers' militias in Saxony—and when this was refused, the order was given for the Reichswehr to march. The limited number of soldiers already in Saxony plastered the streets with the text of a letter from General Müller, the Reich's special commissar in Saxony, to the Prime Minister of Saxony, E. Zeigner. Müller, this said, had been ordered to deploy military units so as 'to restore constitutional and orderly conditions in Saxony'. E.H. Carr writes: 'The Reichswehr had done what Brandler had shrunk from doing. It had fixed the date on which the Communists must either act or confess their impotence.'[21]

All over Germany the Communist organisations were put on alert and awaited the signal for the rising. Brandler spent Sunday, 21 October, in a conference of workers' organisations in Chemnitz aimed at organising resistance to General Müller.

> Brandler insisted that now was the time for the workers of Saxony to call for assistance from the rest of Germany. Otherwise they would be destroyed. The only salvation lay in the immediate call for a national general strike of solidarity. He called on the Social Democrats to drop their vain hope of a peaceful settlement with Berlin. Only an immediate, unanimous vote for the general strike could save the situation.
>
> Brandler seems to have expected the Social Democratic leaders to agree enthusiastically. Instead he was greeted with stunned silence.
>
> Then the Social Democratic minister Graupe took the floor. The present conference, he said, could not by itself decide the response of the workers of Saxony to the army's threats. The defence of Saxony was the task of the 'Government of Republican and Proletarian Defence' and the Social Democratic-Communist majority in the state parliament. It

would be quite wrong for the present conference to usurp the power of such official bodies. If a motion was put to do so, the whole Social Democratic delegation would walk out.

Brandler had got himself—and the German revolution—into an impossible position. He had expected the Left Social Democrats to agree to a project that they well knew meant civil war...[22]

The decision was taken there and then by the KPD Zentrale to abandon the general strike—and with it the German revolution.

Emissaries were dispatched to the different parts of Germany with orders to call off the rising. By a tragic blunder the message did not reach Hamburg, and so there a few hundred Communists took up arms and fought desperately against police and troops for 48 hours. The Zeigner government abandoned office without raising a finger to defend itself. The German revolution ended in a debacle. Trotsky drew the lesson from the debacle of the German revolution in **The New Course** with these words:

> If the Communist Party had abruptly changed the pace of its work and had profited by the five or six months that history accorded it for direct political, organisational, technical preparation for the seizure of power, the outcome of the events could have been quite different from the one we witnessed in November... The proletariat should have seen a revolutionary party at work, marching to the conquest of power.
>
> But the German party continued, at bottom, its propaganda policy of yesterday, even if on a larger scale.[23]

Trotsky developed the argument further in an essay written in September 1924, **The Lessons of October**. (See Chapter Four of the present volume).

Zinoviev looked for a scapegoat for the debacle, and found it in Brandler: he removed him from the leadership of the KPD. Trotsky, who had criticised Brandler's conduct consistently, nevertheless objected in principle to Moscow instituting a guillotine for foreign Communist leaders. He wrote some time after the event:

> In this case, as in others, I fought against the inadmissible system which only seeks to maintain the infallibility of the

central leadership by periodic removals of national leader-
ships, subjecting the latter to savage persecutions and even
expulsions from the party.[24]

If the excitement of the German revolution had gripped the
mass of the workers of Russia, its defeat had a shattering impact.
Quite rightly Trotsky could write a few years later:

> The smashing of the German revolution was a most severe
> blow to our workers, weighed down upon them, put off their
> hopes for a change in their destinies until a more distant
> future. It intensified a narrow concern with local job issues,
> increased atomisation and passivity, and allowed a
> regurgitation of chauvinism, Black Hundredism, etc., to
> occur. And in response to this (although not only to this, to
> be sure) there came down from on high the theory of
> socialism in one country.[25]

Looking back, the failure of the German Revolution in 1923
can be seen to have been a turning point in world history. It was
probably the best single opportunity to seize power presented to
any working class and any Communist Party after October 1917.
The loss of this opportunity brought to an end the European-wide
revolutionary wave that followed the Russian revolution and the
First World War. It thus simultaneously consigned Russia to a
period of isolation, reinforced the tendency to bureaucratic
degeneration, permitted international capitalism to restabilise
itself and paved the way for the triumph of fascism ten years later.

Victory for the German working class would have been an
enormous, perhaps decisive, step on the road to international
socialism. Defeat signified, if not inevitably, then in all likelihood,
the postponement of the world revolution for a whole historical
period.

Chapter four
The Lessons of October

Trotsky uses history to castigate Zinoviev and Kamenev

TROTSKY COULD not reopen the controversy with Zinoviev and Kamenev without incurring the charge of violating party discipline. He kept silent throughout the summer of 1924 on the issues which separated him from the Troika. When in June he was specifically invited by the Presidium of the Fifth Congress of the Comintern to open a debate on the differences in the Russian Party, he declined on the ground that the discussion had been closed by the decision of the Russian Party Congress.[1]

But the harassment of Trotsky did not cease. Frunze, a staunch supporter of the Troika and opponent of Trotsky on the question of military doctrine, succeeded Skliansky as Deputy People's Commissar for War. In September Trotsky's private secretary, M.S. Glazman, persecuted by the Party authorities, committed suicide. Still Trotsky could not bear being branded as a semi-Menshevik, guilty of 'petty bourgeois deviation from Lenin'. Unable to discuss his differences with the Troika in terms of current issues of policy, he fell back on history to vindicate himself.

The opportunity presented itself when in the autumn of 1924 the State Publishers prepared for press a book containing his speeches and writings of 1917. He prefaced it with a long essay entitled **The Lessons of October**. Written under the influence of the recent defeat in Germany, the essay re-examined the crucial points of the Russian revolution, and related the German events to the leadership's failure to grasp the lessons of the October revolution.

Trotsky's speeches and writings of 1917 provide a sturdy reply to the accusation of his being a Menshevik, for they reminded everyone of his role in the revolution. In his review of the history of the Bolshevik Party during the October revolution, he exposed the sad role played by Zinoviev and Kamenev.

The party history, Trotsky wrote, fell into three distinct periods: the years of preparation for 1917; the decisive trial of 1917; and the post-revolutionary era. Each of these periods had problems and significance of its own.

> Numerous documents and considerable material have been issued bearing on the pre-October history of the revolution and the pre-October history of the Party. We have also issued much material and many documents relating to the post-October period. But October itself has received far less attention.[2]

It is in the second period, during 1917, that the Bolsheviks proved their claim: a revolutionary party is tested in actual revolution just as an army is tested in actual war. A Bolshevik should not be judged by what he said or did before 1917, in the course of the confused and in part 'irrelevant period of emigre politics', but what he said and did in 1917. Thus Trotsky played down his past, when he was outside the ranks of the Bolshevik Party, and emphasised his position as leader of the October revolution. By the same criterion the record of his adversaries, the 'Old Bolsheviks', Zinoviev, Kamenev (and Stalin) was evidence against them: they may have been good party members during the years of preparation, but they failed the test of 1917.

The gist of the argument in **The Lessons of October** was that a decisive leadership was crucial for the victory of the revolution. The revolutionary situation is a fleeting opportunity which the revolutionary party misses if it is paralysed by conservative inertia. Shrinking from decisive action at the decisive moment could cause the moment of workers' victory to be missed. Trotsky elaborated this theme by the experience of 1917.

He paints a picture of the conflicts in the leadership of the Bolshevik Party at the different focal points of 1917. The focal points were:

...the position of the party and of the party press in the first period after the overthrow of Tsarism and prior to the arrival of Lenin; the struggle around Lenin's thesis; the April Conference; the aftermath of the July days; the Kornilov period; the Democratic Conference and the Pre-Parliament; the question of the armed insurrection and seizure of power (September to October); and the question of a 'homogeneous' socialist government.[3]

He describes the stand of **Pravda** in March 1917 thus:

...an extreme confusion of political perspectives. As a matter of fact, during the March days, **Pravda** held a position much closer to revolutionary defencism than to the position of Lenin.

...During this same period, and even weeks earlier, Lenin, who had not yet freed himself from his Zurich cage, was thundering in his 'Letters from Afar' (most of these letters never reached **Pravda**) against the faintest hint of any concessions to defencism and conciliationism.[4]

A sad role was played by many leaders of the Bolshevik Party in April, after Lenin returned to Russia.

The problem of the conquest of power was put before the party only after April 4, that is, after the arrival of Lenin in Petrograd. But even after that moment, the political line of the party did not by any means acquire a unified and indivisible character, challenged by none. Despite the decisions of the April Conference in 1917, the opposition to the revolutionary course—sometimes hidden, sometimes open—pervaded the entire period of preparation.[5]

Trotsky turns on Zinoviev and Kamenev the imputation of Menshevism levelled against him by the Troika.

The speech which Lenin delivered at the Finland railway station on the socialist character of the Russian revolution was a bombshell to many leaders of the party. The polemic between Lenin and the partisans of 'completing the democratic revolution' began from the very first day.[6]

Trotsky points to the vacillation of Zinoviev and Kamenev on the eve of the October insurrection.

The resolution for an armed insurrection was adopted by the Central Committee on October 10. On October 11 [Lenin's] letter 'On the Current Situation'...was sent out to the most important party organisations. On October 18, that is, a week before the revolution, **Novaya Zhizn** [New Life] published a letter of Kamenev. 'Not only Comrade Zinoviev and I', we read in this letter, 'but also a number of practical comrades think that to assume the initiative of an armed insurrection at the present moment, with the given correlation of forces, independently of and several days before the Congress of Soviets is an inadmissible step ruinous to the proletariat and to the revolution'... On October 25 power was seized in Petrograd and the Soviet government was created. On November 4, a number of responsible party members resigned from the Central Committee of the party and from the Council of People's Commissars and issued an ultimatum demanding the formation of a coalition government composed of all Soviet parties.[7]

And Trotsky rounds on these opponents: 'those Bolsheviks who... were opposed to the seizure of power by the proletariat were, in point of fact, shifting to the pre-revolutionary positions of the Mensheviks'.[8]

He brings the argument up to date by contrasting the Bolshevik strategy of 1917 with what the Communists did in Germany in 1923. Germany was ripe for revolution, but the Communist leaders missed the opportunity because they succumbed to similar inertia and timidity as was shown by Zinoviev and Kamenev in 1917.

Trotsky criticises Zinoviev for playing down the crucial role of the revolutionary party. He refers to a statement by Zinoviev in his role as President of the Comintern that in Britain the proletarian revolution could come through channels other than the party. He writes:

There has been some talk lately in our press to the effect that we are not, mind you, in a position to tell through what channels the proletarian revolution will come in England. Will it come through the channel of the Communist Party or through the trade unions? Such a formulation of the question makes a show of a fictitiously broad historical outlook; it is radically false and dangerous because it obliterates the chief lesson of the last few years. If the triumphant revolution did not come at the end of the war, it was because a party was lacking....

Without a party, apart from a party, over the head of a party, or with a substitute for a party, the proletarian revolution cannot conquer. That is the principal lesson of the past decade.[9]

In this too Zinoviev deviated from the core of the Bolshevik concept of the role of the revolutionary party.

An avalanche of abuse falls on Trotsky's head

The Troika reacted to **The Lessons of October** with a savage attack involving propagandists and historians, including foreign Communist writers. The most important articles were collected in a large volume, **Za Leninizm**, the contributors being Stalin, Zinoviev, Kamenev, Bukharin, Rykov, Sokolnikov, Krupskaya, Molotov, Bubnov, Andreev, Kviring, Stepanov, Kuusinen, Kolarov, Gusev and Melnichansky.

The main line of argument was that Trotsky exaggerated the errors of Zinoviev and Kamenev in 1917, and exaggerated the importance of the role Trotsky played in that year. A major contribution was made by Kamenev, who bore the brunt of Trotsky's attack. As the editor of Lenin's **Collected Works** he had special authority. The main theme of Kamenev's outpouring was the role of Trotsky *prior* to 1917: 'From the moment of the birth of Menshevism down to its final collapse in 1917' Trotsky had played the role of 'the agent of Menshevism in the working class'. In 1905 Trotsky had made an attempt to escape from 'Menshevik negation' and 'expounded in his own words Parvus's idea of "permanent revolution" '; but the adoption of this 'Leftist phrase' did not hinder his continued collaboration with the Mensheviks. Kamenev quoted widely from Lenin's writings against Trotsky, concerning the period 1904 to 1917.

Kamenev claimed the Trotsky who entered the Bolshevik Party in 1917 was still an enemy of Leninism, of Bolshevism. His four errors after 1917 all resulted from his theory of 'permanent revolution', which led to an underestimation of the peasantry. Trotsky's policy at Brest-Litovsk had been 'an underestimation of the role of the peasantry masked by revolutionary phraseology'; Trotsky's line in the trade union controversy was an attempt to tighten the screws of War Communism in the face of peasant resistance; Trotsky's insistence on planning was inspired by a desire to establish 'the dictatorship of industry'; and Trotsky's attack in the autumn of 1923 on 'the fundamental framework of the dictatorship' through his denunciation of the party leadership and the party apparatus had been due to 'an underestimation of the conditions in which we have to realise the dictatorship in a peasant country'.

The theory of permanent revolution robbed the October revolution of historical justification (thus Kamenev predates Stalin's argument for 'socialism in one country'):

> If Trotsky's theory had proved correct, then it would mean that the Soviet power had long ago ceased to exist. Ignoring the peasantry and not giving any consideration to the decisive question of the alliance of the proletariat and the peasantry, this theory of 'permanent revolution' places the workers' government in Russia in exclusive dependence on the immediate proletarian revolution in the West.[10]

Kamenev ended with a statement: 'The party must choose between Leninism and Trotskyism'.

Zinoviev in his article denied the existence of a right wing in the Bolshevik Party opposing Lenin in 1917:

> Was there a right wing in the Bolshevik Party...? It was not possible—because the fundamental structural principles of the Bolshevik Party according to Lenin excluded the possibility of a right or left wing. [There were only] episodal differences of opinion.[11]

Zinoviev also attacked,

> the notorious theory of the permanent revolution which Comrade Trotsky is now attempting to impose upon Bolshevism. This theory was regarded by Comrade Lenin and all the Bolsheviks as a variety of *Menshevism*... The whole of Trotskyism with its theory of 'permanent' revolution was

nothing else than a cleverly thought out intellectual scheme which was developed according to the requirements of Menshevism.[12]

What is needed?

What is needed is that the party *should guarantee* itself against a repetition of 'assaults' on Leninism. Serious party guarantees are needed that the decisions of the party shall be binding on Comrade Trotsky. The party is no discussion club, but a *party*—and a party operating in the complicated environment in which ours finds itself. The watchword of the day is:

Bolshevisation of all strata of the party!

Ideological struggle against Trotskyism!

Above all, enlightenment, enlightenment and once more enlightenment![13]

Probably the most important intervention was that of Stalin. He himself was not directly attacked in **The Lessons of October**, but he felt the need to support Kamenev and Zinoviev against Trotsky. He began by arguing that Trotsky exaggerated the mistakes of Zinoviev and Kamenev in October 1917. Had the dissension been profound a split in the party could not have been avoided. 'There was no split, and the disagreements lasted only a few days, because, and only because, Kamenev and Zinoviev were Leninists, Bolsheviks.'[14]

Stalin went on to deal with Trotsky's own record. Here for the first time Stalin rewrote Trotsky's role in 1917.

I am far from denying Trotsky's undoubtedly important role in the uprising. I must say, however, that Trotsky did not play any special role in the October uprising, nor could he do so; being chairman of the Petrograd Soviet, he merely carried out the will of the appropriate Party bodies, which directed every step that Trotsky took.[15]

To play down Trotsky's role in the revolution, Stalin quoted from still unpublished minutes of a meeting of the Central Committee on 16 October of the decision to appoint a 'centre' which Stalin now described as a,

practical centre... for the organisational leadership of the uprising. Who was elected to this centre? The following five: Sverdlov, Stalin, Dzerzhinsky, Bubnov, Uritsky. The functions of the practical centre: to direct all the practical organs of the uprising in conformity with the directives of the Central Committee. Thus, as you see, something 'terrible' happened at this meeting of the Central Committee, i.e., 'strange to relate,' the 'inspirer,' the 'chief figure,' the 'sole leader' of the uprising, Trotsky, was not elected to the practical centre, which was called upon to direct the uprising. How is this to be reconciled with the current opinion about Trotsky's special role?[16]

It is interesting to note that this centre never met and was never referred to in any book, article or speech prior to the above statement of Stalin. There is no trace in the party records of any meeting of the 'centre' or of anything done or proposed by it.

Stalin goes on to play down Trotsky's role in October.

Granted, we are told, but it cannot be denied that Trotsky fought well in the period of October. Yes, that is true, Trotsky did, indeed, fight well in October; but Trotsky was not the only one who fought well in the period of October. Even people like the Left Socialist Revolutionaries, who then stood side by side with the Bolsheviks, also fought well.[17]

Stalin went further to attack the legends about Trotsky's role in the civil war.

Among these legends must be included... the very widespread story that Trotsky was the 'sole' or 'chief organiser' of the victories on the fronts of the civil war. I must declare, comrades, in the interests of truth, that this version is quite out of accord with the facts... Perhaps it will not be out of place to quote a few examples. You know that Kolchak and Denikin were regarded as the principal enemies of the Soviet Republic. You know that our country breathed freely only after those enemies were defeated. Well, history shows that both those enemies, ie., Kolchak and Denikin, were routed by our troops *in spite* of Trotsky's plan.[18]

Then Stalin threw a real bombshell. He introduced two quotations from Trotsky's hitherto unpublished letter of 1913 to the Menshevik leader Chkheidze which was intercepted by the Tsarist police and discovered in the archives in 1921 by the Commission of Party History. Trotsky wrote to Chkheidze: 'The entire edifice of Leninism at the present time is built on lies and falsification and bears within itself the poisonous elements of its own decay.' Trotsky also described Lenin as 'a profound exploiter of every kind of backwardness in the Russian working class movement'.[19]

Stalin went on to define the three basic elements of Trotskyism: (1) permanent revolution, which meant a 'revolution without taking into account the peasantry as a revolutionary force'. (2) 'Lack of faith in the party essence of Bolshevism, in its monolithic character', and (3) 'lack of faith in the leaders of Bolshevism', and especially in Lenin. Stalin concludes with a call for war on Trotskyism.

> It is the duty of the Party to bury Trotskyism as an ideological trend.
> There is talk about repressive measures against the opposition and about the possibility of a split. That is nonsense, comrades. Our Party is strong and mighty. It will not allow any splits. As regards repressive measures, I am emphatically opposed to them. What we need now is not repressive measures but extensive ideological struggle against renascent Trotskyism.[20]

Bukharin contributed his tuppence worth. He accused Trotsky of underestimating the peasantry, endangering the *smychka*—the union of the proletariat and peasantry in the building of socialism under the leadership of the party. 'The question of the worker-peasant bloc is the central question; it is the question of all questions'. Trotskyism was 'dynamite under the foundations of the party'. 'We must ideologically liquidate Trotskyism and conquer the whole party under the Leninist banner no matter what'.[21]

To undermine Trotsky's military reputation, Gusev wrote an article which, no doubt ironically, borrowed the title of Trotsky's own collection of articles and speeches on the civil war—'How the Revolution Armed'—and gave examples of Trotsky's high-handed behaviour during the civil war.

Krupskaya, while expressing doubts as to whether Trotsky

had 'really committed all the mortal sins of which he is accused', still joined in criticising him, writing: 'Marxist analysis was never Comrade Trotsky's strong point. This is the reason why he so underestimates the role played by the peasantry.' At the same time Krupskaya was not ready to forget Trotsky's past contributions: 'Comrade Trotsky devoted the whole of his powers to fight for Soviet power during the decisive years of the revolution. He held out heroically in his difficult and responsible position. He worked with unexampled energy and accomplished wonders in the interests of safeguarding the victory of the revolution. The party will not forget this.'[22] Despite all the reservations in her article, the criticism of Krupskaya, who was Lenin's widow, had the most damaging impact on Trotsky's standing among the mass of the rank and file.

1923 Opposition shattered

Support for Trotsky was completely broken. While in the previous winter Moscow had been the principal centre of his support—with about half the party members behind him—this support now completely collapsed.

In September 1924, at the insistence of Zinoviev and Kamenev, a new secretary, N.A. Uglanov, was appointed to the Moscow party, with a mandate to clean up the party organisation. He quickly showed radical results. A party conference of the Moscow region, attended by over 1,100 delegates, unanimously condemned Trotsky.[23] The Opposition failed to capture a single cell or district organisation in Moscow.[24] In all the districts of Moscow the Opposition was practically annihilated. Thus, for instance, in the Baumanskii district, while in 1923, 40 per cent of the organisation supported Trotsky, in 1924 the figure was a mere 1 per cent.[25] Other party organisations followed: the Ukrainian and Belorussian parties hastened to denounce Trotsky. So did the Leningrad city and provincial party committees, the Kharkov provincial party committee, and many, many others. The Central Committee of the Komsomol followed suit.

The stream of literature denouncing Trotsky met with practically no resistance. Trotsky's **The Lessons of October** was published in an edition of only 5,000 copies, and when the discussion was at its height, was virtually unobtainable, fuelling a rumour that it was officially banned.[26]

Foreign Communist Parties were also mobilised in the campaign against Trotsky. The German, French, Polish, Czech, Balkan and American parties joined in his denunciation. The most crushing blow of the whole campaign was the publication in **Pravda** on 9 December of the full text of Trotsky's 1913 letter to Chkheidze. Years later, in his autobiography Trotsky wrote:

> ...the masses of the people were torn with grief over the death of their leader... With no idea of the yesterdays of the party, the people read Trotsky's hostile remarks about Lenin and were stunned. It is true that the remarks had been made twelve years before, but chronology was disregarded in the face of the naked quotations. The use that the epigones made of my letter to Chkheidze is one of the greatest frauds in the world's history.[27]

Very few party members remembered the conditions in the movement in 1913. By 1923 only 10,000 of the old Bolsheviks remained[28] and not all of them were still active. As only 1 per cent of the party members were members before 1917, the fact that the Bolsheviks and Mensheviks did belong to the same party for many years was practically unknown. Few party members now remembered what had happened when Lenin returned to Petrograd in April 1917. Fewer still knew the details of the controversies before and after the seizure of power in October. The fact that Trotsky did not belong to the Bolshevik Party prior to 1917 was a complete shock. The masses were astonished to hear that Trotsky was once a Menshevik or semi-Menshevik, and accepted the Troika's argument that once a Menshevik always a Menshevik.

Trotsky's reaction to the assault

Trotsky's reaction to the savage assault was very unsure. In November 1924 he wrote a document which was a lengthy point-by-point rejoinder to his critics. It was headed 'The Purpose of this Explanation' with a subtitle 'Our Differences'. He repeated previous admissions that he was wrong in his opposition to Lenin in the years before he joined the Bolshevik Party. But he then went on to accuse Kamenev of unfair use of quotations from Lenin:

> Comrade Kamenev has gathered together with great care all

the quotations from Lenin that expose the error of my views. Kamenev turns the polemical blows dealt by Lenin over a number of years into the definitive characterisation of my politics. But the reader is bound to get the impression that this characterisation is incomplete. Thus the reader will find absolutely no answer here to the question of whether my revolutionary activity (before 1914 or before 1917) consisted only of mistakes, or whether there were features that linked me with Bolshevism, pointed toward it, and led me to it. Without an answer to that question, the character of my later role in party work remains totally inexplicable. Besides that, Kamenev's characterisation unavoidably gives rise to questions of another order, ones of a purely factual nature. *Are what Kamenev compiled the only things Lenin said or wrote on the subject? Aren't there other comments by Lenin as well, comments that are based on the experience of the revolutionary years? Is it really fair and honest now, in late 1924, to tell the party only about the comments of pre-revolutionary years, and and say nothing about the comments flowing from our joint work and struggle?* These are questions that must inevitably occur to every serious reader. Old quotations will not suffice. They will only encourage people to conclude that tendentiousness and bias are involved.[29]

Trotsky repeated his criticism of Kamenev's errors in 1917. He defended himself against the charge of ignoring the peasantry, and argued that the danger to the *smychka* was two-fold. It might result from an attempt to put too great a burden on the peasant. But there was also an opposite danger:

If conditions develop in such a way that the proletariat is forced to bear too many sacrifices in order to preserve the alliance, if the working class came to the conclusion over a number of years that in the name of preserving its political dictatorship it had been forced to agree to excessive self-denial of its class interests, that would undermine the Soviet state from the other direction.[30]

The tempo of industrialisation was subject to objective limitations which must be observed.

...no less danger would arise if industry *lagged behind* the economic upturn of the rest of the country. That would give rise inevitably to the phenomena of a goods famine and high retail prices, which would inevitably lead in turn to the enrichment of private capital.[31]

Trotsky did not publish the document 'Our Differences' because he was worried that it might promote an even further escalation of the accusations against him. He wrote:

> If I thought that my explanation might add fuel to the fire of the discussion, or if the comrades on whom the printing of this essay depends were to tell me so openly and directly I would not publish it, however burdensome it may be to remain under the charge of liquidating Leninism. I would tell myself that my only recourse was to wait until a calmer flow of party life allowed the opportunity, if only a belated one, to refute the untrue accusation.[32]

As neither this memorandum nor anything penned by Trotsky was published, **Pravda** could publish a brief editorial note stating: 'In response to questions from a number of comrades, no articles have been received from Trotsky or his closest associates in reply to the published criticism of Trotskyism.'[33]

In the years 1917 to 1923 there was no mention of Trotskyism. Trotskyism was now being invented by Zinoviev, Kamenev and Stalin. The discussions which took place at this time among the Troika and their supporters were partially disclosed two years later when the Troika split up. Zinoviev explained: **'The Lessons of October** served only as a pretext. Failing that a different motive would have been found, and the discussion would have assumed somewhat different forms, nothing more'. 'The trick was to string together all disagreements with new issues. For this purpose "Trotskyism" was invented.' Kamenev explained 'how and why the Trotskyist danger had been invented for the purpose of an organised struggle against Trotsky'. Lashevich stated: 'We invented "Trotskyism" in the struggle against Trotsky'.[34]

It seems that the fierceness of the assault on him and his own isolation paralysed Trotsky's will to fight. In his autobiography he wrote:

> Lying in bed, I went over my old articles, and my eyes fell on these lines written in 1909, at the peak of the reactionary

regime under Stolypin:

'When the curve of historical development rises, public thinking becomes more penetrating, braver and more ingenious. It grasps facts on the wing, and on the wing links them with the thread of generalisation... But when the political curve indicates a drop, public thinking succumbs to stupidity. The priceless gift of political generalisation vanishes somewhere without leaving even a trace. Stupidity grows in insolence, and, baring its teeth, heaps insulting mockery on every attempt at a serious generalisation. Feeling that it is in command of the field, it begins to resort to its own means.'

One of its most important means is slander.

I say to myself that we are passing through a period of reaction. A political shifting of the classes is going on, as well as a change in class consciousness... The deep molecular processes of reaction are emerging to the surface. They have as their object the eradicating, or at least the weakening, of the dependence of the public consciousness on the ideas, slogans and living figures of October. That is the meaning of what is now taking place.[35]

Gigantic social forces were condemning Trotsky to defeat, and he was too clear-sighted not to see this.

Some of my friends used to say to me: 'They will never dare to come out against you in the open. In the minds of the people you are too inseparably bound to Lenin's name. It is impossible to erase the October revolution or the Red army or the civil war'. I did not agree with this. In politics, and especially in revolutionary politics, popular names of acknowledged authority play a very important, sometimes gigantic, but yet not decisive part. In the final analysis, the fate of personal authority is determined by the deeper processes going on in the masses. During the rising tide of the revolution the slanders against the Bolshevik leaders only strengthened the Bolsheviks. During the ebb tide of the revolution the slanders against the same men were able to provide the weapons of victory for the Thermidorean reaction.[36]

'Socialism in one country'

The campaign against Trotsky's permanent revolution acted as a springboard for Stalin's launching of the concept of 'socialism in one country'.

On 20 December 1924 **Pravda** and **Izvestiia** carried an article by Stalin entitled 'October and Comrade Trotsky's Theory of Permanent Revolution' which for the first time contained his formulation of the new doctrine of 'Socialism in One Country'.[37]

Until Lenin's death, no one in the Bolshevik Party suggested that Russia could build socialism by her own unaided effort. Lenin himself repeatedly emphasised the opposite. 'The Russian revolution', he wrote on 4 June 1918, 'was due not to the special merits of the Russian proletariat, but to the course of historic events, and this proletariat was placed temporarily in the leading position by the will of history and made for a time the vanguard of the world revolution.'[38]

'We always staked our play upon an international revolution and this was unconditionally right... we always emphasized...*the fact that in one country it is impossible to accomplish such a work as a socialist revolution.*[39]*

Even after Lenin's death Stalin, who later propounded the idea of 'socialism in one country', said:

> ...to overthrow the power of the bourgeoisie and establish that of the proletariat in a single country is still not to assure the complete victory of Socialism. The chief task, the organisation of Socialist production, is still to be accomplished. Can we succeed and secure the definitive victory of Socialism in one country without the combined effort of the proletarians of several advanced countries? Most certainly not. The efforts of a single country are enough to overthrow the bourgeoisie: this is what the history of our revolution proves. But for the definitive triumph of Socialism, the organisation of Socialist production, the efforts of one country alone are not enough, particularly of an essentially rural country like Russia; the efforts of the proletariat of several advanced countries are needed.[41]**(see next page)

---

*My emphasis. These words are struck out of the fourth edition of Lenin's **Sochineniia**.[40]

Marxism has always envisaged socialism in international terms, because it held that historical advance is associated with greater and greater economic integration on an ever larger scale. The rising bourgeoisie overcame local particularism and established the national market and the national state. The development of the productive forces under capitalism outgrew the national boundaries. As Marx and Engels wrote in the **Communist Manifesto**:

> Modern industry has established the world market...[which] has given an immense development to commerce, navigation, and communication by land... The need of a constantly expanding market for its products chases the bourgeoisie over the whole surface of the globe... The bourgeoisie has given...a cosmopolitan character to production and consumption in every country. *To the great chagrin of reactionaries, the bourgeoisie has drawn from under the feet of industry the national ground on which it stood... In place of the old local and national seclusion and self-sufficiency we now have the many-sided intercourse of nations and their universal interdependence.* [My emphasis] [43]

If capitalism could not restrict itself to national boundaries, then socialism certainly could not.

The doctrine of 'socialism in one country' was cobbled up by Stalin as a weapon against Trotsky's permanent revolution. Trotsky himself accepted the antithesis: 'The theory of socialism in one country...is the only theory that consistently and to the very end opposes the theory of the permanent revolution.'[44]

Bukharin was the first to pick up Stalin's formula and give it theoretical support.[45] For the first time the concept of 'socialism in one country' was included in the text of a party resolution at the Fourteenth Party Congress (December 1925) where it called for 'the struggle against the lack of faith in the building of socialism in one country'.[46] At this stage, as we shall see later, the

---

In the second Russian edition of Stalin's book, **The Theory and Practice of Leninism, which appeared in December 1924, the above section is omitted, and instead one reads: 'Having consolidated its power, and taking the lead of the peasantry, the proletariat of the victorious country, can and must build society... Such, in general, are the characteristic features of the Leninist theory of the proletarian revolution'.[42]

doctrine was opposed by Zinoviev and Kamenev.

Stalin and Bukharin completely distorted Trotsky's position on the question of socialism in one country. They pretended that Trotsky 'had no faith' in socialism, and in socialist construction in the Soviet Union, distorting Trotsky's argument that 'for the construction of a socialist society in the Soviet Union a victory of the proletarian revolution is necessary in one or more of the advanced capitalist countries and that the final victory of socialism in one country, and above all a backward country, is impossible.'[47]

To Trotsky it was clear that the doctrine of 'socialism in one country' fitted the mood of the rising bureaucracy which longed for 'business as usual' not complicated by revolutionary 'adventures'. As he put it:

> The large-scale defeats of the European proletariat, and the first very modest economic successes of the Soviet Union suggested to Stalin, in the autumn of 1924, the idea that the historic mission of the Soviet bureaucracy was to build socialism in a single country... It expressed unmistakably the mood of the bureaucracy. When speaking of the victory of socialism, they meant their own victory.[48]

Some of Stalin's supporters saw in the theory of 'socialism in one country' an opiate for the workers. Thus the economist E. Varga, always adaptable, told Trotsky in 1926: 'Obviously, this theory is false, but it gives the Russian worker a view of the future and sustains his morale. If the Russian worker were sufficiently mature to be inspired by international perspectives, we would not have needed the theory of socialism in one country.'[49]

The mood of the bureaucracy was not out of step with that of the rank and file of the party and the mass of the working class, who had become wary of the expectation of international revolution, which had been dashed in 1917, 1918 and 1920, to rise again in 1923 and shatter once more with the German defeat. Now Stalin appealed to stability, to the longing for peace which dominated the tired workers who had gone through years of war and civil war.

Stalin called Trotsky an 'adventurer', an epithet which stuck among those who were looking for a quiet life. He described Trotsky as the Don Quixote of Communism who might involve the party and government in the most dangerous escapades. The

Russian workers were tired and could not but reject the sweeping historical perspective Trotsky held out before them.

The debate around **The Lessons of October** massively damaged Trotsky's authority and standing. It also had a great effect on the members of the Troika. It badly discredited Zinoviev and Kamenev while leaving Stalin untouched. As a matter of fact, his prestige was enhanced as a result. Trotsky concentrated his attack on Zinoviev and Kamenev who had openly opposed the October revolution, while Stalin's position was far more elusive. Indeed Zinoviev and Kamenev now needed Stalin's testimonial that they were good Bolsheviks. This helped Stalin to establish himself as the senior member of the Troika. Thus, unintentionally, Trotsky helped to defeat his future allies and to promote his most dangerous adversary.

A Pause

On 15 January 1925 Trotsky broke his silence. He addressed a letter to the Central Committee in preparation for its forthcoming session. In it he made it clear that he did not intend to continue with the struggle to influence the party.

> I have not spoken once on the controversial questions settled by the Thirteenth Congress of the party, either in the Central Committee or in the Council of Labour and Defence, and I certainly have never made any proposal outside of leading party and Soviet institutions that would directly or indirectly raise questions that have already been decided.[50]

> Even now, weighing the whole progress of the discussion and in spite of the fact that throughout it many false and even monstrous charges have been brought forward against me, I think that my silence was correct from the standpoint of the general interests of the party.[51]

Trotsky also distanced himself from the theory of permanent revolution.

> ...the formula 'permanent revolution'...applies wholly to the past... If at any time after October I had occasion, for private reasons, to revert to the formula 'permanent revolution' it

was only a reference to party history, ie., to the past, and had no reference to the present-day political tasks.[52]

He ended his letter with an offer to resign from the post of People's Commissar of War.

At the Plenum of the Central Committee and the Central Control Commission Zinoviev pushed for the expulsion of Trotsky from the party. When this move failed he and Kamenev proposed to expel Trotsky from the Politburo. This was opposed by Stalin, Bukharin, Kalinin, Voroshilov and Ordzhonikidze.

At the Fourteenth Party Congress (December 1925)—after Zinoviev and Kamenev broke with Stalin, Stalin explained what had happened at the July 1925 Plenum:

> The group of Leningrad comrades [led by Zinoviev] at first proposed that Trotsky be expelled from the Party... We disagreed with Zinoviev and Kamenev because we knew that the policy of amputation was fraught with great dangers for the Party, that this method of amputation, the method of blood-letting—and they demanded blood—was dangerous, infectious: today you amputate one limb, tomorrow another, the day after tomorrow a third—what will we have left in the Party?[53]

This explanation is very interesting in the light of future 'amputations' and 'blood-letting' carried out by Stalin.

Trotsky's resignation from the chairmanship of the Commissariat of War was unanimously accepted.[54] The justification for this was given in a long resolution drafted by Zinoviev, charging Trotsky with 'anti-Bolshevism', supporting the theory of permanent revolution, and factionalism. It warned Trotsky that it would be impossible for him to remain on the Political Bureau if he continued to violate party discipline. The resolution was passed with two abstentions by members of the Central Committee, Rakovsky and Piatakov, and one abstention by a member of the Central Control Commission, Pravdin. Krupskaya was a member of the Central Control Commission and evidently voted for the resolution.

After the resignation there was a lull in Trotsky's inner-party struggle. This lasted throughout the year 1925 and into the summer of 1926.

The 1923 Opposition practically disbanded. 'For the moment we must not act at all', Trotsky advised his followers, 'no showing ourselves in public but keep our contacts, preserve our cadres of 1923, and wait for Zinoviev to exhaust himself...'[55]

Trotsky completely gave up any immediate struggle. He became so detached from party affairs that he spent his time in the Central Committee sessions reading books—French novels![56]

How desperately anxious he and his adherents were to avoid any renewal of struggle can be seen from the following incident.

At the beginning of 1925 Max Eastman—the American Communist sympathiser who had been in Moscow from the autumn of 1923 to June 1924, was known as a sympathiser of Trotsky and had received information about the struggle in the party from Trotsky himself—wrote a book entitled **Since Lenin Died**. Eastman began by recalling Trotsky's intimate relations with Lenin since 1917; mentioned a letter received by Trotsky from Krupskaya a few days after Lenin's death, in which she assured Trotsky that Lenin's attitude to him had not changed since the time of their first meeting in London in 1902 till the day of Lenin's death; described and quoted from Lenin's Testament, and then gave a detailed account of the struggle of the Troika against Trotsky, beginning in December 1923 and ending with Trotsky's removal from the leadership of the Red Army in January 1925.

The Politburo insisted that Trotsky sign a statement denying the story about Lenin's Testament. In order to prevent a renewal of the inner-party struggle, Trotsky complied, denied what he knew to be true, and thus aided the campaign of falsification directed against himself. He wrote:

> Eastman asserts in several places that the Central Committee has 'concealed' from the party a large number of documents of extraordinary importance, written by Lenin during the last period of his life. (The documents in question are letters on the national question, the famous 'Testament', etc.) This is pure slander against the Central Committee of our party. Eastman's words convey the impression that Lenin wrote these letters, which are of an advisory character and deal with the inner-party organisation, with the intention of having them published. This is not at all in accordance with the facts. Comrade Lenin has not left any 'Testament'... All talk with

regard to a concealed or mutilated 'Testament' is nothing but a despicable lie, directed against the real will of Comrade Lenin and against the interests of the party created by him.[57]

And Trotsky ends his statement with these words:

Whatever Eastman's intentions may be, this botched piece of work is none the less objectively a tool of the counter-revolution, and can only serve the ends of the enemies incarnate of communism and of the revolution.[58]

Three years later, on 11 September 1928, in a letter from Alma-Ata to N.I. Muranov, Trotsky described what had actually led him to sign the above statement:

During the time when the Opposition still figured on correcting the party line by strictly internal means without bringing the controversy out in the open, all of us, including myself, were opposed to steps Max Eastman had taken for the defence of the Opposition. In the autumn of 1925 the majority in the Politburo foisted upon me a statement concocted by themselves containing a sharp condemnation of Max Eastman. Insofar as the entire leading group of the Opposition considered it inadvisable at that time to initiate an open political struggle, and steered toward making a number of concessions, it naturally could not initiate and develop the struggle over the private question of Eastman who had acted, as I said, on his own accord and at his own risk. That is why, *upon the decision of the leading group of the Opposition*, I signed the statement on Max Eastman *foisted upon me by the majority of the Politburo* with the ultimatum: either sign the statement as written or enter into an open struggle on this account.[59]*

Caught on the horns of a dilemma—how to fight the bureaucracy while avoiding factionalism, with the workers tired and passive and himself very isolated—Trotsky gave way to the pressure of the Troika and tragically he denounced Eastman. He thus strengthened Stalin's hand and further weakened his own.

---

*Sadly, Krupskaya was inveigled into discrediting Eastman (and at the same time Trotsky). In a letter to the British left wing paper **The Sunday Worker** she denounced Eastman's book as, 'a collection of all sorts of common slanders'. She wrote the following about Lenin's 'Letters to the Party Congress':

'Max Eastman relates all sorts of fables about these letters (calling them a 'testament'). M. Eastman completely misunderstands the spirit of our party... [Lenin's] speeches at congresses were always marked by special seriousness and thoughtfulness. His letters on internal party relations (the 'testament') were also written for the party congress... This letter contained among other things character sketches of some of the most respected party comrades. The letters imply no kind of lack of confidence in those comrades to whom Lenin was bound by long years of common work... The letters were intended to help the comrades who remained to direct the work along the right line, and for this reason the shortcomings of these comrades, including Trosky, were noted, side by side with their merits, since these had to be taken into account in order to organise the work of the leading group of the party. All the members of the congress were acquainted with the letters, as V.I. desired.'

Krupskaya ended rather abruptly by recalling her own past differences with Trotsky. She had been against him and for the Central Committee in the controversy started by **The Lessons of October**.[60]

Chapter five
Trotsky on culture

WE HAVE seen that Trotsky was forced again and again to hold back from direct confrontation with the ruling group. But even with his hands tied behind his back he did not give up the struggle. Instead he used Aesopian language and also took the fight into fields peripheral to the main struggle. Even then his brilliance and the strength of his analysis made a valuable contribution to Marxist thought.

The proletariat that took power in 1917 was tiny, a mere three million industrial workers in a population of 160 million. Over 70 per cent of the population were illiterate. Cultural pauperism of this dimension, without massive aid from more advanced countries after their own successful socialist revolutions, is incompatible with the masses' ability to emancipate themselves and construct a socialist society.

The aim of socialism is the maximum all-round development of human potential; human needs and desires are its motive force (as against profit under capitalism).

After millennia of suppression of the toiling masses' personality, the revolution saw its first stirrings. Indeed, according to Trotsky, the prime achievement of the revolution was the 'awakening of human personality in the masses—who were supposed to possess no personality'.[1] The revolutionary government saw it as its task to nurture this awakening upon which the future of socialism depended. The preamble to the first systematic Education Act of 16 October 1918 echoed Trotsky in stating: 'The personality shall remain as the highest value in the socialist culture,'[2] and towards its development the Bolshevik government gave whatever resources it could spare to education—for people of all ages—which, after the war effort, was given one of the largest shares of the budget.

The awakening personality of the revolutionary vanguard of the proletariat unleashed a great thirst for knowledge, eagerness for experiment, imaginative leaps and immense creativity. But these heroic efforts were small islands in the vast sea of illiteracy and obscurantism which swamped most of the country. How to bridge the vast chasm between the immensely idealistic aims of the revolution and the barbarous backwardness of the masses that hampered their ability to shape society in their own interests, inevitably became a key problem for the Bolshevik leaders. It is not surprising therefore that passionate debates on the way forward for culture and art formed a prominent feature of the early post-revolutionary period until the late 1920s, and that most of the leading Bolsheviks participated with vehemence in this fight for the 'soul' of the revolution.

Foremost among these was Trotsky. He had always been interested in a wide variety of cultural and artistic activities, even stealing time to read novels when, as commander of the Red Army during the civil war, he raced round the country in his armoured train. When the guns fell silent and the ruling group constrained his political expression he turned to serving the revolution 'not by politics alone', but by applying himself to cultural, artistic, educational, social and other activities relevant to the elimination of Russia's historic barbarism and the cultivation of the 'human personality' of the masses.

The debates around culture and art exposed two main problems arising from the huge contradiction between Russia's highest political achievement and lowest cultural level in Europe (neatly encapsulated in an observation by Trotsky that the Soviet Union had from its heritage both the largest library in the world in Leningrad—through expropriation by the revolution of private libraries—and the lowest level of literacy in Europe). The first was that the backwardness and lack of confidence of the masses could encourage the growth of bureaucracy which found its *raison d'etre* in and thrived on just such a situation. This would push the masses back into passivity and lead to the degeneration of the revolution. The second was the apparently opposite danger of voluntarism— declaring the creation of a new proletarian culture while the masses were still illiterate. In fact this dovetailed with the first problem, suggesting a form of cultural 'socialism in one country'.

Trotsky took on board both these problems, insisting on the need for the peasants and workers to struggle to raise their cultural level, thereby holding back bureaucratic arrogance; and denouncing voluntarism in culture expressed in the Proletkult movement, as he had denounced voluntarism in military affairs expressed in the Proletarian Military Doctrine, and in other areas of life.

The first problem he dealt with both in a series of articles written in the summer of 1923, which were collected in a book called **Problems of Everyday Life** and subsequent publications, and in speaking to meetings of workers in many varied fields on aspects of the subject. The range of topics he covers is astonishingly broad. He takes up questions of philosophy, science, technology, bibliography, philology, stenography, religion, social and individual psychology, literature, library work, the position of women and the family, and much more. All problems are separately dealt with in concrete, often grubby, detail, while taken together the whole book reaches for the stars. This work is unique in Marxist literature, both as the Russian revolution alone exposed concrete examples of the extremes of greatness and smallness, and because few of the revolutionary leaders could span the gulf conceptually.

The proletariat had carried out a successful revolution on the economic and political fronts. But, while this would provide the necessary base for the rise of culture among the masses, and would be untrammelled by capitalist obstructions, a passive wait for the new organisation of the labour process by itself to achieve change would not solve the problems of building socialism. What was needed was constant, active agitation among the masses to consciously reconstruct the mode of life—in effect a cultural revolution.

The active initiative of the masses in cultural change is Trotsky's constant theme in **Problems of Everyday Life**. From that it follows that his criterion for society's cultural advance is the progress of the weakest, most backward elements of society. The revolution, he says, is marked with a growing respect for the personal dignity of every individual, with an ever-increasing concern for those who are weak. Referring to 'the average colourless individual of the working masses' he says: 'The greater his helplessness, ie, the greater his ignorance and illiteracy, the greater attention should be accorded him.'[3] In a speech to workers who wrote reports to newspapers he repeats: 'To arouse the slumbering minds of their most backward fellow workers is the first and foremost task for all worker correspondents'.[4] Without this, the major objective of the soviet state—'to draw the broad popular masses into government and to teach them to rule', an objective 'we must not under any circumstances lose sight of'—would be unattainable.[5]

To help the awakened personality grow and become cultured Trotsky stresses the importance of not relying on the state alone. 'The fetish of the state, even though it be a proletarian state, does not become us Marxists,'[6] he observes, 'No government, even the most alive and enterprising, can possibly transform life without the broadest initiative of the masses'.[7] The state prepares the essentials of a plan, but cannot use one hundredth of the interests, forces, energies that the masses of the population can bring to bear on its evolution. The viability, verification, vitality and concrete benefit of the plan depend upon the extent that the voluntary initiatives of the worker and peasant masses have been put into its drawing up and carrying out. Writing of this in August 1923, he cites examples of successful local or federal voluntary groups and associations which had already been set up in the domains of industry, of daily custom, of worker correspondents, of proletarian and peasant writers. Close to his heart was a 'Society of Friends of the Red Cinema' which he hoped would become a powerful revolutionary institution,[8] successfully competing with the tavern and the Church for the workers' entertainment and desire for celebration. It could thus combat drunkenness and religious obscurantism.

It is in the more intimate problems of everyday living that there is an urgent need to, firstly, break the silence surrounding them, then for agitation among the masses 'through their vanguard elements to examine their way of life, to think about it critically, to *understand* the need for change and to firmly *want* to change.'[9]

Trotsky does not merely preach active participation of the masses, struggle from below, rousing the weakest and most backward in society. He goes into great detail in attempting to show how these goals may be achieved. The titles of some of his articles indicate this attention to detail: 'Civility and Politeness as a Necessary Lubricant in Daily Relations', 'The Struggle for Cultured Speech', 'How to Begin', 'Attention to Trifles', 'Alas, We are not Accurate Enough', 'Big and Small', 'A Few Words on How to Raise a Human Being'.

This element of active struggle by the masses against Russia's barbaric heritage runs like a red thread through all Trotsky's pronouncements on culture. Its validity lies not only in the fact that it is in itself the quickest and surest way of raising social consciousness and securely implanting higher cultural standards in the masses, but also in that it holds back the further encroachment of the bureaucracy, which at the time had already entrenched itself to some considerable degree. Imperative is a 'remorseless struggle against red tape, against official contempt for the living human being and his affairs'.[10] He mentions a practical step that could be taken against bureaucratic arrogance:

> ...single out a hundred civil servants—single them out thoroughly and impartially—a hundred who showed a rooted contempt in their duties for the working masses, and publicly, perhaps by trial, chuck them out of the state machine, so that they could never come back again. Do not expect miracles as a result, but it would be a good beginning—a small change from the old to the new is a practical step in advance, which is of greater value than the biggest talk.[11]

Giving another example of progressive action in 'The Struggle for Cultured Speech', he looks hopefully at the inititive of the Paris Commune shoe factory workers who passed a motion to abstain from swearing, imposing fines for bad language, etc. If this were taken up in the working class, it could have telling consequences for the advance of cultured speech.Trotsky goes on to analyse why the Russian language was so outstanding among languages in its 'loose, sticky and low terms of abuse'.

> Abusive language and swearing are a legacy of slavery, humiliation, and disrespect for human dignity—one's own and that of other people...

He then differentiates between the swearing of the different classes:

Russian swearing in the 'lower depths' was the result of despair, embitterment, and, above all, slavery without hope, without escape. The swearing of the upper classes, on the other hand, the swearing that came out of the throats of the gentry, the authorities, was the outcome of class rule, slaveowner's pride, unshakeable power.

In this context, the Paris Commune's decision was 'a small incident in the turmoil of the present day—but a very telling small incident'.[12]

In all the gatherings Trotsky addressed in the early and middle 1920s his purpose was not to praise or censure the workers, but to show how through their particular job they could influence other workers and advance their culture. For instance, in a speech to the First All-Union Congress of Librarians in July 1924 he insists 'a librarian is not an official dealing with books but rather he is, must be, must become a cultural warrior... fighting for socialist culture'.[13] He compares the countries of Europe—under the hypnosis of a powerful bourgeois culture—with backward Russia, whose 'bourgeoisie was such a miserable historical epigone that during the last few decades everything grand and important in all classes gravitated not to the bourgeoisie but to the workers'. History bore out the first part of his prophecy that, in consequence, 'In Europe it will be incomparably more difficult for the proletariat to come to power, for the enemy is stronger; but when it does come to power it will be incomparably easier for it to build socialism, for it will receive a much larger inheritance. Greater culture, a greater development of technology...'[14]

Russia was producing less than 500 newspapers with 2 million readers, while the US, with a population 20 million smaller, had 20,000 papers with a circulation of 250 million. It was necessary to work hard at bridging the cultural gap, and the government, untrammelled by bourgeois restrictions, would help. 57 per cent of people even in European Russia were illiterate—not to speak of the far more backward hinterland. Even those who could read were largely not very fluent and lacked the knowledge of which books to read and the skill to find them. 'And since our reader cannot find his book, our book must find its reader. This is a librarian's task!'[15]

He goes on relentlessly urging the library workers to reach out to the working masses:

> That library worker is not a library worker of a socialist country if he is simply in charge of a shelf of books and so does not manage to listen to the requests of his readers and serve as an organ of transmission of what he has heard to higher bodies—to bring pressure to bear on the writer and the publishers.[16]

The librarian thus becomes a shield and friendly intermediary between the awakened but yet unconfident reader and the bureaucracy. To assist the nervous new readers further a complaints bureau should be built in libraries where 'every peasant, male or female—and first and foremost those who fear the Soviet official—will feel he can consult the librarian, the "izbach", without feeling he will be let down or have a dirty trick played on him; a librarian who will advise him, write to a newspaper, make public his grievance, defend him'.

Trotsky engages the librarians' feelings of solidarity by explaining:

> To kill the feeling of defencelessness in a person crushed by centuries of hard labour means killing tyranny in the same stroke, and tyranny, it goes without saying, is incompatible with that regime which we are building but are still a long way from completing.[17]

The 'izbach' referred to above is a librarian running a village reading room in a hut. Trotsky looks to their wide proliferation to spread literacy among the peasants and Red Army men, and earnestly describes, in minutest detail, how the 'izbach', 'having gathered around as many people as possible', could with the newest issue of a newspaper, map on wall, reference book at hand, help and instruct the unlearned. 'Such a hut reading room will be an irreplaceable school of Leninism'.[18]

Trotsky deals in this amount of detail, and with great sympathy and understanding, with a host of everyday problems, seeking always the simplest way to activate the people involved, as workers or citizens, to make changes happen, where necessary against indifference at the higher official level.

On 18 October 1923 he wrote a piece called 'Big and Small'.

The 'Big' was the German revolution just broken out and causing enormous excitement in Russia. The 'Small' was bothering about 'everyday life' and other day-to-day matters. To isolate each, dismissing one because of the importance of the other, was 'to distort history, to make a living revolutionary tradition into an abstract canon'.[19]

Trotsky, in his person, was the living embodiment of 'Big' and 'Small'.

It is natural that Trotsky, looking always at the progress of the most backward, the weakest, among the workers and peasants as the criterion for society's advance towards socialism, should have particular regard for the well-being of the most downtrodden of Russia's oppressed millions—women and children—and constantly seek ways of pulling them out of their age-old bondage through their own efforts and activity, aided by liberating government edicts. In all his exhortations to workers to actively work at changing conditions, the woman, or the mother and child, come in for particular attention.

A few quotations out of a rich multitude will indicate Trotsky's attitude to women's burdened past, the present possibilities, and the need for women themselves to take up the struggle for their future liberation:

> A revolution does not deserve its name if with all its might and all the means at its disposal, it does not help the woman—twofold and threefold enslaved as she has been in the past to get out on the road of individual and social progress.[20]

How to evaluate a society?

> The most accurate way of measuring our advance is by the practical measures which are being carried out for the improvement of the position of mother and child... It will be possible to evaluate a human society by the attitude it has toward woman, toward the mother and toward the child.[21]

And not only evaluate:

> In order to change the conditions of life we must learn to see them through the eyes of women.[22]

> ...woman is the coolie of the family...it is impossible to move

forward while leaving the woman far in the rear... Just as it was impossible to approach the construction of the Soviet state without freeing the peasantry from the tangles of serfdom, so it is impossible to move to socialism without freeing the peasant woman and the woman worker from the bondage of family and household...freeing from bondage the mother in penal servitude... To build socialism means to emancipate women and protect mothers.[23]

While addressing the question of the liberation of all women, Trotsky pays particular attention to the most downtrodden.

The central task in the transformation of everyday life is the liberation of women, forced as they have been into the role of mere beasts of burden by the old conditions of the family, household and economy. In the East, in the countries of Islam, this task is imposed more acutely than anywhere else in the world.[24]

After stating the problem, Trotsky looks into ways of solving it. It needs to be understood that,

The problem of women's emancipation, both material and spiritual, is closely tied to that of the transformation of family life. It is necessary to remove the bars from those confining and suffocating cages into which the present family structure drives women, turning her into a slave, if not a beast of burden.

He then shows the way towards liberation:

There are two paths leading to the transformation of everyday family life: from below and from above. 'From below' denotes the path of combining the resources and efforts of individual families, the path of building enlarged family units with kitchens, laundries, etc., in common. 'From above' denotes the path of initiative by the state or by local Soviets in building group workers' quarters, communal restaurants, laundries, nurseries, etc. Between these two paths, in a workers' and peasants' state, there can be no contradiction; one ought to supplement the other... The work must be carried on simultaneously both from above and from below.[25]

As in other fields he goes into great detail about possible ways of worker and peasant families building family group communities. Because both the material resources and the cultural level is so low, it is impossible to make large-scale changes. The only real way forward towards building these enlarged family units, is first for the families to create model communities which the state should assist: 'The first and indisputable success in this direction, however slight and limited in extent, will inevitably arouse a desire in more widespread groups to organise their life on similar lines.' This is step by step progress: 'no rushing too far ahead or lapsing into bureaucratic fanciful experiments'.[26]

Women's activity must address more general questions too, agitating against habits and customs that shackle.

> Just as we have our army agitators, our industrial agitators, our anti-religious propagandists, so must we educate prop-agandists and agitators in questions of custom. As the women are the more helpless by their present limitations, and custom presses more heavily on their shoulders and backs, we may presume that the best agitators on these questions will come from their ranks.[27]

Gaining confidence in small matters of everyday life will lead to understanding and participating in big ones.

> If we have touched her [a working woman] or can touch her with our cultural and domestic work, then we will construct for her a spiritual bridge from the individual to the social, and the German revolution will become for her a close and kindred thing.

Trotsky quotes the gospel to summarize his outlook: 'Whoever is true in the small matters will also be true in the big.'[28]

On Art and Literature

The second problem raised by the cultural debate concerned the desire to forge a new culture for the new ruling class, the proletariat.

Trotsky had written a number of essays on literary criticism even before the revolution. With the guns silent and the introduction of the New Economic Policy in 1921, art revived. As part of the new mood, a number of Trotsky's pre-revolutionary essays on literary criticism were to be republished in a special volume of his **Works**. In writing the preface during a summer vacation in 1922, Trotsky went far beyond his brief, expanding it into what became, when he managed to finish it in his next vacation in 1923, the book **Literature and Revolution**, a remarkable work of great erudition and insight, showing Trotsky, always a fine stylist, at his most brilliant. It relates all facets of art and literature to the supreme fact of life—the revolution—and the tasks of Russia's new ruling class, the proletariat. Trotsky did not return to the subject of artistic creation in his writings until 1938, when he wrote a letter to the American **Partisan Review** called 'Art and Revolution'.

Trotsky clarified and sharpened his ideas in the course of the fierce polemics taking place in the heated revolutionary atmosphere over the nature, purpose and destiny of literature and art under the dictatorship of the proletariat, and the role of the government and party towards art. In particular he took issue with the Proletkult movement, which paralleled the Military Opposition with its Proletarian Military Doctrine and movements in other spheres of life, such as those promoting 'the struggle for a communist ethic' and so on, claiming that the super-ceremonious christening of these societies did not mean that the advent of communism was drawing any closer, and that they merely adorned the rough preliminary work with false labels.[29] It is principally in the course of polemics against Proletcult that his ideas on the nature of art and society are drawn out, and these form a firm background for the struggle he conducted against the movement.

He takes up a number of the questions that perennially arise regarding the nature of art and society. If a work of art, he asks, is rooted in the ideology of a ruling class of long ago, such as Dante's **Divine Comedy** in the Florentine petty bourgeoisie of the thirteenth century, what makes it able to speak to and move us centuries later in very different class societies?

Trotsky explains that civilisation serves a double purpose: that of humanity growing and conquering nature; and that of division into classes. From the latter it is clear that some elements of the cultural heritage are discardable; from the former that some elements have common, universal features, such as feelings of love or fear of death, which are constant, though they may be differently expressed at different times. When they are expressed so powerfully that they throw into relief features common to people of all times of class society, they rise above the limitations of life in far-off times, enriching people's internal life, refining feelings, generalising experience, helping people's self-awareness and understanding of their position in the universe. That is what makes them speak across the centuries.

Another perennial problem he deals with is the connection between the individual artist and society. He starts with Marx's dictum that 'The mode of production in material life determines the social, political and intellectual life processes in general'. These processes are expressed by the individual. But if there is only individuality in a work of art, there is no purpose in interpreting it. Individuality in fact is the welding together of national, class, temporary and institutional elements. It is expressed in the uniqueness of the welding together, of the proportions of the psycho-chemical mixture of elements. Not only the individual artist, but the individual viewer or reader also has a unique, individual soul. The bridge between soul and soul is not the unique but the common. He puts it thus: 'Only through the common is the unique known'[30]—a beautifully brief expression of the dialectical relationship between the individual artist and society.

It follows from art's being a social servant that the artist cannot be 'without a tendency', that is, a definite relationship to social life, even if this is not expressed in political terms; a relationship created through the everyday cultural and ideological connection of the class and its artists. Bourgeois artists, for instance, breathed the air of the salons, receiving hypodermic inspiration from their class.

Does it then follow that propaganda art is art? Trotsky says that though art is a social servant, the artistic worth of propaganda art should not be exaggerated: it simplifies complex reality to present easy lessons. What raises propaganda to art is a work's deep thought and feeling, rendering reality in all its complexity, whose 'message' is organic, not an obtrusive appendix. In later years he cites as worthy examples the novel **Fontamara** by the Italian Ignazione Silone and the paintings of Diego Rivera.

Trotsky always attested to the specificity of art and its

incompatibility with compulsion, all the more emphatically after Stalin's accession to power and the stifling of all but official propaganda. Even if art consciously serves a social movement, he claimed, it must be judged by its own law, the law of art. Art has to be approached as art, literature as literature, that is, as specific fields of human endeavour. The class criterion must be refracted artistically.

Art cannot tolerate orders, lies, hypocrisy, conformity. It can be an ally of the revolution only if it is faithful to itself, if it struggles for revolutionary truth, not in terms of any school, but of the 'immutable faith of the artist in his own inner self'. 'You shall not lie!'—that is the formula for salvation.

Another requirement of art is abundance. For Trotsky art was the highest test of the vitality and significance of an epoch. Because it is the most complex part of culture, the most sensitive, the most protected, it needs a rich soil.

> 'Culture feeds on the sap of economics and a material surplus is necessary, so that culture may grow, develop and become subtle... Art needs comfort, even abundance.
> And in addition to material requirements, it needs a flexible atmosphere of sympathy.'[31]

Art and revolution

The revolution caused a break in artistic development. The old world died with the October revolution, and the revival of art was possible only from the point of view of October. The whole of culture, from its economic base to its ideology, needed rebuilding after the civil war. Art alone could not do this; in fact all real art was silenced. 'When the sound of weapons is heard the Muses fall silent'. With the best forces of the proletariat expended in the political and military struggle, the rebuilding was a revolutionary task, and the function of art, therefore, was entirely determined by its relation to the revolution. What this revolutionary task of rebuilding meant under the dictatorship of the proletariat was to hold the fort for the European and world revolution which were expected to triumph in the not too distant future. The Russian proletariat were soldiers in a military campaign:

Life in Revolution is camp life. Personal life, institutions, methods, ideas, sentiments, everything is unusual, temporary, transitional, recognizing its temporariness and expressing this everywhere, even in names. Hence the difficulty of an artistic approach.

The difficulty was that the revolution could not be seen in parts, as episodes.

The transitory and the episodic have in them an element of the accidental and the accidental bears the stamp of insignificance. The Revolution, taken episodically, appears quite insignificant.[32]

It is like an ant which, crawling over a statue of Venus, cannot grasp its beauty but sees only the grooves and bumps. The revolution is only grand and mighty when seen in its entirety, with the objective historical tasks which are the goal of its leading forces.

All the agonies, sacrifices, blood, heroism and faith are justifiable only if the great historic event being born is seen. If this is missed, all that is seen is episodes marked by torn boots, lice, blood, but not a revolution.

The turmoil of artistic strivings, gropings and experiments made in this transitory period inevitably gives birth merely to sketches, *études*, rough drafts, many more unsuccessful than successful. But they have a tremendous innate importance, being imbued as never in the world before with one inspiration—the historic task of the revolution, which was the conscious, purposeful construction of a new socialist society.

Attitude to artistic groups

Trotsky evaluated the output of all the literary and artistic groups according to their relation to the revolution. The bourgeois artists of the pre-revolutionary period pretended nothing had happened, that the revolution did not concern them. Their outpourings were therefore like mere 'scribblings in the complaint book of the Berlin Railway Station'[33] (through which they mostly emigrated to the West).

The 'fellow travellers'—a term invented by Trotsky—were young artists moulded by the revolution, who accepted it as a great event in the history of the nation, but were not committed to the communist ideal. They therefore could not organically merge with the revolution, which they looked upon as an elemental power, but not as a purposeful process. Not subscribing to communism and the vanguard position of the working class, they turned to the peasantry; that is, they looked at the revolution from without, romanticising it while bewailing the torn boots and the cockroaches. The revolution is not, however, torn boots plus romanticism. With their ambivalent position, it was not clear whether their reconciliation to the revolution was the starting point of a move forward—or backward. There were facts enough for both, Trotsky says. After all, the peasantry looked both ways: they loved the Bolsheviks who gave them land, and hated the Communists who requisitioned their surpluses.

The fellow-travellers, leaning on the peasantry, also avoided the city. But the heart of the revolution was the city, and its task was planning, modernising the economy, uprooting village idiocy, enriching the personality and making it more complex—through electrification, not the peasant's candle; through materialist philosophy, not woodland superstition and fatalism. Without the leadership of the city Russia would never get to socialism. It was the revolution's peasant foundation and patchiness of culture that made it formless; it was the Bolshevik leadership that made it planful and finished. It was in a combination of these two extremes that the soul, the internal character, the poetry of the revolution lay. This clarity, however, was foreign to the fellow-travellers, because the revolution displaced their organic axis and they lost their self-confident mastery of their art. Trotsky nevertheless, far from spurning them, considered their work useful as manure for the seeds of the new culture, and stoutly defended their right to free artistic expression, against vilification as bourgeois liberals of both the artists and of Trotsky himself for defending their right, by adherents of Proletkult.

The Futurists, by contrast, ardently supported the revolution and yearned to serve the new regime through their art, not by adorning life, but by helping to organise it. The best known of the Futurists was the poet Mayakovsky. Trotsky looked more sympathetically upon the Futurists. They had been rebels against the old order before October—albeit Bohemian rebels; they connected art with technology, they identified with Bolshevism and internationalism; and yet Trotsky was critical. He maintained that they showed contempt for the literary traditions of the past; they were in fact for a complete break with the past and the creation of a new proletarian culture. This Trotsky vehemently opposed, as we shall see below in his polemics with Proletkult.

Also, the Futurist poets, he says, were poets who became communists, not communists who became poets, and so were weakest when singing about communism. Again he stoutly defended their right freely to express themselves, and suggested they could be an important component of current output and a link to future socialist culture.

Trotsky's whole general approach to art and literature argued against the line of Proletkult. He also aimed his barbs specifically at the movement in what was his greatest cultural polemic.

Proletkult organised around a journal of that name on urban, district and factory levels, running literary workshops as well as special sections devoted to poetry, theatre and music. It had a wide measure of support after the revolution, encompassing most of the Futurists and many leading figures in the Bolshevik Party, like Bukharin and Lunacharsky. It appealed to young workers who thirsted for knowledge but were iconoclastic. It insisted on autonomy from Narkompros, the Commissariat of Enlightenment, and set up its own parallel institutions to the government ones.

The fiercest opponents of Proletkult were Lenin and Trotsky.

The reasoning behind the Proletkult attitude was spelled out by Bogdanov, who was its principal theoretician, a person with whom Lenin had long had ideological differences and who was expelled from the Bolshevik Party in 1909.

Bogdanov argued that the dictatorship of the proletariat advanced along three parallel but distinct lines: political, economic and cultural. Its political organ was the party, its economic organ the trade unions, and its cultural organ Proletkult. The economic and political struggles had succeeded in October 1917, but the revolution would not be complete until the cultural revolution succeeded with the construction of proletarian culture. This dictated a specific, organisationally independent form of struggle, particularly as culture was the last refuge of the bourgeoisie in retreat.

The same culture cannot serve different regimes, said Proletkult. The old bourgeoisie had its own culture, the victorious proletariat must build its own, have its own 'class art' as an organising force in the struggle for socialism. The bourgeois culture of Western civilisation was alien to this struggle. It was the very opposite of proletarian culture, which was based on Marxist class consciousness, internationalism, materialism, atheism; and western culture was therefore completely inadmissible for proletarian cultural expression. Bukharin, for instance, thought that the party should have its specific line 'in all fields of ideological and scientific life, even in mathematics'.[34]

Art was not only conditioned by its social environment, in this instance the workers' state, but could in its turn condition and organise the experience of the masses, mobilizing them to action to transform society. It was to this end that Proletkult set up the institutions parallel to but independent of Narkompros, where ordinary workers could practice and forward the development of proletarian culture and proletarian artists could be employed.

The new proletarian culture would be based on social labour and comradely collaboration which would become common to mankind in the future classless society.

Proletkult covered a spectrum of outlooks, particularly in the attitude to the preservation of the culture of the past and the use of specialists. One extreme claimed that all past bourgeois culture had nothing of any worth at all (except in natural science and technological skills), and were impatient to destroy it and create a new proletarian culture immediately. They therefore, like their parallel movement in the armed forces, the Military Opposition, opposed any co-operation with bourgeois specialists who were incapable of serving the interests of the proletariat. Speed was therefore of the essence. The cultural revolution must be accomplished here and now.

Not all the adherents of Proletkult supported the destruction of the past heritage. Bukharin did not, and even Bogdanov understood that the proletariat could not afford entirely to reject the bourgeois culture of the past, and would need to retain the collectivist elements within it.

On the question of the use of bourgeois specialists, Lenin and Trotsky had to refight the battle they had joined with the Military Opposition over the appointment of pre-revolutionary officers and other specialists in the army, from whom the Red Army soldiers had to 'learn to learn', even though they had been their enemies.[35] Lenin was forthright:

The Communist who has failed to prove his ability to bring together and guide the work of specialists in a spirit of modesty, is a potential menace. We have many such Communists among us, and I would gladly swap dozens of them for one conscientious qualified specialist.[36]

Lunacharsky, the Commissar of Enlightenment, supported Lenin and Trotsky in this. He considered the training and experience lodged in the bourgeois specialists to be necessary 'instruments of labour'. And in fact he played the prime role in convincing bourgeois actors, artists, engineers, playwrights, poets, professors, scientists and teachers to accept and work for the new government.

In the heated debates around proletarian culture in the early 1920s Lenin and Trotsky came out implacably against the movement. Already in 1919 Lenin had proclaimed a 'relentless hostility...to all inventions of intellectuals, to all "proletarian cultures" ':[37]

Proletarian culture is not something that suddenly springs from nobody knows where, and is not invented by people who set up as specialists in proletarian culture. Proletarian culture is the regular development of those stores of knowledge which mankind has worked out for itself under the yoke of capitalist society, of feudal society, of bureaucratic society.[38]

Trotsky elaborated on this theme. There was bourgeois class culture and socialist classless culture, but not proletarian culture. Proletarian culture could in no sense be equated with bourgeois culture. The bourgeoisie owned both physical and mental means of production within feudal society centuries before the bourgeois revolutions and their acquisition of state power. They possessed the comfort and abundance necessary for art to grow and become subtle.

The condition of the working class on taking power was the very opposite. It had never owned either the physical or mental means of production within the old society, and emerged from it propertyless, exploited, uneducated—in complete cultural pauperism. It therefore could in no way inaugurate a new and significant phase in the development of the human mind.

In addition the proletariat was not granted the luxury of the centuries-long gestation of class rule like the bourgeoisie. For a workers' state to survive it needed the world socialist revolution, and this, according to Trotsky, involved decades, not centuries, during which transitional period its energies would be taken up by fierce class struggles internationally, which were political rather than cultural. The more the proletariat succeeded and the conditions for cultural creation became favourable, the closer the proletariat would be to ceasing to be a proletariat and dissolving into the socialist community.

The aim of bourgeois revolutions was to perpetuate the domination of the bourgeoisie. The aim of the proletarian revolution was to dissolve the proletariat in a classless society as quickly as possible.

Trotsky argued further that culture is created when the intelligentsia of the class and the class itself interact, as was the case in the bourgeois salons. This fusion was even more vital for the proletariat than the bourgeoisie, as proletarian culture would be based on the creative activity of the masses, not a distinct elite stratum of artists. But the backwardness of the proletariat placed an insuperable obstacle before the fusion of the artists with their class. Unlike the bourgeoisie, the proletariat came to power only with the need to take possession of its cultural heritage, because it had none of its own. This resulted in the unfortunate necessity to promote a special stratum of cultural workers not organically linked with the class.

The demand for today's proletariat to break with tradition sounds hollow when,

> addressed to the working class which does not need and cannot break with any literary tradition because it is not in the grip of any such tradition.

He adds: 'We Marxists have always lived in tradition and we have not because of this ceased to be revolutionaries.'

The proletariat's task is to take over the tradition, commune with it, absorb it and in *that way* transcend it. The task of the revolution is not creating culture but bearing culture to the backward masses.

Trotsky also pointed out the danger of Proletkult's iconoclastic haste, as art matured slowly and needed time to blossom. The different metaphors he uses to make the point are striking: 'The nightingale of poetry, like that bird of wisdom, the owl, is heard only after the sun is set.' 'The political writing of the class hastens ahead on stilts while its artistic creativity hobbles behind on crutches'. 'The mind limps after reality'.[39] He explains why:

> Unlike in politics, in artistic creation an enormous role is played by subconscious processes—slower, more idle and less subjected to management and guidance, just because they are subconscious.

Lenin also pointed to the lag, indirectly criticising a central plank of Proletkult: 'the cultural task cannot be discharged as rapidly as the political and military tasks'.[40] Time, therefore, is of the essence for the blossoming of art.

Trotsky argued, therefore, that,

> It is fundamentally incorrect to contrast bourgeois culture and bourgeois art with proletarian culture and proletarian art. The latter will never exist, because the proletarian regime is temporary and transient. The historic significance and the moral grandeur of the proletarian revolution consist in the fact that it is laying the foundations of a culture which is above classes and which will be the first culture that is truly human.[41]

What there was—the strivings and experiments—was the proletariat putting its stamp on art, breaking up the ground, preparing it for sowing. But that was a far cry from proletarian culture in the sense of a harmonious system of knowledge. The products of pre- and post-October socialist poets were revolutionary documents, political events, not literary ones. The 'inartistic doggerel' that abounded was not new literature. Proletkult says: give us something even pock-marked, but our own. Trotsky decries this: pock-marked art is not art, therefore not necessary for the masses. Shakespeare's works one day will be only historical documents, also **Capital**, but not yet. We still recommend them to the workers.

The danger of Proletkult was that it compressed the future into the narrow limits of today, falsified perspectives, violated proportions, distorted standards, cultivated the arrogance of small circles. All such quests for a philosopher's stone combined despair at our cultural deficiency with a faith in miracles. There is no reason to despair, he says, neither are there miracles.

Bukharin and Lunacharsky claimed Trotsky pessimistically considered the dictatorship of the proletariat as a cultural vacuum; the present as a sterile hiatus between a creative past and a creative future.[42] Trotsky in fact considered the international revolution imminent, at which time Russia would no longer need to pull itself up by its own bootstraps and the emergence of a classless society would herald the possibility of creating a socialist culture. Russia was holding the fort, and its cultural ferment preparing the ground and putting down markers for this eventuality. Stalin and Bukharin, his ideologue of 'socialism in one country'—and with it a 'snail's pace' gestation of the international revolution—could not intellectually tolerate a barren epoch which denied the new bureaucracy omnipotence in all fields including culture. They therefore forced the future into the present, conjuring up a proletarian culture in the here and now, and by-passing history on their way to Utopia.

It is interesting to note that the Communist Party—which had constantly resisted taking sides in the literary disputes, and desired nothing better than to tolerate all the conflicting groups and schools, subject only to the condition of loyalty to the revolution and to the regime, after the proclamation of the doctrine of 'socialism in one country' in December 1925, tilted over in early 1926 to a renunciation of neutrality and a positive attitude to taking decisions about artistic matters—a victory for the view that art and literature were inseparable from politics[43] and a development much approved by Proletkult, which hoped to be and was in fact the recipient of party favour until it was crushed under the dull thud of Socialist Realism's heavy boots in the mid-1930s.

Party attitude to art

Trotsky had a very libertarian attitude to the party's position regarding artistic development. The party could take a position on the political use of art, that is, whether it was pro- or counter-revolutionary, and try to help groups grasp the meaning of the revolution. But it could not rule on its development, its struggle for new forms. Art demanded freedom, it could not tolerate orders. And on this basis the party did indeed permit very extensive freedom in the field of art.

Also the party did not regard as revolutionary and legitimate only that art that spoke to workers of their lives, such as a description of a factory chimney, or a rising against capital. The imagination needed to be lifted by a new *lyric* poetry. What the party should say to the poet is: 'Please write about anything you can think of!' In the depths of reaction, in 1938, Trotsky could boldly say:

> If, for the better development of *material* production the Revolution must build a *Socialist* regime with centralised control, to develop intellectual creation an *Anarchist* regime of individual liberty should from the first be established. No authority, no dictation, not the least trace of orders from above![44]

He ends a **Manifesto Towards of Revolutionary Art** written in 1938 (with André Breton) with the slogans:

> The independence of art—for the revolution.
> The revolution—for the complete liberation of art![45]

Nor will revolutionary art be created only by workers, especially as they would be too busy fighting the class struggle. The fellow-travellers were helpers, not competitors.

The party illuminates the road, but art must make its own way. It was not possible early on to estimate the place of any group, so the party must pay attention to every artistic talent that was not counter-revolutionary and wait patiently. This attitude dictated that while Trotsky fiercely opposed Proletkult, he as fiercely defended its right to exist.

Science and society

As part of the overall cultural debate Trotsky followed his critique of artistic creativity with an incursion into an evaluation of the new society's relation to science, which he described as the 'knowledge that endows us with power',[46] and hence 'the most important lever of culture'.[47] Science had been a youthful interest of his, which he abandoned for the sake of political activity, but renewed when this activity landed him, after he resigned in 1925 as Commissar of War, in the post of head of the Board for

Electro-Technical Development of the Committee for Industry and Technology.

With the scientists, Trotsky considered his task for the most part the opposite of that in the literary and artistic debate. In the latter he felt obliged to take to task the over-eager, impatient young revolutionary poets and artists whose iconoclasm sought to largely destroy the pre-revolutionary heritage in favour of ambitious 'proletarian'-inspired projects of dubious artistic or cultural value, and imbue them with the knowledge of the masses' need not to smash the past but to absorb it to enrich their present endeavours.

While he did rehearse the same arguments against Proletkult for the benefit of those—and there were some, though far fewer than in the artistic fraternity—who believed in a specifically 'proletarian' science, this was not his main aim when dealing with the scientists, for they were by and large not youthful products of the revolution, but bourgeois specialists who stayed and worked for the new regime.

Scientists' practical work constantly proved the veracity of dialectical materialism, yet most of them failed to recognise this and opposed the ideas of Marxism ideologically. Trotsky therefore sat at their feet for the study of different branches of science, but felt obliged to act as their tutor when it came to locating science in the broader philosophic ambiance. So to the scientists he expounded the philosophy and sociology of Marxism.

After all, the definition of science, according to Mendeleyev, the most eminent Russian scientist was: to know so that we may foresee and act. And, taking Mendeleyev as an example, Trotsky shows how, in drawing up his Periodic Table of the Elements, based securely on materialist thinking and research on atomic weights, he brilliantly foresaw the existence of hitherto undiscovered elements. He,

> knocked at one of nature's hitherto closed doors, and from within a voice answered: "Present!" Actually, three voices responded simultaneously, for in the places indicted by Mendeleyev there were discovered three new elements. A marvellous triumph for thought, analytical and synthesizing![48]

Yet this same Mendeleyev, so knowledgeable and far-seeing

in chemical scientific research, was clueless in social scientific matters. His chemical prediction was made in 1871, the year of the Paris Commune. Far from analysing the causes or motives of this great social upheaval, he was simply hostile, and it fell to the German exile Karl Marx to shed the light of scientific dialectical materialism on this social event, whose rays penetrated through to the actions of the Russian October and beyond.

While trying to draw the scientists out of the parochialism of science in general by looking at social development too in a scientific Marxist way, Trotsky was careful to avoid some Marxists' attempts 'to transmute the theory of Marx into a universal master key and ignore all other spheres of learning'. Trotsky remembers that if anyone did this in Lenin's presence,

> Vladimir Ilyich would rebuke him with the expressive phrase 'Komchvanstvo' ('communist swagger'). This would mean in this particular case—communism is not a substitute for chemistry. But the converse theorem is also true. An attempt to dismiss Marxism with the supposition that chemistry (or the natural sciences in general) is able to decide all questions is a peculiar 'chemist swagger', which in point of theory is no less erroneous and in point of fact no less pretentious than communist swagger.[49]

Just as he had earlier pointed to the specificity of art as a particular field of human endeavour, so he points to the specificity of the different branches of science: 'each science covers a particular field, ie., a field of complex combinations of elementary phenomena and laws that require a special approach, special research technique, special hypotheses and methods.'[50]

Trotsky thus aimed for the scientists to combine 'professional specialization with an all-encompassing synthesis of the processes and problems of our life and work.'[51]

Results and Prospects

Isaac Deutscher recounts the fate of Trotsky's cultural critique of the mid-1920s:

> The whole 'Trotskyist' conception of culture and art soon came under fire. It offended the half-educated party man by its very breadth and complexity. It outraged the bureaucrat

to whom it denied the right to control and regiment intellectual life. It also antagonised the ultra-revolutionary literary sects whose pretensions it refused to accept. Thus a fairly wide anti-Trotskyist 'front' formed itself in the cultural field; and it was kept in being, reinforced, and eventually absorbed by the political front. The struggle against Trotsky's influence as a literary critic became part of the endeavour to destroy his political authority; and so his opponents declared his views on art to be part and parcel of the wider Trotskyist heresy.[52]

Far from the pessimism he was accused of by Bukharin and others, Trotsky evinced an eternal optimism about the future of socialism, even in the darkest days of Stalinism and his own persecution. With his deep understanding of historical materialism and sensitive feeling for artistic creativity, he conjured up a prophetic vision of future socialist society, with which he ends **Literature and Revolution**. Solidarity will be the basis of society:

> All the emotions which we revolutionaries, at the present time, feel apprehensive of naming—so much have they been worn thin by hypocrites and vulgarians—such as disinterested friendship, love for one's neighbour, sympathy, will be the mighty ringing chords of socialist poetry.[53]

With political struggle eliminated (because of the elimination of classes), and three or four hours of labour per day sufficient to satisfy all material needs, the powerful force of competition—in bourgeois society market competition—will assume higher forms: struggle for one's opinion, one's project, one's taste.

Collective interests and individual competition—which will have a profoundly ideal and unselfish character—will give rise to opposing tendencies in all spheres. There will be struggles over, for instance, a new canal, the distribution of oases in the Sahara, regulation of the climate, pedagogical systems, new theatres, chemical hypotheses, competing tendencies in music, best systems of sports. The human personality will grow into full bloom.

Art will become the most perfect method of the progressive building of life in every field. The walls will come down between art and industry, between art and nature. People will reorganise nature, relocating mountains and rivers, improving on nature, rebuilding the earth according to their own taste. There will also be a redistribution of humanity. The city will dissolve and the village rise to the plane of the city.

Then people will also refashion themselves through collective experiment, subjecting physical, subconscious and psychological processes to the control of reason. **Literature and Revolution** ends with the words:

> The average human type will rise to the heights of an Aristotle, a Goethe or a Marx. And above this ridge new peaks will rise.

Chapter six
Split in the Troika

Rise of the kulaks puts pressure on Zinoviev, Kamenev and Stalin

AFTER TROTSKY left the Commissariat of War in January 1925 there followed a long pause in his inner-party struggle. It lasted throughout 1925 and into the summer of 1926. Not only did he not express any criticism of official policy in public, but he kept quiet even in the sessions of the Central Committee and the Political Bureau. We saw how in the Eastman case he capitulated to the pressure of the Troika. There was a general tiredness among the working class and a lack of fighting spirit. In addition there was a cohesion in the party apparatus and Trotsky still believed this was *the* party he had to relate to and accepted the ban on factions. As long as these conditions existed then the path of action was closed to him. He had to bide his time.

After these months of keeping quiet, even when things started changing—with the Troika breaking as Zinoviev and Kamenev split from Stalin—Trotsky was slow to react.

A number of factors led to fissures in the Troika. First of all, the defeat of Trotsky in 1924 weakened the bond that kept the triumvirate together.

Then developments in Russia's economy led to tensions in the Troika. Now Zinoviev and Kamenev moved to repeat the arguments Trotsky had used since 1923. These concerned two main points: the tempo of Russia's industrialisation and the government's attitude towards the kulak. Trotsky argued that the slow recovery of industry threatened socialism, and that speedy industrialisation was needed, the funds for which would largely come from levies on the rich peasants.

In June 1924 a serious drought threatened the harvest, with ruin facing the Volga Basin and South-Eastern Russia. In July the price of grain began to soar. In August grain prices were a hundred per cent above the level of August 1923.[1]

Toward the end of 1924 and throughout 1925 the problem of the kulak came to the fore. As E.H. Carr explains:

> By December 1924 the state had collected only 118 million puds of grain out of the projected 380 millions; and the grain stocks held by the state, which had amounted to 214 million puds on January 1, 1924, stood at only 145 millions on January 1, 1925. The situation was now critical. The estimate for the total collection was cut from 380 million to 290 million puds, the share of the Ukraine being reduced from 34 to 26 per cent of the total. All thought of grain exports went by the board, and an import of 30 million puds was authorised. In November the official maximum price for rye had been raised to 85 kopeks a pud. The attempt to maintain the maximum prices was then abandoned. In December the price to the grower of a pud of rye rose to 102 kopeks, and thereafter rose by leaps and bounds till it reached 206 kopeks in May 1925. This price-fixing policy had been defeated. The *kulak* had proved victorious. The cities were once more being held to ransom.
>
> The rise in grain prices was alarming... It threatened to rekindle the discontents, so recently allayed, of the industrial proletariat... the rise in prices also threatened relations in the countryside. In the existing structure of rural society, the price question sharply divided the peasants themselves. Only the well-to-do peasants consistently had grain surpluses and were primarily interested in high prices.
>
> ...the poor peasants who lived wholly or in part by hiring out their labour were normally on balance buyers, not sellers, of grain... High prices following a bad harvest tended therefore to benefit the well-to-do peasants, to press hardly on the poor peasants, and to drive more and more of the middle peasants into the category of poor peasants who could subsist only by hiring out their labour. Such was the situation which developed in the winter of 1924-1925.[2]

The class differentiation of the peasantry was accelerating.

This was facilitated in three main ways: through the leasing of land, through the loaning of draught animals and agricultural machines and implements, and through the hiring of labour.

It was very common,

> for the rich peasant, who possessed horses and implements in sufficient quantity, to rent land from his poorer neighbour, who, giving up the unequal struggle to cultivate his land on his own account, leased it to the kulak in return for a share of the harvest and, for the rest, lived by hiring out his labour. This practice was everywhere on the increase. Figures from two areas in the northern Caucasian region showed that, in one, two-and-a-half times as much land was leased in 1925 as in 1924, and in the other nearly twice as much...
>
> The number of poor peasants eager to dispose of land which they had not the capacity to cultivate was so large as to depress rents for such land to a very low figure. Where from 8 to 13 roubles a year had been paid for a *desyatin* of land in the northern Caucasus before the war, it was now worth only from 50 kopeks to 3 roubles a *desyatin*...[3]

> The loaning of working animals and agricultural implements and machines was probably an even more important factor than the leasing of land in the growth of rural capitalism.[4]

While the rural rich became richer the middle and poor peasants became poorer.

> A popular estimate for the whole of USSR, frequently repeated at this time, put the proportion of 'horseless' peasants in 1924 at 40 per cent.

In the Ukraine the proportion of peasants without working animals and without agricultural implements rose from 19 per cent in 1921 to 34 per cent in 1922, 45 per cent in 1923 and 46 per cent in 1924.[5]

> The third factor in the process of differentiation—the hiring of labour—was a corollary and concomitant of the other two. The increasing concentration in the hands of a well-to-do group of peasants of the ownership or control of the means of production meant, at the other end of the scale, an increasing number of poor peasants whose only resource was

to sell their labour. The *batrak* or hired agricultural worker, was the counterpart of the kulak.[6]

Between 1922 and 1924 the lot of the *batraks* steadily worsened. As the number of potential workers grew under pressure of the natural population increase, with declining reserves of land and animals, and the closing, through unemployment in industry, of the most obvious avenue of escape, the conditions of employment deteriorated.[7]

In the spring of 1925 the party and government authorities were bent on aiding the kulaks. Thus on the question of the fixing of the agricultural tax for 1925-1926 the Central Executive Committee of the Soviets in March 1925 decided to reduce the total assessment from 470 million roubles in 1924-1925 to 300 million roubles for the coming year.[8] It was also decided to reduce the rating of animals for assessment by one-third: this was definitely a concession to the well-to-do peasant, who alone possessed animals in any quantity.[9] On 21 April 1925 the Presidium of the Central Executive Committee of the RSFSR allowed the leasing of land, as the employment of hired labour had been allowed before.[10] On 14 March 1925, in conversation with a delegation of village correspondents, Stalin argued for making concessions to the peasants' private ownership of land.

> Stalin agreed that without security the peasant would not manure his land and asked for how many years the land should be allocated; and, when the peasant replied, 'For 20 years', Stalin is said to have inquired: 'And suppose for longer, for 40 years, or even forever?' This boldness evidently surprised the peasant, who replied: 'Perhaps for longer, perhaps forever, but this would need thinking over by more than one head'. Stalin then wound up the discussion by saying that this would not be ownership, since the land could not be sold, but that it would be possible to utilise it with confidence.[11]

A similar tune was sung by Kamenev. In a speech to the Moscow Provincial Congress of Soviets which met in April 1925 he said:

> *We shall also have to review our legislation about the utilisation*

*of land, about hiring of labour and about leasing, since we have
many juridical restrictions which are in fact of a kind to hold
back the development of productive forces in the countryside,*
exacerbating class relations instead of leading them into the
right channel...

We are for the development of productive forces, we are
against those survivals which impede the development of
productive forces... We are for peasant accumulation—the
Soviet power must take its stand on this point of view—but
we are for the regulation of this accumulation.[12]

To put the cap on the pro-kulak policy, Bukharin pronounced
in a speech at a mass meeting in Moscow on 17 April 1925:

Our policy in relation to the countryside should develop in
the direction *of removing, and in part abolishing, many
restrictions which put the brake on the growth of the well-to-do
and kulak farm.*

To the peasants, to all the peasants, we must say: *Enrich
yourselves...* As long as we are in tatters, the kulak may defeat
us economically. But he will not do so if we enable him to
deposit his savings in our banks. We shall assist him but he
will also assist us. Eventually the kulak's grandson will be
grateful to us for our having treated his grandfather in this
way.[13]

Lenin had argued for the 'alliance of workers and peasants',
but he never offered support to the wealthy peasants; he treated
the middle peasants, and even the poor peasants, as unreliable
allies whom the lure of property might turn against the
proletariat. Bukharin translated the *smychka* into an alliance with
all the peasants, hence he turned his back on organising the poor
peasants against the rich.

It was in April 1925, at the Fourteenth Party Conference, that
the Troika stood united for the last time in arguing for a policy of
concessions to the peasants: reduction in the agricultural tax and
sanction given to the leasing of land and the hiring of labour.
Zinoviev again repeated the hoary myth of Trotsky's underestimation of the peasantry.

The Conference declared:

By ensuring conditions for free accumulation in kulak households, the tempo of accumulation in the whole economy is raised, the national income grows more rapidly, the material possibilities of real economic support for weak and poor households are increased, the possibilities of absorbing surplus population are broadened, and, finally, a more favourable atmosphere is created for the growth of co-operatives and the guiding of peasant savings into the co-operative channel.[14]

Thus the conference staked on the kulak the prospect of the revival of the whole economy.

Following the conference, the Central Committee,

sanctioned 'the broader utilisation of the right of leasing land by peasants' up to a maximum period of two rotations, or, where the three-field or four-field system was still in operation, of 12 years. Even this limit might be exceeded in the case of state lands leased to peasants.

Also,

the resolution recommended the abandonment of 'the recently existing practice of limiting prices of grain and agricultural products', and the adoption of the practice of agreements through 'state and co-operative purchasers' without 'compulsory prices for peasant sellers'. This registered the victory of the well-to-do peasants who had broken the attempt to impose fixed prices for grain after the 1924 harvest.[15]

At the All-Union Congress of Soviets which met in May 1925, it fell to Kamenev to defend the,

official economic policy. He spoke of the need for measures 'which will take the shackles off the peasant economy': this meant to extend the period for which security of tenure of land was given by the existing law (in the Ukraine, nine years) and to remove restrictions on the leasing of land and the hiring of labour.[16]

Zinoviev and Kamenev turn on Bukharin and Stalin

The publication on 1 June 1925 of the speech of Bukharin delivered on 17 April rang alarm bells.

Krupskaya, angered by what she regarded as a perversion of her late husband's views, wrote an article attacking the Bukharin line and the policy of indulgence for the kulak, and sent it to **Pravda** for publication. Bukharin, the editor of **Pravda**, wrote a counter-article defending himself, and submitted both articles to the Politburo. It was a delicate situation. To veto the publication in **Pravda** by Lenin's widow still seemed invidious and shocking to party consciousnesses. But the argument against a public airing of differences between leading party members on so explosive a subject was also strong, and eventually prevailed. By a majority the Politburo decided that neither Krupskaya's article nor Bukharin's reply should be published. The minority consisted of Zinoviev and Kamenev.[17]

The break-up of the Troika was very sudden indeed. Now Zinoviev and Kamenev faced an alliance of Stalin and Bukharin.

In 1923-4, it was Zinoviev who raised the slogan, 'face to the countryside' in the course of the campaign against Trotsky.

For some two years no-one was more vocal than Zinoviev in criticising Trotsky for his alleged 'underestimation of the peasantry'. It was only in the second half of 1925 that Zinoviev changed his tune.

On 30 July 1924 he published an article entitled 'The harvest failure and our Tasks', the keynote of which was an emphasised phrase: 'It is time, high time, to compel a number of our organisations *to turn their face more to the countryside'*. From this time onwards, throughout the autumn and winter, the exhortation 'face to the countryside' was constantly reiterated in Zinoviev's speeches and articles and became the catchphrase of party policy. A volume of Zinoviev's articles and speeches was published in 1925 under the title **Litsom k Derevne** (Face to the Countryside).

However, the irresolute and impressionistic Zinoviev changed his stance under the pressure of events.

Victor Serge was correct to describe Zinoviev as 'Lenin's biggest mistake'.[18] He was weak and cowardly. Trotsky, in a letter to Ivan Smirnov written in Alma Ata in 1928, relates a conversation he had with Lenin soon after the October revolution:

I told Lenin: 'What surprises me is Zinoviev. As for Kamenev,

I know him well enough to be able to predict where the revolutionary in him will end and the opportunist begin. Zinoviev I don't know personally at all, but from descriptions of him and a few of his speeches it seemed to me that he was a man who would be stopped by nothing and who feared nothing.' To this V.I. [Lenin] replied: 'He fears nothing where there is nothing to fear'. With that the conversation ended.[19]

Now Zinoviev used his slogan in a completely different sense as an argument against Stalin and Bukharin.

On 21 June 1925, in a speech in Leningrad to a conference of party workers in the Red Army, Zinoviev declared:

'Face to the countryside' meant 'Face to the middle and poor peasants'; some peasants had apparently interpreted it as 'a turning towards the well-to-do strata in the countryside', as a proof of the determination of the leadership to rely, not on 'the wretched nag', but on 'the fat kulak horse'. The decisions on leasing and on hired labour had, in fact, been a 'serious concession to the rich top stratum in the countryside': to pretend otherwise was to offer the party a dose of 'sugared water.

...the kulak in the countryside is more dangerous, far more dangerous, than the NEPman in the town.[20]

In October Zinoviev published a 400-page volume entitled **Leninizm**, in which he argued that the danger was 'complacency, when it turns into glossing over of the class struggle in the countryside and playing down of the danger from the kulak'.[21]

Next Zinoviev turned his guns on the doctrine of 'socialism in one country'.

The final victory of socialism is impossible in one country. The victory of the socialist order over the capitalist will be decided on an international scale.[22]

Zinoviev backed up this assertion with a large number of quotations from Lenin on the impossibility of building socialism in one country.[23]

Lenin was from head to foot an *international* revolutionary. His teaching was applicable not only to Russia but to the whole world. We, disciples of Lenin, must banish as a hallucination the mere thought that we can remain Leninists if we weaken by a single jot the international factor in Leninism.[24]

It was the first time that the concept of 'socialism in one country' had been openly assailed. In the same book Zinoviev argued very strongly for inner-party democracy, repeating practically word for word what Trotsky had argued in **The New Course**: 'The structure of the Leninist party must be such as to guarantee *under all conditions the maximum inner-party proletarian democracy*'.[25]

Paradoxically, the conflict between Zinoviev and Kamenev on the one side and Stalin and Bukharin on the other was sharpened by what, after early fears, proved to be an excellect harvest in 1925.

E.H. Carr writes:

> The troubles of 1925 began not, like those of 1924, from a partial failure of the harvest, but from unexpected difficulties in marketing it. The largest harvest since the revolution was paradoxically followed not by abundance, but by stringency on the internal grain market, and by a strong upward pressure on prices. In the previous year the fixed prices of the state purchasing organs had held their own throughout the autumn in spite of competition from higher prices in the free market. In 1925 the 'directive' prices of the state purchasing organs failed to bring out buyers and were almost at once forced up in an unequal struggle to compete with the free prices.[26]

The beneficiaries of the high prices were the rich peasants. To quote the statement of the Central Executive Committee of the Soviets:

> The less prosperous peasants bring in their grain in the autumn, the more prosperous in the spring. The more prosperous peasants and the middle peasants sometimes buy grain in the autumn and keep it till the spring in the hope of making money on it.
>
> From the Urals and from Siberia, from the Ukraine and from the North Caucasus reports came in of a deliberate holding back of grain by the well-to-do peasants.

The well-to-do peasant, no longer pressed for money, and with little in the way of available supplies of industrial goods on which to spend it, found himself in the position of being able to hold the state to ransom.

In December,

The full gravity of the situation became apparent. The grain collection of the year 1925-1926 was likely to fall short by 200 million puds of the estimated 780 millions; and a decision of the Politburo suspended all exports. The vision of industrial expansion on a broad front financed on the proceeds of ample grain surpluses faded away. The kulak had shown himself master of the situation.[27]

Break-up of the Troika

Towards the end of 1925 Zinoviev and Kamenev drew conclusions similar to those Trotsky had held in 1923 about the kulaks threatening socialist construction, and enriching themselves at the expense of other classes: they paid low wages to labour, squeezed the poor peasants, bought up or leased the land, and charged the poor peasants and urban workers high prices for food. They avoided taxation and sought to pass their burden onto the shoulders of the poor. They strove to accumulate capital at the expense of the state, and thus slowed the accumulation within the state sector of the economy, consequently holding back the industrialisation of the country.

On 5 September, when the Central Committee was discussing the arrangements for the coming Fourteenth Party Congress, four members of the Central Committee—Zinoviev, Kamenev, Sokolnikov and Krupskaya—came out with a joint statement demanding a free debate throughout the party on all the controversial issues that had arisen. This document was afterwards known as 'The Platform of the Four'. It was never published and no clear account of its contents has ever appeared in print. At the October Central Committee meeting Zinoviev and Kamenev made a direct attack on the Bukharin-Stalin peasant policy which they accused of making concessions to the kulaks at the cost of the poor peasants and agricultural workers. But still old habits didn't die easily. The leadership continued manoeuvring. The Central Committee *unanimously* passed a number of resolutions on economic policy—including one on the peasantry—that covered over the widening differences behind the scenes.

Still, between October and December Moscow and Leningrad were engaged in an intense, bitter and barely concealed war. In both capitals the elections of delegates to the congress were rigged; Moscow elected only Stalin's and Bukharin's nominees, Leningrad only Zinoviev's.

The Fourteenth Party Congress opened on 18 December and was dominated by conflict between Stalin and Bukharin on the one side and Zinoviev and Kamenev on the other. The debate was stormy. The fundamental issues were: the doctrine of 'socialism in one country', the attitude towards the peasantry, industrialisation policy and planning. Zinoviev and Kamenev disclosed the unscrupulous measures which they, together with Stalin, had used to crush the 1923 Opposition.

Krupskaya deplored the lack of inner-party democracy: 'Individual opinions were not expressed in the pages of our central organ, and, thanks to this omission, the party was not prepared for the discussion which descended on it like a bolt from the blue two weeks before the congress.' She ended with a favourite quotation from Lenin: 'There have been occasions in history when the teaching of great revolutionaries have been distorted after their death. Men have made them into harmless icons, and, while honouring their name, they blunted the revolutionary edge of their teaching'.[28]

Krupskaya's voice carried a lot of weight with party members who knew how long and how closely she had been associated with Lenin, not only as his wife, but as a co-worker.

Zinoviev warned of the danger threatening socialism from the kulak, NEPman and bureaucrat. He recalled Lenin's Testament and its warning about Stalin's abuse of power.

Kamenev protested very strongly against the establishment of autocratic rule over the party. He urged the restoration of freedom for minorities to state their views. 'Back to Lenin. We are against creating a theory of the *Vozhd* [leader]. We are against making a *Vozhd*. We are against the Secretariat, which has in practice combined both policy and organisation, standing over the political organ. We are for our upper layers being organised in such a fashion that there would be a really all-powerful Politburo, uniting all the policies in our party, and, together with that, subordinating to itself the Secretariat'. Kamenev concluded: 'I have come to the conviction that Comrade Stalin cannot fulfil the role of unifier of the Bolshevik staff [*disturbance; applause from the Leningrad delegation; jeers and applause for Stalin*]'. Amidst the din, Kamenev finished: 'We are against the theory of one-man rule; we are against creating a *Vozhd*'.[29]

Stalin went out of his way to defend the concept of 'collective leadership' of the party: 'To lead the party otherwise than collectively is impossible. Now that Ilyich is not with us it is silly to dream of such a thing (*applause*), it is silly to talk about it.'[30] Stalin turned the tables on Zinoviev and Kamenev by referring to their demand in 1923 that Trotsky should be expelled from the party. He again argued against 'the method of amputation, the method of blood-letting'.[31]

He asked what the meaning of the platform of Zinoviev and Kamenev was.

'It means to lead the Party without Rykov, without Kalinin, without Tomsky, without Molotov, without Bukharin... It is impossible to lead the Party without the comrades I mentioned.'*
'What in fact do they want of Bukharin? They demand the blood of Comrade Bukharin. That is what Comrade Zinoviev demands when in his concluding speech he sharpens the issue of Bukharin. You demand the blood of Bukharin? We shall not give you that blood, be sure of that. [*Applause*].'[33]**

Stalin now levelled against Zinoviev and Kamenev all the charges from which he defended them the year before when they were made by Trotsky. They were the 'deserters' and 'strike-breakers' of October. Stalin stood by his new partners Bukharin, Rykov and Tomsky, in the same way as he had previously stood by Zinoviev and Kamenev.

Stalin's machine was victorious. When the vote was taken on the question of endorsing the Central Committee reports delivered by Stalin and Molotov, 559 voted for and 65 against.[34]

---

*As Rykov, Tomsky and Bukharin were murdered by Stalin in the purges of the 1930s, in the more recent editions of this speech, one reads: '...to lead the Party without Kalinin, without Molotov'.[32]

Stalin, having himself got Bukharin's blood in 1938, found this passage embarrassing, and therefore expurgated it from his **Works.

This congress was a turning point in the party history. It not only represents the last occasion on which the Central Committee position was challenged by a co-report, but also the last time an opposition group was represented by delegates at the party congress.

Collapse of Zinoviev's stronghold, Leningrad

The Fourteenth Congress issued a declaration to the Leningrad Organisation deprecating the behaviour of Zinoviev and other Leningrad representatives at the Congress.[35]

On the face of it Leningrad looked like an unassailable citadel for Zinoviev. He controlled the administrative machinery of the city and the province, the press and the party. It looked as though he had a large body of ardent followers. However, when it came to the crunch, it took Stalin less than two months to take complete control of the party organisation in Leningrad, from the *uezd*, to the *raion*, to the *guberniia*.

The historian T.E. Nisonger writes:

> In overall summary, it may be stated that as the impending conflict with the Stalin group approached, Zinoviev, on the surface at least, appeared firmly in command of the Leningrad party structure. Zinoviev's adherents dominated the Leningrad provincial committee, the gubkom bureau; the gubkom secretariat; five of Leningrad's six *raikomy* and their bureaus; the komsomol organisation; the *guberniia* control commission; and the *guberniia* trade union council in addition to the Leningrad press. Zinoviev himself was apparently extremely self-confident concerning the security of his position in Leningrad.[36]

Victor Serge, who lived at the time in Leningrad, observed:

> Zinoviev, whose demagogy was quite sincere, believed every word he said about the warm support of Leningrad's working class masses for his own clique. 'Our fortress is impregnable', I heard him say.[37]

The 1 January 1926 plenary session of the Central Committee took a decision to cease any further discussion of the issues which were disputed at the Congress, to which end no member or candidate member of either the Central Committee or the Central

Control Commission who had sided with the opposition at the Congress, could participate in any way in the post-Congress discussion.[38]

However, in order to demonstrate that they enjoyed the support of the Leningrad party masses, the Zinovievites convened special sessions of the Central City, Volodarskii, Moskovsko-Narvskii and Vasileostrovskii *raion* party *aktivs* on 28 December for the specific purpose of endorsing the Leningrad delegation's stance at the Fourteenth Congress.

The pro-opposition resolutions were carried by over-whelming majorities. For instance, only 20 of the more than 2,500 activists present at the Moskovsko-Narvskii session opposed the Zinovievite resolution. An analagous resolution was adopted by 490 to 12 in the central city *raion*, by nearly 800 to 22 in the Vasileostrovskii *raion*, and by 815 to 81 with 4 abstentions in the Volodarskii *raion*.[39] On 5 and 6 January 1926 an eight-member delegation of the Central Committee made up of Molotov, Kirov, Voroshilov, Kalinin, Andreev, Tomsky, Petrovsky and Shmidt, arrived in Leningrad. With them came four members of the Presidium of the Central Control Commission.

On 7 January the Central Committee nominated Kirov as provisional First Secretary of the Leningrad provincial committee, and on 8 January the Moscow Central party apparatus reorganised the North West Bureau, entirely by-passing the Leningrad organisation[40], and appointed a new Bureau Secretariat which was also headed by Kirov.

Once the apex of the Leningrad party organisation was conquered by the Stalinists, they removed the Zinovievites from key positions in the lower and middle levels of the Leningrad apparatus.

The victory of the Stalinists in the lowest levels of the party was swift. On 21 January 1926, 652 of the 717 party collectives in Leningrad held special meetings to discuss the Fourteenth Congress. These 652 collectives embraced 73,268 of the 77,056 members and candidate members (96 per cent) of the Leningrad organisation. Of these, 70,228 (96 per cent) voted in favour of the resolutions passed by the Fourteenth Congress which condemned the opposition; 2,190 voted against (3.5 per cent) and 275 (0.5 per cent) abstained. These figures do not include the 11,356 party members in the Red Army and Fleet then stationed in Leningrad. It was reported that 10,129 (89 per cent) of the military personnel attended meetings of this nature; 10,028 (99 per cent) voted in favour of condemning the opposition, 54 supported the opposition, while 47 abstained.

Resolutions supporting Stalin were reported to have been adopted *unanimously* at all the conferences of the *raions* except the Moskovsko-Narvskii *raion* conference, where one abstention was recorded.[41] The Egorov collective which had adopted a pro-Zinoviev resolution on 31 December 1925 by 55 votes to 2, now, on 3 February 1926 adopted an anti-opposition resolution by 500 votes with none against.[42]

On 10 February 1926 an Extraordinary Leningrad Provincial Conference was held. After a three hour political report by Bukharin on the Fourteenth Congress, the Conference unanimously adopted a resolution condemning the opposition. This conference represented the final consolidation of the Stalinist victory in the Leningrad organisation.[43]

The Stalinists used the same methods against the Zinovievites that the Zinovievites had used to consolidate their own power previously. Nisonger writes:

> ...the Zinovievites' chief adherents used various types of coercion or threats thereof to thwart active Stalinist sympathisers or punish Zinovievite defectors (and hence serve as a warning to other would-be defectors). Individuals who invoked the Zinovievites' displeasure were removed from party positions, dismissed from their employment, arrested and/or threatened with sanctions by the *guberniia* control commission. In a similar vein, the Zinovievites attempted to discharge hostile newspaper editors and employees from the *guberniia*-level press. Moreover, they endeavoured to prevent the convocation of party meetings at which it was anticipated that anti-opposition resolutions would be adopted. Other stratagems employed by the Zinovievites included denying Stalinist agitators access to Leningrad's industrial enterprises, issuing edicts in the name of the gubkom prohibiting Leningrad's newspapers from publishing anti-opposition material...[44]

Now the Stalinists employed the same tactics. According to Nisonger:

...a great many parallels existed between the Stalinist strategy and the Zinovievite counter-strategy. Both groups sought to create the impression that they were supported by the mass of rank and file Communists, both undertook to remove hostile newspaper editors, both claimed that their opponents were violating party unity, both used to their own advantage the power of appointing and discharging party officials, and the Zinovievites employed the *guberniia* control commission against the Stalinists just as the Stalinists utilised the Central Control Commission against the opposition.[45]

The swift and easy victory of the Stalinists in Leningrad shows how shallow had been the commitment of the activists and rank and file of the party to Zinoviev.

Trotsky maintains silence

Throughout the fortnight that the Fourteenth Party Congress was in session Trotsky sat silent. He did not react to Krupskaya's appeal for real democratic discussion and against the stultifying effect of the Lenin cult. He said nothing when Zinoviev recalled Lenin's Testament and its warning against Stalin's abuse of power, or when he dealt with the threat to socialism posed by the kulaks, NEPmen and bureaucrats.

He kept quiet when Kamenev protested against the establishment of autocratic rule over the party. He stood aside from the vicious, well-orchestrated attack by the Stalinists on the Leningrad opposition. He did not protest when Bukharin put the case for 'socialism in one country' in opposition to Zinoviev's attack on the doctrine. Trotsky kept aloof from the dispute in the party leadership.

Thirteen years later, when he appeared before the Dewey Commission in Mexico, he confessed that at the Fourteenth Congress he was astonished to see Zinoviev, Kamenev and Stalin clashing. 'The explosion was absolutely unexpected by me', he said. 'During the congress I waited in uncertainty, because the whole situation changed. It appeared absolutely unclear to me.'[46]

These words, uttered many years after the event, were confirmed in unpublished notes Trotsky wrote on the eve of the Fourteenth Congress and during the Congress.

Although Trotsky must have been aware of the differences

within the Troika before the Congress, he underestimated their scope and importance. Preoccupied with his duties in the Supreme Council of the National Economy and in writing his book **Towards Capitalism or Socialism?** in August 1925, he had not been following the growth of dissent in the Politburo. The fact that both sides in the debate twisted and turned in an effort to hide the differences from the party, that even after the sharp debate on economic policy in the Central Committee in October they still managed to pass a unanimous resolution, must have led Trotsky to assume that the conflict in the Troika was mere shadow boxing. The fact that it was Zinoviev, hitherto the most vicious member of the Troika and the most outspoken representative of its policies, who was now leading the attack on the right in the Conference, must have made the split in the Troika look like a mere intra-bureaucratic squabble. Zinoviev's conversion from the principal proponent to the main opponent of the peasantry policy within a few weeks, could only confirm Trotsky's estimate of him as very unstable.

The adherence of G.Y. Sokolnikov to the Zinoviev-Kamenev partnership must have further encouraged Trotsky to see the new grouping as an unprincipled clique. Sokolnikov had joined the Zinoviev opposition merely because of his antipathy towards Stalin: on economic policy he stood with Bukharin, i.e., on the extreme right of the party. This is what Trotsky wrote about Sokolnikov in his diary notes on the fourth day of the Congress:

> The fact that today Sokolnikov appears as one of the leaders of the Leningrad Opposition is unprincipled politics of a purely personal kind and at the same time it is a great curiosity. He was and remains the theoretician of the economic disarmament of the proletariat in relation to the countryside.[47]

Still, Trotsky's lack of awareness of the depth of the conflict in the party leadership was really astonishing. Zinoviev's attack on the doctrine of 'socialism in one country' had been carried on in public for months. Isaac Deutscher was correct in describing Trotsky's state of mind: even if Zinoviev, Kamenev, Krupskaya and Sokolnikov had not raised the demand for an open debate in the party as long ago as the plenary session of the Central Committee in October, and even if the public controversy over socialism in a single country had given no indication of the new cleavage, it would still be something of a puzzle how an observer as close, as interested, and as acute as Trotsky could have remained unaware of the trend and blind to the many omens. How could he have been deaf to the rumblings that had for months been coming from Leningrad?

His surprise, we must conclude, resulted from a failure of observation, intuition and analysis. Moreover, it is implausible that Radek, Preobrazhensky, Smirnov, and his other friends should not have noticed what was happening and that none of them tried to bring matters to Trotsky's attention. Evidently his mind remained closed. He lived as if in another world, wrapped up in himself and his ideas. He was up to his eyes in his scientific and industrial pre-occupations and literary work, which protected him to some extent from the frustration to which he was exposed. He shunned inner-party affairs.[48]

One significant factor that probably blinded Trotsky to the changes in Zinoviev and Kamenev was that these two were his harshest opponents in 1923-4. In **The Lessons of October** they appeared as the leaders of the party's right wing; both in 1917 in Russia and during the revolution in Germany in 1923. Hence Trotsky was incredulous when they appeared as spokesmen of a new left.

He had, however, noted changes.

On 9 December (that is, nine days before the beginning of the Fourteenth Congress) Trotsky wrote notes in his diary about the dispute between the Leningrad organisation and the Central Committee:

Neither side has made any specific, practical proposals that would alter in one way or another the economic and political relationship of forces between the proletariat and the peasantry. The legalisation of the leasing of land and the hiring of farm labour were carried out, to the best of the party's knowledge, without any internal struggle. The reduction of the agricultural tax went through in the same way.

But still he felt that there must be something behind the conflict between Zinoviev and Kamenev on the one hand and Stalin and Bukharin on the other.

> The party discussion which is now unfolding between the Leningrad organisation and the Central Committee and which is becoming more and more heated, has its social roots in the relations between the proletariat and the peasantry under conditions of capitalist encirclement...

Unfortunately the conflict between the two sections of the leadership was distorted by the fact that the bureaucratic regime in the party determined the forms and methods of the dispute.

> The extraordinary difficulty, at least at the present stage, in determining the real class essence of the differences, is engendered by the absolutely unprecedented role of the party apparatus; in this respect it has gone far beyond what existed even a year ago. One need only consider the significance of the fact that in Leningrad a resolution directed against the Central Committee was adopted unanimously or virtually unanimously at the same time that the Moscow organisation unanimously—without a single abstention—adopted a resolution against Leningrad.

Still, however heavy the hand of the bureaucracy, the conflict between sections of the bureaucracy did express pressure from the masses,

> Certain mass moods, which have no chance of being represented at all accurately through the mass organisations, trade unions, or party, make their way through to the upper party circles by obscure and roundabout means...thus setting into motion certain lines of thinking and subsequently either gaining a firm foothold or not, depending on the wishes of the apparatus in charge of a particular area... it is no accident that Leningrad ended up as the site of the apparatus's opposition to the Central Committee.
> ...the position taken by the upper circles in Leningrad is a bureaucratically distorted expression of the political anxiety felt by the most advanced section of the proletariat.[49]

Trotsky could not forget that Leningrad—the cradle of

October—had the strongest Marxist and Bolshevik traditions. It was the most proletarian of Soviet cities. Its workers felt very strongly the need for a bold industrial policy. The city engineering plants and shipyards, starved of iron and steel, were idle. It suffered badly from the scourge of unemployment. The Leningrad party organisation, however bureaucratic, still could not help reflecting the discontent of the workers of the city.

Four days after the beginning of the Congress, on 22 December, Trotsky wrote in a note 'On the Leningrad Opposition' that 'the Leningrad Opposition [was] the continuation and development of the 1923-4 Opposition'.

> The central theme of the Leningrad Opposition is to blame the official policy, or its right-wing manifestation, for the fact that the peasantry is beginning to push the proletariat into the background, and for the fact that within the ranks of the peasantry the kulak is edging out the middle peasant and the middle peasant is edging out the poor peasant.
>
> ...It is not at all accidental that the Leningrad organisation turned out to be the most sensitive to the voices of warning, just as it is no accident that the leaders of that opposition were forced, in the struggle for self-preservation, to adapt themselves to the class sensitivity of the Leningrad proletariat. The result of this is a paradox, quite shocking on the surface but at the same time totally in accord with the underlying forces at work: The Leningrad organisation—having gone to the furthest extent in its struggle against the Opposition, having inveighed against the underestimation of the peasantry, and having raised the slogan 'Face to the countryside' loudest of all—was the first to recoil from the consequences of the noticeable turnabout that has occurred in the party, the ideological source of which was the struggle against so-called Trotskyism.[50]

But Trotsky could not overlook the fact that Zinoviev's left turn was 'a bureaucratic and demagogic adaptation of the apparatus higher-ups to the anxiety of the advanced section of the working class.' At the same time Leningrad workers were alienated from the local party bureaucracy and from Zinoviev. Herein lay the actual weakness of Zinoviev's social base, as events would prove in the coming days and weeks.

That the Leningrad methods of party and economic leadership, the shrill agitational style, the regional arrogance, etc., built up an enormous amount of dissatisfaction with the ruling group in Leningrad; and that the intense resentment against the Leningrad regime felt by many, many hundreds of workers who have at one time or another been thrown out of Leningrad and dispersed throughout the country, has added to this dissatisfaction—these facts are absolutely incontestable and their importance must not be under-estimated.[51]

The swift collapse of Zinoviev's Leningrad citadel which we have dealt with, proved how brilliant was Trotsky's grasp of the issue. After the Fourteenth Congress Trotsky's illness recurred, and it was not until the spring of 1926 that he managed to meet Zinoviev and Kamenev to form the United Opposition. When the bloc between Trotsky and Zinoviev was set up, the Leningrad Opposition had of course already been shattered.

The United Opposition is created

The only record we have of the first meeting between Trotsky and members of the Zinoviev Opposition is a short passage in Trotsky's autobiography. Kamenev said to Trotsky:

'It is enough for you and Zinoviev to appear on the same platform and the party will find its true Central Committee'. I could not help laughing at such bureaucratic optimism. Kamenev obviously underestimated the disintegrating effect on the party of the three years' activity of the trio. I pointed it out to him without the slightest concession to his feelings. The revolutionary ebb-tide that had begun at the end of 1923—that is, after the defeat of the revolutionary move-ment in Germany—had assumed international proportions. In Russia, the reaction against October was proceeding at full speed. The party apparatus more and more was lining itself up with the right wing. Under such conditions it would have been childish to think that all we need do was join hands and victory would drop at our feet like a ripe fruit. 'We must aim far ahead', I repeated dozens of times to Kamenev and Zinoviev. 'We must prepare for a long and serious struggle.'[52]

It was following a joint plenum of the Central Committee and Central Control Commission that took place on 6-9 April 1926 that the United Opposition—composed of the members of the 1923 Opposition and the Leningrad followers of Zinoviev and Kamenev—was formed.

This was the first time in two years that Trotsky participated actively in a major party organ. It was on this occasion that Stalin poured scorn on Trotsky's suggestion to build a hydro-electric power station on the Dnieper. Trotsky later published Stalin's words:

> 'The means required here are enormous, some hundred millions. We should be falling into the position of a peasant who had saved up a few kopeks, and, instead of repairing his plough or renewing his stock, bought a gramaphone and ruined himself.'[53]

In the discussion at the plenum Kamenev supported Trotsky, particularly in his prediction of the potential adverse consequences of a bumper harvest, if industry lagged behind, and in his demand for increased taxation of the wealthy peasants.

However Kamenev, as former head of the Council of Labour and Defence, felt some responsibility for the industrial policy which Trotsky criticised. And he baulked at supporting Trotsky completely. 'I am not able to associate myself with that part of them [ie, Trotsky's amendments to Rykov's draft resolution] which assesses the past economic policy of the party which I supported one hundred per cent'.[54] Kamenev also made some scoffing remarks about Trotsky. When the Central Committee rejected Trotsky's amendment, Kamenev and Zinoviev, it seems, abstained. But then, when Kamenev's amendment was put to the vote, Trotsky supported it. This was a step towards establishing the bloc.

After the plenum the three met and agreed to join forces. Zinoviev and Kamenev agreed to make a public admission that Trotsky was right all along when he warned the party against the bureaucracy. In return Trotsky was ready to state that he was wrong in assailing them as the leaders of the bureaucracy when the real leader was Stalin.

However, before the three managed to make precise plans, or even to formulate clear policies, a mere day or two after meeting together, Trotsky had to leave Russia for medical treatment in Germany. The malignant fever from which he had suffered in the last years, recurred, incapacitating him completely.

Chapter seven

The United Opposition

The United Opposition is launched

AFTER TROTSKY'S return to Russia, in the latter part of May 1926, he, Zinoviev and Kamenev set out to unite their factions. This was not easy. First of all, the Trotskyist faction had been dispersed and had to be brought together again. When this took place it became clear that it was far weaker than it had been in 1923. Secondly there was great resistance in the two factions to unity. Among Trotsky's associates some favoured unity with the Zinovievites, but others—Radek and Antonov-Ovseenko— preferred an alliance with Stalin. Still others declared a plague on both their houses. Mrachkovsky, a hero of the Ural battles, declared: 'Stalin will deceive us, and Zinoviev will sneak away'.[1] Victor Serge, a member of the Leningrad group of Trotskyists, said that this group was far from enthusiastic about merging with the Zinovievites.

> We were taken aback by the news that Trotsky had concluded an agreement with the Leningrad Opposition. How could we sit at the same table with the bureaucrats who had hunted and slandered us... We hesitated to hand over the list of our leading members to them. What would they be up to tomorrow?[2]

Among the Zinovievites there was also great resistance to the merger. After all it was Zinoviev and Co. who had made the most vicious assault on Trotsky over the past two years.

Zinoviev and Kamenev had to explain to their adherents that Trotskyism was a bogey that they themselves had invented.

Finally, embarrassed by the charge that they had surrendered to Trotskyism, Zinoviev and Co. asked Trotsky to help. To accommodate them Trotsky made a rotten compromise: he renounced the theory of permanent revolution.

Trotsky felt, and continued to feel, that the creation of the bloc with the Zinovievites was justified even after his allies betrayed him and capitulated to Stalin at the end of 1927. Trotsky writes in his autobiography:

> Zinoviev and Kamenev openly avowed that the 'Trotskyists' had been right in the struggle against them ever since 1923. They accepted the basic principles of our platform. In such circumstances it was impossible not to form a bloc with them, especially since thousands of revolutionary Leningrad workers were behind them.[3]

As we have mentioned, Kamenev and Zinoviev were ecstatically optimistic, but Trotsky felt differently. Victor Serge remembers:

> I had no confidence that we would win: I was even sure in my own heart that we would be defeated. I remember saying this to Trotsky... In the old capital we could count on only a few hundred militants, and the mass of the workers was indifferent to our case. Leon Davidovich spread his hands wide: 'There is always some risk to be run. Sometimes you finish like Liebknecht and sometimes like Lenin'.[4]

In the end the United Opposition struggled against Stalin and Bukharin for about eighteen months.

The first time the United Opposition leaders acted in concert was at the joint plenum of the Central Committee and the Central Control Commission of 14-23 July 1926. There Zinoviev made a statement admitting that the Trotskyist Opposition of 1923 had been right, and Trotsky withdrew the charge of opportunism levelled at Zinoviev and Kamenev in **The Lessons of October**.

Zinoviev stated:

> 'I have made many mistakes, but I consider two mistakes as the most important ones. My first mistake of 1917 is known to all of you... The second mistake I consider *more dangerous* because the first one was made under Lenin. The mistake of

1917 was corrected by Lenin and made good by us within a few days with the help of Lenin. But my mistake of 1923 consisted in...'

Ordzhonikidze (*interrupting*): 'Then why did you dupe the entire party?'

Zinoviev: 'We say, there can no longer be any doubt now that the main nucleus of the 1923 Opposition, as the development of the present ruling faction has shown, correctly warned against the dangers of the departure from the proletarian line, and against the alarming growth of the apparatus regime... Yes, in the question of suppression by the bureaucratised apparatus, Trotsky proved to be right as against us.'[5]

At the same session Trotsky declared:

> There is no doubt that in **The Lessons of October** I associated the opportunist shifts in policy to the names of Zinoviev and Kamenev. As experience of the ideological struggle in the Central Committee testifies, that was a gross mistake. This mistake is to be explained by the fact that I had no opportunity of following the ideological struggle among the seven [of the Politburo] and of ascertaining in time that the opportunist shifts proceeded from the group headed by Comrade Stalin, in opposition to Comrades Zinoviev and Kamenev.[6]

The major document of the United Opposition was a declaration signed by thirteen Opposition members of the Central Committee, including Zinoviev, Kamenev, Krupskaya and Trotsky. This document embraced the essential principles of the Opposition case for the whole period from 1923 to 1927.

The United Opposition defined its attitude as that of the Bolshevik left, defending the interests of the working class against the kulaks, NEPmen and bureaucracy. The declaration starts with an assault on the bureaucracy of state and party:

> The immediate cause of the increasing crises in the party is *bureaucratism*, which has grown appallingly in the period since Lenin's death and continues to grow.[7]

The growth of the bureaucracy was rooted in the economic

backwardness of the country.

The Declaration attributed factionalism to the growth of bureaucratism, which was in turn the product of 'the lowering of the specific weight of the proletariat in our society'.

One crucial criterion for socialist advance is a rise in the level of workers' wages. The government imposed a wage stop, authorising no increase in workers' earnings unless accompanied by a rise in productivity. Workers' wages were still lower than before the war and they were not paid punctually.

> Inefficiency and sloppiness in setting pay rates and work norms, which make life hard for the workers, are nine times out of ten the direct result of bureaucratic indifference to the most elementary interests of the workers and of production itself. These can also be considered the source of non-punctual payment of wages, ie., the relegation to the background of what should be the foremost concern.[8]

Workers' wages should be improved, as also should the housing conditions of workers. Taxation had to be reformed. State revenue came increasingly from indirect taxes, the brunt of which was borne by the poor. This burden had to be lightened, and the kulaks and NEPmen made to carry a heavier burden of taxes.

The climax of the Declaration was the demand for more rapid industrialisation:

> The year just passed has shown with full clarity that state industry is lagging behind the economic development of the country as a whole. The new harvest again catches us short of reserves of industrial goods. But progress towards socialism can be assured only if the rate of industrial development, instead of lagging behind the overall movement of the economy, draws the rest of the economy along after it, systematically bringing the country closer to the technological level of the advanced capitalist countries. Everything should be subordinated to this goal, which is equally vital for both the proletariat and the peasantry. Only on the condition of a satisfactory powerful development of industry can both higher wages for the workers and cheaper goods for the village be assured.

The lagging of industry threatened the *smychka* of the proletariat and the peasantry.

If the upper layers in the village were able to hold back last year's harvest until this spring, thereby cutting into both exports and imports, increasing unemployment and causing retail prices to rise, that means that the economic and tax policies that gave the kulaks the chance to pursue such a course against the workers' and peasants' interests, were in error. Under these conditions, correct tax policies, along with correct price policies, are an essential part of socialist management of the economy. Several hundred million roubles accumulated and concentrated in the hands of the upper strata of the villages even now go to promote the debt bondage of the rural poor to the loan sharks and usurers. The merchants, middlemen, and speculators have already piled up many hundreds of millions of roubles, which have long since been parlayed into billions. It is necessary to apply the tax screws more energetically in order to extract a significant portion of these resources to nourish industry, to strengthen the system of agricultural credit, and to provide the lowest strata in the villages with support in the form of machinery and equipment on advantageous terms. The question of the *smychka* between agriculture and industry under present circumstances is above all a question of industrialisation.[9]

The Declaration denounced the policy of relying on the kulaks.

In questions of agricultural policy, the danger of a *shift toward the upper strata in the village* has become more and more plainly delineated... The alliance with the middle peasant is more and more transformed into an orientation toward the 'well-to-do' middle peasant, who more often than not proved to be a junior edition of the kulak. One of the primary tasks of the socialist state is, through the formation of cooperatives, to bring the poor peasants out of their dead-end situation.

...the fact is that under the pretext of an alliance of the poor with the middle peasants we everywhere observe the political subordination of the poor to the middle peasants and through them to the kulaks.[10]

The Declaration criticises the policy of the Comintern, inspired by the theory of 'socialism in one country', and leading to reliance for the defence of peace on British trade union leaders, in the Anglo-Russian Committee. (See further on this point in the next chapter.)

Finally the Declaration turns to the issue of factionalism and denounces the persecution of the Opposition: to lead the party forward 'does not mean strangling it'.

The United Opposition retreats and capitulates

Again and again we see the same unfolding of events. The Opposition moves forward, meets massive resistance from the Stalinists, and retreats.

The reaction of the Central Committee majority to the Opposition's Declaration was vehement. The debate at the Central Committee Plenum was heated, and this was exacerbated by the unfortunate occurrence of a grim incident: Dzerzhinsky, the Chairman of the Supreme Economic Council, upheld the official economic policy and reputedly threatened the Opposition with 'fresh gunpowder'. After two hours of a shrieking speech he left the rostrum, suffered a heart attack, collapsed and died in the lobby before the eyes of the Central Committee.

The Central Committee completely rejected all the Opposition demands. It repudiated the demand for a review of the wage scales; it refused to exempt poor peasants from taxation and impose heavier taxes on the better-off peasants; it resisted the demand for accelerated industrialisation. Finally it reaffirmed its support for the Bukharin-Stalin Comintern policy, and in particular for the Anglo-Russian Committee.

Stalin violently assaulted the Opposition, not dealing with the essence of the controversy, but concentrating on the issue of party discipline. He accused the Opposition of forming a faction—thus violating the Leninist decision of the Tenth Congress—and Zinoviev of abusing his position as President of the Comintern for factional purposes, attacked Lashevich and a group of less prominent oppositionists for holding a clandestine meeting in the woods outside Moscow, and finally laid into one

Ossovsky, who had expressed the view that the Opposition should constitute itself as an independent party.

The Central Committee resolved to expel Ossovsky from the party, to dismiss Lashevich from the Central Committee and the Commissariat of War where he was Deputy Commissar, and to deprive Zinoviev of his seat on the Politburo.[11] As Kamenev had been only an alternate member of the Politburo since the Fourteenth Congress, Trotsky alone of all the Oppositionists now remained on this body.

It was now clear to Trotsky that to restrict the discussion to the Central Committee and Politburo—where the Opposition was in a tiny minority—was hopeless. Hence the Opposition decided to appeal to the rank and file of the party against the Politburo and the Central Committee. Accordingly in the summer of 1926 the adherents of the Opposition brought their arguments to the notice of all party members. They distributed policy statements, tracts and 'theses', and spoke at party cells.

Trotsky's first speech was to a Party cell of workers on the Kazan railway on 30 September 1926. On the following day, Radek, Piatakov, Zinoviev and Trotsky spoke at a party meeting in the Aviapribor factory in Moscow.[12]

However, the party machine went in to full steam to stop the Opposition in its tracks. All its meetings were disrupted by jeering and heckling, which often made it impossible for the speakers to be heard. Deutscher writes:

> For the first time in nearly thirty years, for the first time since he had begun his career as revolutionary orator, Trotsky found himself facing a crowd helplessly. Against the scornful uproar with which he was met and the obsessive hissings and hootings, his most cogent arguments, his genius for persuasion, and his powerful and sonorous voice were of no avail. The insults to which other speakers were subjected were even more brutal. It was clear that the Opposition's first concerted appeal to party opinion had met with failure.[13]

On 2 October the Moscow Party Committee passed a resolution condemning the meeting at Aviapribor accusing Trotsky, Zinoviev and Piatakov, who spoke at it, of factionalism, and inviting the Central Committee to call the Opposition to account.

The failure of the Opposition campaign became evident, and so, on 4 October, the leaders of the Opposition made what was really an appeal for terms of surrender. It was the Zinovievites who put the pressure on Trotsky to do this. Trotsky was not surprised. He knew Zinoviev. In a different context years later he wrote: 'Zinoviev...was inclined, as everybody knew, to fall into panic whenever a difficult situation arose.'[14]

In return for the Opposition's agreement to abstain from 'factionalism', Stalin was supposed to call off the campaign of hounding the Opposition before the approaching Fifteenth Party Conference. Of course, Stalin did not abide by this agreement. At a meeting of the Politburo on 11 October he dictated draconian terms to the Opposition:

> The opposition must consent to these conditions if it desires peace in the Party.
> What are our conditions?
> The first point is that it must publicly declare that it will unreservedly obey the decisions of our Party bodies.
> The second point is that the Opposition must openly admit that its factional activity was erroneous and harmful to the Party.

The third point was that the Opposition must distance itself from former members of the Workers' Opposition like Shliapnikov and Medvedev.

The fourth point was that the Opposition must dissociate itself from opposition groups in Communist parties abroad.[15]

The Opposition leaders capitulated. On 16 October they issued a statement declaring:

> We categorically reject the theory and practice of 'freedom of factions and groupings' and recognise that such theory and practice are contrary to Leninism and the decisions of the party. We consider it our duty to carry out the decisions of the party regarding the impermissibility of factional activity. At the same time, we consider it to be our duty to admit openly before the party that we and our supporters, in putting forward our views on a number of occasions after the Fourteenth Congress, have committed acts which violated party discipline and that we have followed a factional course

which goes beyond the limits of ideological struggle within the party laid down by the party. In recognising these acts as wrong, we declare that we emphatically 'denounce factional methods of propagating our views, as these methods endanger the unity of the party, and we call upon all comrades who share our views to do the same. We call for the immediate dissolution of all factional groupings which have been formed around the views of the 'Opposition'.

At the same time, we admit that by our appearances in Moscow and Leningrad in October, we violated the decision of the Central Committee on the impermissibility of a discussion, in that we opened such a discussion against the decisions of the Central Committee.

...we consider it absolutely impermissible to support either directly or indirectly the factionalism of any group in the various sections of the Comintern against the line of the Comintern...

The statement ends with these words:

> ...we pledge ourselves to render every possible assistance to the party in the liquidation of factional struggle and to combat new breaches of discipline.[16]

Stalin's conditions were accepted completely. The Opposition's statement appeared in **Pravda** on 17 October. **Pravda** declared: this was 'the complete, absolute and magnificently sustained victory of the party over the United Opposition'.

The United Opposition found itself trapped by its own acceptance of the banning of factions.

The banning of factions was not a part of the Bolshevik tradition, but on the contrary, was at complete variance with it, as Trotsky explained many years later. He wrote on 15 July 1939:

> The entire history of Bolshevism was one of free struggle of tendencies and factions. In different periods Bolshevism passed through the struggle of pro- and anti-boycottists, 'otzovists', ultimatists, conciliationists, partisans of 'proletarian culture', partisans and opponents of the armed insurrection in October, partisans and opponents of the Brest-Litovsk treaty, left communists, partisans and opponents of

the official military policy, etc. etc. The Bolshevik Central Committee never dreamed of demanding that an opponent 'abandon factional methods', if the opponent held that the policy of the Central Committee was false. Patience and loyalty towards the opposition were among the most important traits of Lenin's leadership.

It is true that the Bolshevik Party forbade factions at the Tenth Party Congress in March 1921, a time of mortal danger. One can argue whether or not this was correct. The subsequent course of development has in any case proved that this prohibition served as one of the starting points of the party's degeneration. The bureaucracy presently made a bogey of the concept of 'faction', so as not to permit the party either to think or to breathe. Thus was formed the totalitarian regime which killed Bolshevism.[17]

Now, the acceptance by Trotsky and the other leaders of the United Opposition in October 1926 that they would restrict their arguments to the party's leading bodies alone without appealing to the rank and file, committed them to complete impotence. In addition, they disavowed all the foreign groups and individuals who had declared support for the Russian Opposition and paid for this by expulsion from their own parties.

The Yugoslav Communist observer Ante Ciliga, a supporter of the Opposition, wrote about Trotsky's 'prudence and diplomacy':

> Whereas the majority, led by Stalin and Bukharin, manoeuvred to obtain the total exclusion of the Opposition, the latter constantly sought for compromises and amicable arrangements. This timid policy of the Opposition was instrumental, if not in bringing about its defeat, certainly in weakening its resistance.[18]

It was the pressure of the Zinovievites and the fear of a split in the United Opposition, and above all the feeling of tragic helplessness that led Trotsky to go along with the statement of 16 October. He also hoped that this would give the Opposition some breathing space. The leaders of the Opposition hoped that Stalin would stop the organisational reprisals against it after they issued the statement of 16 October, but in vain. On 18 October a bombshell exploded. Max Eastman published Lenin's Testament in the **New York Times**. This was the first time that the full text saw the light of day. A year earlier Eastman had published excerpts from the Testament in his book **Since Lenin Died**, and Trotsky, under Politburo pressure, disavowed Eastman and denied the authenticity of the Testament. As Zinoviev and Kamenev at the Fourteenth Party congress (December 1925) had demanded the publication of the Testament and repeated this demand again and again, it seemed to Stalin that Eastman's article in the **New York Times** was inspired by the leaders of the Opposition.

When on 21 October the Politburo met, newspapers all over the world were full of the sensational disclosure of Lenin's Testament. This enraged Stalin and Bukharin who now launched a vicious attack on the Opposition. In theses for the coming Fifteenth Party Conference the Politburo accused the Opposition of not renouncing its 'errors of principle', and of not denouncing Trotskyism, which was a 'Social-Democratic deviation', despite its formal submission to party discipline.

Trotsky must have felt that Stalin had tricked the Opposition into committing suicide, and so at an angry scene at the Politburo he called Stalin 'the gravedigger of the revolution'. This vehement outburst horrified its hearers, even including some of the Trotskyists.

Natalia Sedova describes this scene:

Muralov, Ivan Smirnov and the others came to our flat in the Kremlin one afternoon, waiting for Leon Davidovich to return from a Politburo meeting. Piatakov arrived first, very pale and visibly upset. He poured himself a glass of water, gulped it down and said, 'I have been under fire, but this—this was worse than anything I've ever seen! Why, oh why, did Leon Davidovich say that? Stalin will never forgive him or his children for generations to come!' Piatakov was so overwrought that he was unable to tell us clearly what had happened. When Leon Davidovich finally came into the dining-room, Piatakov rushed up to him. 'Why, why did you say that?' Leon Davidovich brushed the question aside; he was exhausted but calm.[19]

The Central Committee deprived Trotsky of his seat on the

Political Bureau, and announced that Zinoviev would not represent the Soviet Communist Party on the Executive of the Comintern, thus removing him, in practice, from the presidency of the Comintern.

The Fifteenth Party Conference

When the conference opened on 26 October the Opposition leaders hoped to salvage something from the ceasefire by prudent behaviour; so they refused to participate in the discussion for six days, even during the debate on the economic theses, which were presented by Rykov.

On the seventh day, 1 November, Stalin presented his theses on the Opposition, which contained the nastiest possible attack on it.

Stalin recalled all that Zinoviev had said about Trotsky as the enemy of Leninism, and Trotsky's description of Zinoviev and Kamenev as the 'strike-breakers of October'. He ridiculed the 'mutual amnesty' they guaranteed each other. He repeated *ad nauseam* the history of Trotsky's antagonism to Lenin's ideas, and accused Zinoviev and Kamenev of 'surrendering to Trotskyism'. He denounced the Opposition for inciting the party against the peasantry in the interests of excessive industrialisation which 'would condemn millions of workers and peasants to impoverishment', and would not be different to the capitalist method of industrialisation. Instead Stalin put forward the policy of the party majority, the 'socialist' method of industrialisation:

> What is the principal merit of the socialist method of industrialisation? It is that it leads to unity between the interests of industrialisation and the interests of the main mass of the labouring sections of the population, that it leads not to the impoverishment of the vast masses, but to an improvement of their living standards, not to an aggravation of the internal contradictions, but to the latter being evened out and overcome.[20]

Again and again Stalin denounced the Opposition as Menshevik, 'Social-Democratic'.

Finally, he called on the conference to give the Opposition a unanimous rebuff.

Zinoviev, Kamenev and Trotsky all spoke in reply.

Both Zinoviev's and Kamenev's speeches were plaintive and pleading. Both tried to exonerate themselves from the charge that they had 'surrendered to Trotskyism', claiming that they had united with Trotsky only for a definite and limited purpose, as Lenin had often done.

Zinoviev said that had he been told that it was undesirable 'in the interests of peace' for the Opposition to offer an explanation, he would not have spoken. Trotsky's speech was brilliant in content and form, although moderate in tone—the latter probably as a concession to his Zinovievite allies.

Trotsky argued the Opposition's case for industrialisation as the key to strengthening the coalition of the workers and peasants. What was 'Social-Democratic' in this policy? He pointed out the speedily increasing social differentiation of the peasantry. The Opposition asked that the well-to-do pay higher taxes and that the poor be granted relief. 'What is there in it that is Social-Democratic?' The Opposition was against a credit policy which favoured the kulak. Was this Social-Democratic?

> There have been differences of opinion on the question of wages. In substance, these differences consisted of our being of the opinion that at the present stage of development of our industry and economy, and at our present economic level, the wage question must not be settled on the assumption that the workers must first increase the productivity of labour, which will then raise the wages, but that the contrary must be the rule, that is, a rise in wages, however modest, must be the prerequisite for an increased productivity of labour... This may be right or it may not, but it is not 'Social-Democratic'.[21]

The Opposition did not share Bukharin's view that capitalism had regained stability. Was that Social-Democratic? Was the Opposition's criticism of the Anglo-Russian Committee Social-Democratic?

Trotsky recalled his service in the Comintern, his close collaboration with Lenin, and especially his support for Lenin in the transition to NEP, the NEP he is allegedly wishing to destroy. He was charged with 'disbelief' in the building of socialism.

Yet had he not written:

...the advantages of our system over capitalism...will enable us in the next few years to increase the coefficient of our industrial expansion not only to twice the figure of 6 per cent attained in the prewar period, but to three times that figure, and perhaps to even more.[22]

Trotsky then went on to refute the theory of 'socialism in one country'. He quoted liberally from Lenin in his support. Particularly withering was his criticism of Bukharin's defence of the theory.

In his last article in **Bolshevik**, which I must say is the most scholastic work which has ever issued from Bukharin's pen [*laughter*], he says: 'the question is whether we can work towards socialism, and *establish* it, *if we abstract this from the international factors*'....

...Just listen to this: 'Whether we can work towards socialism, and establish it, if we abstract this question from the international factors'. If we accomplish this 'abstraction', then of course the rest is easy. But we *can not*. That is the whole point. [*Laughter*].

It is possible to walk naked in the streets of Moscow in January, if we can abstract ourselves from the weather and the police. [*Laughter*]. But I am afraid that this abstraction would fail, both with respect to weather and to police, were we to make the attempt. [*Laughter*].

'We repeat once more: *it is a question of internal forces and not of the dangers connected with the outside world. It is therefore a question of the character of the revolution*'. [He said, quoting Bukharin]...

The character of our revolution, independent of international relations! Since when has this self-sufficing character of our revolution existed? I maintain that our revolution, as we know it, would not exist at all but for two international prerequisites: firstly, the factor of finance capital, which, in its greed, has fertilised our economic development; and secondly, Marxism, the theoretical quintessence of the international labour movement which has fertilised our proletarian struggle. This means that the revolution was being prepared, before 1917, at those crossroads where the great forces of the world encountered one another. Out of this clash of forces arose the 'Great War', and out of this the October Revolution. And now we are told to abstract ourselves from the international situation and to construct our socialism at home for ourselves. That is a metaphysical method of thought. There is no possibility of abstraction from the world economy.

Trotsky goes on to deal with foreign trade.

> What is export? A domestic or an international affair? The goods to be exported must be produced at home, thus it is a domestic matter. But they must be exported abroad, hence it is an international transaction. And what is import? Import is international! The goods have to be purchased abroad. But they have to be brought into the country, so it is a domestic matter after all. [*Laughter*]. This example of import and export alone suffices to cause the collapse of Comrade Bukharin's whole theory, which proposes an 'abstraction' from the international situation. The success of socialist construction depends on the speed of economic development, and this speed is now being determined directly and more sharply than ever by the imports of raw materials and machinery... The whole of our constructive work is determined by international conditions.[23]

In the same speech Trotsky made a very serious concession to the Zinovievites: he denounced the theory of permanent revolution.

> I have no intention, comrades, of raising the question of the theory of permanent revolution. This theory—in respect both to what has been right in it and to what has been incomplete and wrong—has nothing whatever to do with our present contentions. In any case, this theory of permanent revolution, to which so much attention has been devoted recently, is not the responsibility in the slightest degree of either the Opposition of 1925 or the Opposition of 1923, and even I myself regard it as a question which has long been consigned to the archives.[24]

The Fifteenth Party Conference was marked by defections from the United Opposition. In his closing speech Stalin announced that Krupskaya had broken off relations with the Opposition. This defection must have had a shattering impact. In addition Shliapnikov and Medvedev, having been disowned by the Opposition leadership, now signed recantations of their views, which Stalin broadcast as a sign of the 'futher collapse of the Opposition bloc'. Finally Stalin played the leaders of foreign Communist Parties against the Opposition. On their behalf Clara Zetkin, the veteran German Communist, criticised Trotsky and Zinoviev.[25]

By far the nastiest attack on the Opposition was carried out by Bukharin. Deutscher describes the scene

> Now [Bukharin] stood by Stalin's side, as Zinoviev had stood there two years earlier, and assailed the Opposition with reckless virulence, exulting in its plight, bragging, threatening, inciting, sneering, and playing up to the worst elements in the party. The kindly scholar was as if transfigured suddenly. The thinker turned into a hooligan and the philosopher into a thug destitute of all scruple and foresight. He praised Stalin as the true friend of the peasant smallholder and the guardian of Leninism; and he challenged Trotsky to repeat before the conference what he had said at the Politburo about Stalin 'the grave-digger of the revolution'. He jeered at the restraint with which Trotsky had addressed the conference, a restraint due only to the fact that the party had 'seized the Opposition by the throat'. The Opposition, he said, appealed to them to avert the 'tragedy' that would result from a split. He, Bukharin, was only amused by the warning: 'Not more than three men will leave the party. This will be the whole split!', he exclaimed amid great laughter. 'This will be a farce, not a tragedy.' He thus scoffed at Kamenev's apology.
>
> 'When Kamenev comes here and...says: "I, Kamenev, have joined hands with Trotsky as Lenin used to join hands with him and lean on him", one can only reply with Homeric laughter: what sort of a Lenin have they discovered! We see very well that Kamenev and Zinoviev are leaning on Trotsky in a very odd manner. (*Prolonged laughter; and applause*) They "lean" on him in such a way that he has saddled them completely (*giggling and applause*), and then Kamenev

squeals: "I am leaning on Trotsky". (*Mirth*) Yes, altogether like Lenin! (*Laughter*)'... self-assured and complacent, juggling and jingling with quotations from Lenin, [Bukharin] returned to the attack on permanent revolution, on Trotsky's 'heroic postures', hostility towards the *muzhik*, and 'fiscal theory of building socialism'; and again and again he extolled the steadfastness, the reliability, and the caution of his own and of Stalin's policies which secured the alliance with the peasantry. When the Opposition 'screamed' about the strength of the kulak and the danger of peasant strikes and of famine in the towns, it was trying to frighten the people with bogeys. The party should not forgive them this and the 'chatter about the Soviet Thermidor', unless they came with their heads bowed to repent, confess, and beg: 'Forgive us our sins against the spirit and the letter and the very essence of Leninism!' Amid frantic applause he went on:

'Say it, and say it honestly: Trotsky was wrong when he declared that ours was not a *fully* proletarian state! Why don't you have the plain courage to come out and say so?... Zinoviev has told us here how well Lenin treated oppositions. Lenin did not expel any opposition even when he was left with only two votes for himself in the Central Committee... Yes, Lenin knew his job. Who would try and expel an opposition when he could muster two votes only? (*Laughter*) But when you get all the votes and you have only two against you and the two shriek about Thermidor, then you may well think about expulsion.'

The conference was delighted with this display of cynicism and shook with merriment. From the floor Stalin shouted: 'Well done, Bukharin. Well done, well done. He does not argue with them, he slaughters them!'[26]

The Opposition was routed. The Conference sanctioned the expulsion of Trotsky, Zinoviev and Kamenev from the Politburo, threatening them with reprisals if they dared to reopen the controversy.

The harassment of the Opposition was continued before an international audience when the Seventh Enlarged Plenum of the Executive Committee of the Comintern met on 22 November. The removal of Zinoviev from presidency of the Executive Committee was confirmed and he was stripped of all his Comintern functions. On 7 December Stalin made a three-hour speech attacking the Opposition leaders. Discussion on the question lasted a week. Bukharin, Kuusinen, Treint, Pepper, Birch, Stern, Brandt, Remmele and many others attacked Trotskyism. Stalin's resolution describing the Opposition as a 'right-wing danger to the party, frequently concealed behind left phrases', connected with other oppositions both in Russia and abroad, passed unanimously. The Executive Committee of the Communist International approved the expulsion of Trotskyists and Zinovievites from foreign Communist Parties.[27]

Again lying low

In the winter of 1926-27 the United Opposition reached a fate similar to that of the 1923 Opposition after its defeat. With the banning of factions the choice was either to go on fighting and risk expulsion from the party or accept defeat. The Zinovievites were inclined to lie low. Zinoviev and Kamenev went so far as to advise their followers to keep their views to themselves, and if need be even to deny their association with the Opposition. Such advice, of course, could not but demoralise those to whom it was given. They began to desert and recant.

The Trotskyists, who had already gone through a similar experience in 1923-4, knew they could gain nothing from a policy of passivity. Trotsky, in a memorandum written on 26 November, re-examined the recent experience, and with complete realism still argued that however difficult the situation, however depressed the workers' mood, revolutionaries should not give in to that. In the memorandum Trotsky analyses the reasons for the strength of the bureaucracy and the weakness of the Opposition. He finds the main cause in the conservative mood of the workers.

It would be wrong to ignore the fact that the proletariat today is considerably less receptive to revolutionary perspectives and to broad generalisations than it was during the October Revolution and in the ensuing few years...

...the masses, especially the older generation...have grown more cautious, more sceptical, less directly responsive to revolutionary slogans, less inclined to place confidence in broad generalisations. These moods, which unfolded after the ordeals of the civil war and after the successes of economic reconstruction and have not yet been undone by the new shifts of class forces—these moods constitute the basic political background of party life. These are the moods which bureaucratism—as an element of 'law and order' and 'tranquility'—relies on. The attempt of the Opposition to put the new problems before the party ran up against precisely these moods.

The older generation of the working class, which made two revolutions, or made the last one, beginning with 1917, is suffering from nervous exhaustion, and a substantial section of it fears any new upheavals, with their attendant prospects of war, havoc, epidemic, and so on.

The attack on the theory of permanent revolution fed on workers' spiritual exhaustion.

A bogey is being made out of the theory of permanent revolution precisely for the purpose of exploiting the psychology of this substantial section of the workers, who are not at all careerists, but who have put on weight, acquired families. The version of the theory which is being utilised for this is of course in no way related to the old disputes, long relegated to the archives, but simply raises the phantom of new upheavals—heroic 'invasions', the disruption of 'law and order', a threat to the attainments of the reconstruction period, a new period of great efforts and sacrifices.

The youth are not exhausted, but are far too inexperienced:

The young generation, only now growing up, lacks experience in the class struggle and the necessary revolutionary tempering. It does not explore for itself, as did the previous generation, but falls immediately into an environment of the most powerful party and governmental institutions, party tradition, authority, discipline, etc. For the time being this renders it more difficult for the young generation to play an independent role. The question of the correct orientation of the young generation of the party and of the working class acquires a colossal importance.[28]

This explanation of the objective causes for the weakness of the Opposition could have become an excuse for giving up the struggle.

Nothing was further from Trotsky's thinking.

To repeat what Trotsky said: a revolutionary has to fight, no matter whether he is destined to end as Lenin did—to live and see his cause triumph—or to suffer the fate of Liebknecht who served his cause through martyrdom.

The winter of 1926-7 passed with the Opposition paralysed by irresolution brought about by Zinoviev's panic and Trotsky's efforts to prevent the dissolution of the partnership with Zinoviev. But one thing workers do not like is nebulousness, half measures and diplomatic evasions.

Two great events taking place outside the Soviet Union had a big impact on the inner-party struggle: the general strike in Britain in May 1926, and the rise and fall of the Chinese revolution. The Chinese revolution gave a new fillip to the United Opposition. As Trotsky wrote in his autobiography:

> As early as the beginning of 1927, Zinoviev was ready to capitulate, if not all at once, at least gradually. But then came the staggering events in China. The criminal character of Stalin's policy hit one in the eye. It postponed for a time the capitulation of Zinoviev and of all who followed him later.[29]

Chapter eight
The General Strike in Britain

The Anglo-Russian Committee

IN THE WINTER and spring of 1925, while Trotsky was recuperating in the Caucasus he wrote a book, **Where is Britain Going?** Just then the leadership of the Comintern was attaching great importance to a new link established between the Soviet and British trade unions.

A delegation of Russian trade unionists attended the Hull Congress of the TUC in September 1924, following which in November six delegates of the TUC went to Russia. These discussions resulted in an agreement to set up an Anglo-Russian Committee to work for international trade union unity. At a conference held in London the following April, a Joint Declaration was issued, and the Committee established. At the Scarborough TUC of September 1925 the policy was endorsed, and Tomsky was received as a fraternal delegate.

The Congress buzzed with revolutionary fervour. Alonzo Swales in his Presidential address said:

> We are entering upon a new stage of development in the upward struggle of our class... The new phase of development which is world-wide has entered upon the next and probably the last stage of revolt. It is the duty of all members of the working class so to solidify their movements that, come when the time may be for the last final struggle, we shall be wanting neither machinery nor men to move forward to the destruction of wage slavery and the construction of a new order of society based upon co-ordinated effort and work with mutual goodwill and understanding.

A large number of extreme left speeches and resolutions followed. The British Empire was condemned; the Dawes Plan for the reconstruction of Europe with American capital was opposed; plans for united work with the Russian trade unions were endorsed. The Communist Party's **Workers' Weekly** was very impressed with the proceedings:

> The Congress was intent on its work from start to finish. When Swales delivered his opening speech the real temper of the Congress began to manifest itself. The more militant became the mood, the more the delegates responded to his fighting challenge.[1]

A general offensive by the mine owners was expected shortly, and the language of speeches and resolutions at the Congress seemed to indicate that the official union leaders were preparing for the showdown in a few months' time.

> Everyone looked to the General Council to give the lead... In many places it was assumed that the General Council was secretly making the full preparations. The presence on the council of a left wing (comprising Purcell, Swales, Hicks, Tillet, Bromley and others) lent colour to this idea.[2]

It was against this background that Trotsky wrote his book **Where is Britain Going?** In essence it was directed against the Russian leadership's mistaken hope that the General Council of the TUC would swing leftward under the influence of the Anglo-Russian Committee and that Communist influence would gradually transform the Labour Party.

The left turn of the British trade union leadership was very shallow. It was largely a result of the disgust felt throughout the trade union movement, even among the right wing of the bureaucracy, with the policies of the first Labour government of 1924.[3] The first months of 1924 saw a rash of strikes, principally in transport. Workers wanted to use the partial economic recovery and the existence of the government they themselves had elected to advance their position. But the MacDonald government acted as scabs.

The Comintern leadership, above all Zinoviev, was very impressed with the left phraseology of the TUC leaders. Zinoviev even came to the conclusion that in Britain the revolution could be victorious without the Communist Party playing a crucial role. At the Fifth Congress of the Comintern (June-July 1924), Zinoviev, referring to the leaders of the Communist Party of Great Britain, such as Bob Stewart and Arthur MacManus, made this cryptic comment:

> In England, we are now going through the beginning of a new chapter in the labour movement. We do not know whither the Communist Mass Party of England will come, whether only through the Stewart-MacManus door—or through some other door. And it is entirely possible, comrades, that the Communist Mass Party may still appear through still another door—we cannot lose sight of that fact.[4]

Zinoviev was looking for a short cut. By talking of this mysterious 'other door', he implied that a mass revolutionary party could be built by the current around the Labour and TUC lefts.

There followed a policy of manoeuvring and unprincipled flirting with the leaders of the TUC and the lefts of the Labour Party.

Where is Britain Going?

Trotsky's book starts from a conviction that Britain was moving towards a social crisis of the first magnitude. The decline of British capitalism had been continuous since the end of the nineteenth century. Britain was squeezed by German capitalism, and since the First World War by that of the United States.

> Britain today stands at a critical point...
> The powerful and ever-growing world pressure of the United States makes the predicament of British industry, British trade, British finance and British diplomacy increasingly insoluble and desperate...
> During the war the gigantic economic domination of the United States had demonstrated itself wholly and completely. The United States' emergence from overseas provincialism at once shifted Britain into a secondary position.[5]

The decline of British industry and the strains in the empire added to the deepening crisis of British capitalism.

For a time Britain's decline, accelerated by the First World

War, was hidden by the disruption of the German economy. But Germany, aided by the United States, was now manifestly recovering its strength and reappeared as Britain's most dangerous competitor in the world market.

The crisis of British capitalism showed itself at its most extreme in the coal industry. This old, technically backward industry was in sharp competition with the German mining industry. As Trotsky wrote elsewhere, in a letter of 5 March 1926:

> The present miners' wages are maintained by a subsidy from the state, burdening an already crippling budget. To continue the subsidy means to accumulate and deepen the economic crisis. To withdraw the subsidy means to produce a social crisis.[6]

Britain, Trotsky argued, was drifting into a massive industrial dispute in the mining industry.

> With regard to the [future] miners' strike, it is not of course a question of an isolated strike, however big it may be, but the commencement of a whole series of social conflicts and crises.[7]

The economic crisis would bring with it a sharp political crisis in the workers' movement: a crisis of Labourism, of Fabianism.

The struggle for workers' emancipation demanded a break with the traditional ideas that dominated workers' thinking. Trotsky therefore launched a massive and brilliant assault on these traditions. The traditions, to which Trotsky returns again and again, could be summed up under four headings: religion, pacifism, gradualism and parliamentary democracy. All these in essence were one: submission to the ruling class.

Trotsky gave a brilliant analysis of Labourism, stripping it of its social pretensions and showing it to be dependent on the traditions of the Conservatives and Liberals. He pointed out its acceptance of the prevailing bourgeois ideas—its fetishism of religion, monarchy and empire, its insularity, its ignorance and narrow mindedness, and its pacifist hypocrisy while supporting the aims of state and empire. These difficulties were all sharply exposed:

> The outlook of the leaders of the British Labour Party is a sort

of amalgam of Conservatism and Liberalism, partly adapted to the requirements of the trade unions, or rather their top layers. All of them are ridden with the religion of 'gradualness'. In addition they acknowledge the religion of the Old and New Testaments. They all consider themselves to be highly civilised people, yet they believe that the Heavenly Father created mankind only then, in his abundant love, to curse it, and subsequently to try, through the crucifixion of his own son, to straighten this highly knotty affair a little. Out of the spirit of Christianity there have grown such national institutions as the trade union bureaucracy, MacDonald's first ministry and Mrs. Snowden. Closely tied to the religion of gradualness and the Calvinist belief in predestination is the religion of national arrogance.[8]

Trotsky then goes on to quote Ramsay MacDonald: 'Socialism is based upon the gospels'. 'It is an excellently conceived [sic] and resolute attempt to Christianise government and society'.

Trotsky's polemic against Fabian pacifism is unsurpassed. He starts by quoting MacDonald:

Socialism does not believe in force... Socialism is a state of mental health and not a mental sickness... and therefore by its very nature it must repudiate force with horror. It fights only with mental and moral weapons.

And Trotsky comments:

MacDonald is against revolution and for organic evolution. He carries over poorly digested biological concepts into society. For him revolution, as a sum of accumulated partial mutations, resembles the development of living organisms, the turning of a chrysalis into a butterfly and so forth; but in this latter process he ignores just those decisive, critical moments when the new creature bursts the old casing in a revolutionary way.

Trotsky deflates the Fabians with sarcasm.

Even the chick which has taken shape in the egg has to apply force to the calcareous prison that shuts it in. If some Fabian chick decided out of Christian (or any other) considerations to refrain from acts of force the calcareous casing would inevitably suffocate it. British pigeon fanciers are producing a special variety with a shorter and shorter beak, by artificial selection. There comes a time, however, when the new offspring's beak is so short that the poor creature can no longer pierce the egg-shell. The young pigeon falls victim to compulsory restraint from violence; and the continued progress of the short-beak variety comes to a halt. If our memory serves us right, MacDonald can read about this in Darwin. Still pursuing these analogies with the organic world so beloved of MacDonald, we can say that the political art of the British bourgeoisie consists of shortening the proletariat's revolutionary beak, thereby preventing it from perforating the shell of the capitalist state. The beak of the proletariat is its party. If you take a glance at MacDonald, Thomas and Mr. and Mrs Snowden then it must be admitted that the bourgeoisie's work of rearing the short-beaked and soft-beaked varieties has been crowned with striking success—for not only are these worthies unfit to break through the capitalist shell, they are really unfit to do anything at all.[9]

That the ruling class, faced with its overthrow, would resort to violence, was for Trotsky glaringly obvious, and the pacifism of the Labour leaders both stupid and harmful.

What does the renunciation of force in the final resort signify? Only that the oppressed must not adopt force against a capitalist state: neither workers against the bourgeoisie, nor farmers against landlords, nor Indians against the British administration and British capital. The state, constructed by the violence of the monarchy against the people, the bourgeoisie against the workers, the landlords against the farmers, by officers against soldiers, Anglo-Saxon slave owners against colonial peoples, 'Christians' against heathens—this bloodstained apparatus of centuries-long violence inspires MacDonald with pious reverence. He reacts 'with horror' only to the force of liberation.[10]

'Gradualism' can on the surface appear as slow progress, while in reality it is an adaptation to the existing order.
Rejecting revolutionary force means complete surrender to

the bourgeoisie, servility to the existing state, to bourgeois legality and force. It certainly does not mean opposing the bourgeois state's violence in Britain and in the Empire.

Fabianism prided itself on its peculiar British tradition which was unadulterated with alien Marxism. Trotsky retorted that the Fabians cultivated only the conservative national traditions while completely overlooking their progressive strands.

> From Puritanism the MacDonalds have inherited—not its revolutionary strand but its religious prejudices. From the Owenites—not their communist enthusiasm but their reactionary Utopian hostility to the class struggle. From Britain's past political history the Fabians have borrowed only the spiritual dependence of the proletariat on the bourgeoisie. History has turned its backside on these gentlemen and the inscriptions they read there have become their programme.[11]

Trotsky goes on to consider the two major British revolutionary traditions: that of Cromwell and of the Chartists.

> The British social crisis of the seventeenth century combined in itself features of the German Reformation of the sixteenth century with features of the French Revolution of the eighteenth century.[12]

The Puritans rose magnificently to face the social crisis of the time.

> Cromwell was a great revolutionary of his time, who knew how to uphold the interests of the new bourgeois social system against the old aristocratic one *without holding back at anything*. This must be learnt from him, and the dead lion of the seventeenth century is in this sense immeasurably greater than many living dogs.
> ...Cromwell was in no case a 'pioneer of labour'. But in the seventeenth century drama, the British proletariat can find great precedents for revolutionary action...
> It can be with some justice said that Lenin is the proletarian twentieth-century Cromwell.[13]

The British proletariat should be inspired by Cromwell and his followers:

...the British proletariat should borrow this spirit of self-confidence and aggressive courage from the old Independents. The MacDonalds, Webbs, Snowdens and others have taken from Cromwell's comrades-in-arms only the religious prejudices and combined them with a purely Fabian cowardice. The proletarian vanguard has to combine the Independents' revolutionary courage with a materialist clarity of world-outlook.[14]

The working class movement of Britain has another great national tradition—Chartism.

The era of Chartism is immortal in that over the course of a decade it gives us in condensed and diagrammatic form the whole gamut of proletarian struggle—from petitions in parliament to armed insurrection. All the fundamental problems of the class movement of the proletariat—the inter-relation between parliamentary and extra-parliamentary activity, the role of universal suffrage, trade unions and co-operation, the significance of the general strike and its relation to armed insurrection, even the inter-relation between the proletariat and the peasantry—were not only crystallised out of the progress of the Chartist mass movement, but found in it their principled answer. Theoretically this answer was far from always irreproachable in its basis. The conclusions were not always fully drawn, and in all the movement as a whole and its theoretical expression there was much that was immature and unfinished.

But then Chartism was the rising movement of a young class.

It can be said that the Chartist movement resembles a prelude which contains in an undeveloped form the musical theme of the whole opera. In this sense the British working class can and must see in Chartism not only its past but also its future... Chartism did not win a victory not because its methods were incorrect but because it appeared too soon. It was only an historical anticipation.[15]

Trotsky goes on to deal with the nature of the trade union bureaucracy. He was very precise in locating the specific role of this bureaucracy in the political wing of reformism.

The Labour Party... is only a political transposition of the... trade union bureaucracy. The Labour Party and the trade unions—these are not two principles, they are only a technical division of labour. Together they are the fundamental support of the domination of the British bourgeoisie.[16]

The Fabian leadership of the Labour Party and bureaucracy of the trade unions were the greatest bulwarks of capitalism. Trotsky writes of the Fabian leaders:

These pompous authorities, pedants and haughty, high-falutin' cowards are systematically poisoning the labour movement, clouding the consciousness of the proletariat and paralysing its will. It is only thanks to them that Toryism, Liberalism, the Church, the monarchy, the aristocracy and the bourgeoisie continue to survive and even suppose themselves to be firmly in the saddle. The Fabians, the ILPers and the conservative trade union bureaucrats today represent the most counter-revolutionary force in Great Britain, and possibly in the present stage of development, in the whole world.[17]

Trotsky does not see any *qualitative* difference between the MacDonalds and the 'Lefts'—A. Purcell, G. Hicks, A.J. Cook.

The left wing of the Labour Party represents an attempt to regenerate centrism within MacDonald's social-imperialist party. It thus reflects the disquiet of a part of the labour bureaucracy over the link with the leftward moving masses. It would be a monstrous illusion to think that these left elements of the old school are capable of heading the revolutionary movement of the British proletariat and its struggle for power. They represent a historical stage which is over. Their elasticity is extremely limited and their leftness is opportunist through and through. They do not lead nor are capable of leading the masses into struggle. Within the bounds of their reformist narrowness they revive the old irresponsible centrism without hindering, but rather helping, MacDonald to bear the responsibility for the party's leadership and in certain cases for the destiny of the British Empire too.

The crucial task of the Communist Party is to fight the Labour leaders including the 'Lefts'. They,

> convert the political feebleness of the awakening masses into an ideological mish-mash. They represent the expression of a shift but also its brake.[18]

> The path of the Communist Party, as the future great party of the masses, lies not only through an implacable struggle against capital's special agency in the shape of the Thomas-MacDonald clique but also through the systematic unmasking of the left muddleheads by means of whom alone MacDonald and Thomas can maintain their positions.[19]

A couple of years after the general strike Trotsky returned to dealing with the trade union bureaucracy.

> If there were not a bureaucracy of the trade unions, then the police, the army, the courts, the lords, the monarchy would appear before the proletarian masses as nothing but pitiful ridiculous playthings. The bureaucracy of the trade unions is the backbone of British imperialism. It is by means of this bureaucracy that the bourgeoisie exists, not only in the metropolis, but in India, in Egypt and in the other colonies.[20]

A particularly unsavoury role is played by the Labour 'Lefts'.

> ...the highest post in the mechanism of capitalist stabilisation is no longer occupied by MacDonald and Thomas, but by Pugh, Purcell, Cook and Co. They do the work and Thomas adds the finishing touches. Without Purcell, Thomas would be left hanging in mid-air and along with Thomas also Baldwin. The chief brake upon the British revolution is the false, diplomatic masquerade 'Leftism' of Purcell which fraternises sometimes in rotation, sometimes simultaneously with churchmen and Bolsheviks and which is always ready not only for retreats but also for betrayal.[21]

Trotsky brilliantly foresaw the pathetic role of the 'Lefts' in the coming General Strike. On 5 March 1926, two months before the General Strike, he wrote:

> ...both the rights and the lefts, including of course both Purcell and Cook, fear to the utmost the beginning of the

denouement. Even when in words they admit the inevitability of struggle and revolution they are hoping in their hearts for some miracle which will release them from these perspectives. And in any event they themselves will stall, evade, temporise, shift responsibility and effectively assist Thomas over any really major question of the *British* labour movement.[22]

Trotsky saw through the tinsel and glitter of the 1925 Scarborough TUC Congress that had so mesmerised the leaders of the Communist Party of Great Britain as well as Zinoviev.

The resolutions of the congress were the more to the left the further removed they were from immediate practical tasks... to think that the leading figures at Scarborough might become the leaders of a revolutionary overthrow of power would be to lull oneself with illusions... It must be clearly understood: this sort of leftism remains only as long as it does not impose any practical obligation. As soon as a question of action arises the lefts respectfully surrender the leadership to the rights.[23]*

Whatever the relative strength of the 'Lefts', the Rights were bound to direct them:

The rights win despite the fact that the lefts are more numerous. The weakness of the lefts arises from their disorder and their disorder from their ideological formlessness.[26]

This was written months before the betrayal of the General Strike on 13 May 1926 which so astounded British socialists.

---

*Elsewhere Trotsky pointed out: 'In Marx's era the trade unionists used to adopt radical resolutions in regard to Poland, but put the question of Ireland and India quite differently'.[24]

Now the 'Lefts' showed great sympathy for the Soviet Union. Trotsky was very shrewd in explaining this: '...in the sympathies of many lefts for the Soviet Union (alongside hostility towards their own communists) there is contained a good deal of the deference of the petty bourgeois towards a strong state power... one cannot build revolutionary perspectives on such a deference'.[25]

The 1926 General Strike

The general strike of May 1926 was a watershed in the class struggle in Britain in the inter-war years. Its defeat was decisive for the working class, bringing to an end a long though not uninterrupted period of working class militancy, leading to a prolonged domination of the class-collaborationist right wing of the trade unions, and to entrenched right-reformist domination of the Labour Party.

By the mid-1920s the British ruling class as a whole wanted a readjustment of the economy. As in every capitalist crisis the working class was expected to pay the price. So in some ways the battle of 1926 was no unusual event. The system has always tried, and will always try to make the workers solve its problems. But the very depth of the crisis and scale of the struggle made 1926 exceptional. This was to be battle of Titans, with the ruling class ready to pit its combined economic, political and ideological batallions against the workers and their chief defensive organisations, the trade unions.

On 29 July 1925 Prime Minister Stanley Baldwin told the miners' leaders 'that the government would not grant any subsidy to the industry and that it must stand on its own economic foundations.'[27]

Next day the **Daily Herald** reported a conversation between Baldwin and representatives of the Miners' Federation of Great Britain in which the Prime Minister twice insisted that 'all the workers of this country have got to take reductions in wages to help put industry on its feet.'[28]

On 30 July the mine owners announced that they would end the 1924 agreement, cut wages, abolish the national minimum, revise wage determination from national to district agreements, and maintain standard profits no matter how low wages fell. The same day a special conference of trade union delegates resolved unanimously that the movement should refuse to handle coal.

The next day Baldwin met the miners' executive and a special committee of the TUC jointly. He explained that the coal owners had agreed to suspend lock-out notices, that a Royal Commission into the coal industry would be appointed, and that the government would, in the meantime, guarantee financial subsidies until 30 April 1926. This was 'Red Friday'. Baldwin had no choice but to back off. As he told his biographer, G.M. Young, several years later: 'We were not ready'.[29]

After 'Red Friday' the union leaders sat with folded arms, making no preparations for the future government and employers' offensive against the miners. The historian Alan Bullock, in his biography of Ernest Bevin, writes:

> In the seven months between [October 1925] and the crisis at the end of 1926 which led straight into the General Strike, the full General Council did not once discuss what was to happen when the government subsidy came to an end on 30 April nor concern itself with preparations for the support of the miners—apart, of course, from receiving the reports of the Special Industrial Committee in the normal course of its monthly meetings.
>
> ...the Industrial Committee took no more active steps than the General Council itself. It met twice between 1 October 1925 and 1 January 1926, resolving on the first occasion (25 October) to watch the course of events and meet again in 1926 'if circumstances warrant it', and on the second occasion (18 December) not to seek additional powers as suggested at Scarborough.[30]

Throughout the nine months prior to 1 May 1926 the 'Lefts' on the General Council of the TUC showed not one iota more initiative than the right wingers. When on 1 May 1926 over one million miners were locked out the TUC reluctantly called a national strike.

From the beginning the TUC leaders made it clear that they intended to keep a tight grip on the strike. They took it upon themselves to decide who should stop work and who should not. Not all workers were called out. The TUC strategy was instead framed as a strike in 'waves'—one group of workers was to strike while others waited. Had all trade unionists been called out from the beginning the impact would have been far greater.

The interdependence of different sectors of industry made nonsense of the hastily cobbled together idea of separate waves. Notwithstanding the terrible leadership, throughout the nine days—4-12 May—the strike was rock solid. Workers showed both massive enthusiasm and dogged determination. Everywhere the strike grew in power by the day. More and more of industry ground to a halt. As a matter of fact the bureaucracy was holding back floods of workers who wished to be involved. The chief problem the officials faced was not getting people out but keeping members at work. This was evidence of the really militant spirit of the workers. A large number of non-unionists went on strike when their unionised workmates came out.

During the strike the 'Left' union leaders tail-ended the Right. And the Communist Party tail-ended the 'Lefts'. The central slogan of the Communist Party throughout the strike was, 'All power to the General Council'! This slogan became a cover for the activities of the TUC leadership.

While the strike was going strong, behind the back of the workers the leadership of the TUC and the Labour Party were conspiring with government ministers and officials on how to end it. The secret negotiations started on the fourth day of the strike (7 May) and went on until the strike was brought to an end. Throughout, not only were the rank and file workers kept in the dark but the miners' leaders too were lied to. On 12 May the strike was called off. This was a complete surrender. The decision to surrender was *unanimous*. The two miners' representatives on the 32-strong General Council were absent (Tom Richards was ill and Robert Smillie stayed in Scotland to assist his members there).

The decision of the General Council to call off the strike was taken without consulting the miners. Only afterwards were the miners' representatives notified of it. The 'Lefts' on the General Council behaved no differently to the Rights. Later Ben Turner, a right-winger on the General Council made this highly significant comment in a letter to the Communist Party-influenced **Sunday Worker**:

> I don't think you were just to the General Council of the TUC. You divided us into left-wingers and right-wingers [but] the absolute unanimity of the General Council in declaring the General Strike off did not divide us into left-wingers and right-wingers.[31]

The miners, abandoned, fought on alone for another six months.

After the end of the General Strike, the TUC 'Lefts' were brazen enough to pretend that the general strike had not been sold out at all. Thus on 13 June Purcell wrote in the **Sunday**

Worker that the stoppage was merely a 'preliminary encounter' and,

> more real working-class progress was made in those few days than has been made in as many years previously. Those who talk about the failure of the General Strike are mentally a generation behind the times in which we live.[32]

An even more startling rewrite of events came from the pen of Hicks in the same issue:

> Was the General Strike a victory or defeat?
> I reply: Who has gained the most from it? The working class has gained infinitely more from the General Strike than has the capitalist class... 'A Great Victory'.
> Of course the General Strike has been a success—a great victory. Those who talk about the General Strike being a failure and of the uselessness of the General Strike as a weapon must be living in a world of their own imagining.[33]

Trotsky's reaction to the General Strike

On the third day of the General Strike Trotsky wrote:

> The fundamental importance of the General Strike is that it poses the question of power point-blank...
> We must look facts in the face: the principal efforts of the official Labour Party leaders and of a considerable number of official trade union leaders will be directed not towards paralyzing the bourgeois state by means of the strike but towards paralyzing the General Strike by means of the bourgeois state.

What was necessary for the salvation of the strike was a radical change in leadership:

> ...success is possible only to the extent that the British working class, in the process of the development and sharpening of the General Strike, realises the need to change its leadership, and measures up to that task. There is an American proverb which says that you cannot change horses in mid-stream. But this practical wisdom is true only within certain limits. The stream of revolution has never been

crossed on the horse of reformism, and the class which has entered the struggle under opportunist leadership will be compelled to change it under fire.

...An implacable struggle against every act of treachery or attempted treachery and the ruthless exposure of the reformists' illusions are the main elements in the work of the genuinely revolutionary participants in the General Strike.[34]

The Communist leaders and the collapse of the General Strike

A half confession of error by the leadership of the CPGB followed the collapse of the General Strike.

To lead is to foresee, and the Communist Party leaders foresaw nothing. After the strike they had to admit that they did not expect the betrayal by the General Council. George Hardy wrote:

> Although we knew of what treachery the right-wing leaders were capable, we did not clearly understand the part played by the so-called 'left' in the union leadership. In the main they turned out to be windbags and capitulated to the right wing. We were taught a major lesson; that while developing a move to the left officially, the main point in preparing for action must always be to develop a class-conscious leadership among the rank and file.[35]

The **Workers Weekly**, in aggrieved surprise, said:

> We warned our readers of the weakness and worse of the right wing on the General Council—but here we confess that reality has far exceeded our worst forbodings... The Communist Party had in fact consistently warned the workers that such was likely to happen, but even the Communist Party can be forgiven for not believing it to be possible that once the struggle had begun these leaders should have proved themselves such pitiful paltroons as to surrender at the very moment of victory.[36]

Only after the strike ended, in a flush of insight, did the party leadership understand the role of the 'Left' on the General Council. On 13 May the Communist Party issued a statement stating *inter alia* the following:

...most of the so-called left wing have been no better than the right. By a policy of timid silence, by using the false pretext of loyalty to colleagues to cover up breaches of loyalty to workers, they have left a free hand to the right wing and thus helped to play the employers' game. Even now they have not the courage to come out openly as a minority in the General Council and join forces with the real majority—the workers—against the united front of Baldwin-Samuel-Thomas.[37]

The Eighth Congress of the CPGB repeated: the 'Lefts' were,

apologists for the General Council... aiders and abetters of the right-wing during the strike... unashamed agents of the Trade Union Congress... a set of phrase-mongers who had won easy fame as 'revolutionaries' on the issue of international trade union unity.[38]

There was no mention of who had assisted the 'Lefts' to gain this 'easy fame'. And for many months there was no word of self-criticism for the CPGB or Comintern line.

The Comintern leadership did not indulge in any self-criticism—even semi-criticism—at all. It argued that it was clearly right, that if mistakes were committed it was because of defects in the national leadership in Britain.

Two months before the General Strike, a meeting of the Seventh Plenum of the Executive Committee of the Communist International approved the policies adopted by the CPGB. In his opening speech Zinoviev said that the best results over the past year had been gained in Britain (and China). The policy of the CPGB showed how united front tactics should be used.[39]

Immediately after the General Strike the Comintern leadership started singing a new tune. Now the British Communist leaders were reprimanded for their failure to criticise the TUC openly and sharply enough.

To add to the muddle, Stalin, at a meeting in Tiflis on 8 June, while referring to the leaders of the TUC and the Labour Party as 'downright traitors or spineless fellow-travellers of the traitors', nevertheless affirmed that the attitude of the CPGB was absolutely correct throughout, one of the reasons for its failure in the strike being that it enjoyed little prestige among British workers.

Stalin continued to argue the crucial need to preserve the Anglo-Russian Committee. In July 1926 at a joint Plenum of the Central Committee and the Central Control Commission he said:

> The... task of the [Anglo-Russian Committee] is to organise a broad movement of the working class against new imperialist wars in general, and against intervention in our country by (especially) the most powerful of the European imperialist powers, by Britain in particular.
> ...if the reactionary trade unions of Britain are prepared to join with the revolutionary trade unions of our country in a bloc against the counter-revolutionary imperialists of their country, why should we not welcome such a bloc?[40]

(Trotsky's comment on these words was sharp and to the point: 'Stalin cannot understand that were the "reactionary trade unions" capable of waging a struggle against their own imperialists, they would not be reactionary trade unionists.')[41]

For months after the general strike not a word of criticism was made of the CPGB by the Comintern. However, six months later there was a change. In December the ECCI criticised the Central Committee of the CPGB for a tendency to tone down its attack on the General Council, including its left wing. Bukharin endorsed this criticism in his opening speech to the Plenum of the ECCI: the CPGB was not consistent and severe enough in its criticism of the 'left' leaders.[42]

On every major question in British politics preceding the General Strike Trotsky offered by far the best approach. His brilliant characterisation of the intellectual shallowness, religiosity and vacillating nature of the MacDonalds and Thomases is as fresh today as it ever was. Furthermore, it is just as appropriate to their modern equivalents as it was in 1925 and 1926. Trotsky saw straight through the seeming differences between these right-wing reformists and the more left sounding George Lansbury in the Labour Party or union leaders such as Cook, Purcell and Hicks. Beneath the appearance he divined the common reformist and bureaucratic traits.

Though incorrect in some details, Trotsky's penetrating analysis overcame the great geographical distance and paucity of information which cut him off from Britain.*see next page

His skill came from the depth of his Marxism. Unlike so many who were caught up in the degeneration of the Russian revolution, Trotsky kept a firm grasp of the two fundamental lessons of Bolshevism—that a victorious struggle depended on the leadership which only a revolutionary party could offer, and that the emancipation of the working class could not come through bureaucrats, however radical they might sound, but only through the activity of the working class itself. There was no other way, however much the Communist Party leaders in London and Moscow would have preferred it.[44]

After the formation of the United Opposition Zinoviev, after further vacillation, agreed with Trotsky that the bloc of the Soviet trade unions with the British General Council should be broken. Unfortunately some in Trotsky's own wing, like Karl Radek, still opposed the break-up of the Anglo-Russian Committee.

The ARC Lingers on to Death

Even after the debacle of the General Strike and defeat of the miners, Stalin and Bukharin continued with the policy of a bloc between the top circles of the Soviet trade unions and the General Council. Meetings of the ARC continued to take place—in Paris in July 1926, in Berlin in the following month and in April 1927. On his return from the last meeting Tomsky, the leader of the Russian delegation, reported that all the decisions were unanimous and that the enemies of the working class, who hoped for the dissolution of the ARC, were disappointed. His report was

---

*One important prediction of **Where is Britain Going?** proved completely wrong. Trotsky wrote:

'A certain analogy would appear to arise between the fate of the Communist and Independent [ILP] parties. Both the former and the latter existed as propaganda societies rather than parties of the working class. Then at a profound turning in Britain's historical development the Independent party headed the proletariat. After a short interval the Communist Party will, we submit, undergo the same upsurge. [Therefore] the Communist Party will occupy the place in the Labour Party that is at present occupied by the Independents.'[43]

In no sense did Trotsky suggest that the Communist Party and ILP shared common politics, and the witch hunt of Communists which took off just after Trotsky wrote the book soon put paid to any idea that revolutionaries could lead from inside the Labour Party.

approved by the Russian trade union council. The principal decision had been won on non-intervention in each others' affairs. The ARC had nothing to say about the British government note of 28 February 1927 to the Soviet government that carried the threat of a rupture of diplomatic relations; or about the British navy bombardment of Nanking.

Finally, in September 1927 the TUC decided to break up the ARC. The same Congress decided to enter into a period of close collaboration with the employers, under the Mond-Turner agreement.

Chapter nine
The Chinese Revolution

THE EVENTS in China had enormous influence on the mood of party members in Russia. Serge remembers: 'The Chinese revolution galvanised us all. I have the impression of a positive wave of enthusiasm heaving up the whole Soviet world—or at least the thinking part of it.'[1]

The revolution, however, was decapitated in 1927, when the Shanghai working class was massacred by Chiang Kai-shek, leader of the Kuomintang and chief of its army. A short survey of the Chinese revolution is warranted.

First interventions of Moscow in China

In August 1922 the representative of the Comintern, Maring (the Dutch Communist Sneevliet) arrived in Shanghai, and after meeting with Sun Yat-sen, leader of the bourgeois nationalist party, the Kuomintang, he then met the Communist Party. At the time the Kuomintang was a formless and ineffective body dependent on the tolerance of the local 'progressive' warlord. Maring proposed that the Communist Party should join the Kuomintang. Prominent leaders of the party, including its General Secretary, Ch'en Tu-hsiu, opposed the plan on the ground that it deprived the party of its class independence. Maring countered these objections by advancing the novel view that the KMT was, in fact, a multi-class party representing 'a bloc of four classes'— that is, a bloc of the bourgeoisie, petty bourgeoisie, workers and peasants.[2] When the Central Committee of the CCP continued to resist, Maring invoked the discipline of the Comintern. Under this threat, the Central Committee reluctantly agreed. Although the

CCP was young and inexperienced its leaders still demonstrated a more consistently revolutionary stance than Maring. When Ch'en Tu-hsiu came to Moscow for the Fourth Congress of the Comintern he was upbraided as 'ultra-left' for his resistance to joining the KMT. Karl Radek told the Chinese delegates to the Congress that it was the task of the CCP to 'bring the workers into a rational relationship with the objectively revolutionary elements of the bourgeoisie'.

> You must understand, comrades, that neither the question of Socialism nor of the Soviet Republic are on the order of the day. Unfortunately, even the historic questions of national unity and of the united national republic are not yet on the order of the day in China. The present state of China reminds us of the eighteenth century in Europe, especially in Germany where capitalist development was too weak to allow the establishment of a united national centre.[3]

As the resistance in the ranks of the CCP to joining the KMT was very strong, the ECCI on 12 January 1923 issued a formal resolution on CCP-KMT collaboration, drafted by Zinoviev.

> 1. The only serious national revolutionary group in China is the Kuomintang, which is based partly on the liberal-democratic bourgeoisie and petty bourgeoisie, partly on the intelligentsia and workers.
> 2. Since the independent workers' movement in the country is still weak, and since the central task for China is the national revolution against the imperialists and their feudal agents within the country, and since, moreover, the working class is directly 'interested in the solution of the national-revolutionary problem while still being insufficiently differentiated as a wholly independent social force, the ECCI considers it necessary that action between the Kuomintang and the young CCP should be coordinated.
> 3. Consequently in present conditions it is expedient for members of the CCP to remain in the Kuomintang.[4]

Parallel to Maring's activity on behalf of the Comintern was the activity of the representatives of the Soviet government.

As early as 25 July 1919 the Soviet government had proclaimed its readiness to renounce all the imperialist privileges held by Tsarist Russia in China. It renewed this offer in a further declaration on 27 October 1920, and unofficial Soviet representatives began making efforts in Peking to negotiate a new treaty on this basis. The Russian offer to treat China on a basis of complete equality greatly heightened the prestige of the newly established Soviet power.

In January 1923 the Soviet government sent Adolf Ioffe, one of its first rank diplomats, to establish formal contacts with Sun Yat-sen in Shanghai. On 26 January 1923 Ioffe and Sun Yat-sen issued a joint manifesto, the first part of which stated:

> Doctor Sun is of the opinion that, because of the non-existence of conditions favourable to their successful application in China, it is not possible to carry out either Communism or even the Soviet system in China. M. Ioffe agrees entirely with this view. He is further of the opinion that China's most important and most pressing problems are the completion of national unification and the attainment of full national independence.[5]

This formula was interpreted to mean further support for the subordination of the CCP to the KMT.

Sun Yat-sen was in no doubt that the members of the CCP had to accept the discipline of the KMT. He told Ioffe:

> If the Communist Party enters the Kuomintang it must submit to discipline and not criticise the Kuomintang openly. If the Communists do not submit to the Kuomintang I shall expel them; and if Soviet Russia should give them secret protection, I shall oppose Soviet Russia.[6]

Sun Yat-sen made it clear that he envisaged the relationship between the CCP and KMT to be the relationship of subordinate to master. In December 1923 he wrote: 'If Russia wants to co-operate with China she must co-operate with our Party and not with Ch'en Tu-hsiu. If Ch'en disobeys our Party, he will be ousted.'[7]

The Third Conference of the CCP in June 1923 issued a manifesto stating: 'The KMT should be the central force of the national revolution and should assume its leadership'.[8]

Initially, the KMT encouraged anti-British strikes and nationalist agitation gave an impetus to the mass struggle which the nationalists then tried to stop. It was this which made it very easy for an initially very small and very middle class communist party to liquidate itself into the nationalist movement—ignoring the warning on this in the theses of the Second Congress of the Comintern (as did the bureaucratised Comintern itself).

The Communists gained admittance to the KMT in January 1924 by pledging individual allegiance to its principles and submission to its discipline. Under a system of dual party membership, designed for the occasion, they bound themselves to keep faith simultaneously with Sun Yat-sen's platform negating the class struggle and with their own platform enjoining the class struggle. In the words of the Third Congress of the CCP, this meant '...a two-fold struggle within the national... as well as... the class movement.'[9]

To strengthen the military prowess of the KMT the Russians founded the Whampoa Military Academy in May 1924 to lay the basis for a corps of officers for a new Nationalist Army. The Academy was supplied and run with Russian funds. Before long shiploads of Soviet arms were coming into Canton harbour to supply the KMT armies.

In the military ranks of the KMT a special place was held by Chiang Kai-shek. He was sent by Sun Yat-sen to Moscow to study Red Army methods and the Soviet system. Chiang left China in July 1923 and remained in Russia for six months. On his return to Canton at the end of the year, he became the darling of Mikhail Borodin, the Soviet representative, and the Russian military advisers. He also became director of the Whampoa Military Academy.

The beginning of the Chinese Revolution

In the first month of 1925 strikes spread throughout China. Since the larger factories were almost all directly or indirectly under foreign ownership, this was an anti-imperialist as well as an anti-capitalist movement.

A wave of strikes in Shanghai in the early months of 1925 led to the shooting of a number of workers by the Japanese police on 30 May. This was followed by a mass demonstration in which twelve students were killed by the British police. The reaction to this was a general strike that spread from Hong Kong and Canton in the South, to Shanghai and then further north to Peking. In

Hong Kong and Canton 250,000 workers came out on a strike that lasted a whole year. The general strike was accompanied by a boycott of British goods.

The Communist Party influence grew very rapidly. At the same time the KMT was able to consolidate its power in Kwangtung. At the end of June 1925 it proclaimed itself the National Government of China.

Stalin's and Bukharin's views on the KMT

Stalin and Bukharin argued that because of the national oppression of China by imperialism the national unity of the proletariat, the peasantry and the bourgeoisie was imperative. The coming revolution would be a bourgeois revolution; the bourgeoisie and the Kuomintang were revolutionary. The CP had to maintain unity with the Kuomintang, not to estrange it. In January 1926 Stalin and the other members of the Presidium of the Fourteenth Party Conference of the Soviet Communist Party sent the following telegram to the Presidium of the Second Congress of the KMT:

> To our Party has fallen the proud and historical role of leading the first victorious proletarian revolution of the world... We are convinced that the Kuomintang will succeed *in playing the same role in the east, and thereby destroy the foundation of the rule of the imperialists in Asia*... if the Kuomintang strengthens the alliance of the working class and the peasantry in the present struggle, and allows itself to be guided by the interests of the fundamental forces of the revolution...'[10]

The KMT was admitted into the Comintern as an associate party, and the ECCI, amid loud applause, elected Chiang Kai-shek as an honorary member. This was just a few weeks before Chiang Kai-shek carried out his first anti-Communist coup. Bukharin told a Leningrad Party Conference:

> What is essentially new and original is that now the Chinese revolution already possesses a centre organised into a State power. This fact has enormous significance. The Chinese revolution has already passed the stage of evolution in which

the popular masses struggle against the ruling regime. The present stage of the Chinese revolution is characterised by the fact that the forces of the revolution are already organised into a state power; with a regular disciplined army... the advance of the armies, their brilliant victories... are a special form of the revolutionary process.[11]

Bukharin told the Fifteenth Soviet Party Conference (October 1926) that it was necessary 'to maintain a single national revolutionary front' in China as 'the commercial-industrial bourgeoisie was at present playing an objectively revolutionary role.'

It was necessary to prevent the peasantry from going to excesses in its struggle for land as this could antagonise the bourgeoisie. The over-riding duty of the CCP was to safeguard the unity of all the anti-imperialist forces, the unity of the KMT.[12]

Some time later, on 30 November, Stalin, speaking at the Chinese Commission of the ECCI, extolled Chiang Kai-shek's armies.

The revolutionary armies in China are a most important factor in the struggle of the Chinese workers and peasants for their emancipation... the advance of the Cantonese means a blow at imperialism, a blow at its agents in China; it means freedom of assembly, freedom to strike, freedom of the press, and freedom to organise for all the revolutionary elements in China in general, and for the workers in particular.

The Communists should submit completely to the KMT and its ideology.

The student youth (the revolutionary students), the working class youth, the peasant youth—all this constitutes a force that could advance the revolution with giant strides, if it was subordinated to the ideological and political influence of the Kuomintang.

Stalin went on to warn the Chinese Communists against any attempt to set up soviets.[13]

Stalin and Bukharin invoked Lenin to give the mantle of authority to their theory: in 1905 Lenin urged socialists in Russia to aim at a 'democratic dictatorship of workers and peasants' as the immediate aim of the revolution. Stalin and Bukharin waved the banner of the democratic dictatorship for the CCP.

Trotsky criticises Stalin's and Bukharin's schematism

The assumption of Stalin and Bukharin that the Chinese people, oppressed by imperialism, would be pressurised into a national unity of conflicting classes was completely mechanistic. They argued that under imperialist oppression the bourgeoisie, petty bourgeoisie, peasantry and proletariat, would all feel equally the need for a united anti-imperialist struggle. Thus the internal struggles between the classes would be dampened. Logically following from this was the slogan of a 'Bloc of Four Classes'—the bulwark of the fight against imperialism.

Trotsky tore this argument to pieces, arguing that the pressure of imperialism does not only not weaken the class struggle among the Chinese people but on the contrary strengthens it. He wrote in May 1927:

> It is a gross mistake to think that imperialism mechanically welds together all the classes of China from without... The revolutionary struggle against imperialism does not weaken, but rather strengthens the political differentiation of the classes. Imperialism is a highly powerful force in the internal relationships of China. The main source of this force is not the warships in the waters of the Yangtse Kiang... but the economic and political bond between foreign capital and the native bourgeoisie...
>
> ...everything that brings the oppressed and exploited masses of the toilers to their feet inevitably pushes the national bourgeoisie into an open bloc with the imperialists. The class struggle between the bourgeoisie and the masses of workers and peasants is not weakened, but, on the contrary, it is sharpened by imperialist oppression, to the point of bloody civil war at every serious conflict...
>
> A policy that disregarded the powerful pressure of imperialism on the internal life of China would be radically false. But a policy that proceeded from an abstract conception of national oppression without its class refraction and reflection would be no less false.[14]

Again, Stalin and Bukharin assumed that because the Chinese

bourgeoisie was nationally oppressed it was more progressive than the Russian bourgeoisie, which had belonged to a ruling nation. Trotsky wrote:

> Historical experience bears out the fact that the Polish bourgeoisie—notwithstanding the fact that it suffered both from the yoke of the autocracy and from national oppression—was more reactionary than the Russian bourgeoisie and, in the State Dumas, always gravitated not towards the Kadets but towards the Octobrists. The same is true of the Tartar bourgeoisie. The fact that the Jews had absolutely no rights whatever did not prevent the Jewish bourgeoisie from being even more cowardly, more reactionary, and more vile than the Russian bourgeoisie.[15]

Dampening the class struggle of the proletariat and peasantry, Trotsky argued, would weaken the anti-imperialist struggle. The anti-imperialist revolution could win only if the proletariat, leading the peasantry, crushed the bourgeoisie's attempt to compromise with imperialism.

> The victory over foreign imperialism can only be won by means of the toilers of town and country driving it out of China. For this, the masses must really rise millions strong. They cannot rise under the bare slogan of national liberation, but only in direct struggle against the big landlords, the military satraps, the usurers, the capitalist brigands.[16]

The class struggle of the proletariat would inevitably push the Chinese bourgeoisie into the arms of imperialism:

> The Chinese bourgeoisie is sufficiently realistic and acquainted intimately enough with the nature of world imperialism to understand that a really serious struggle against the latter requires such an 'upheaval of the revolutionary masses as would primarily become a menace to the bourgeoisie itself...
> A democratic or national liberation movement may offer the bourgeoisie an opportunity to deepen and broaden its possibilities for exploitation. Independent intervention of the proletariat on the revolutionary arena threatens to deprive the bourgeoisie of the possibility to exploit altogether.[17]

When Stalin and Bukharin spoke of the revolution in China as being bourgeois democratic, they made even less sense than the Mensheviks did when they made a similar characterisation of the Russian revolution.

There was no separation between capitalists and landlords in China. The Chinese merchants stemmed, to begin with, from the landed gentry. The new wealth accumulated through trade went largely into land. There was an organic link between Chinese capitalism and semi-feudal exploitation. As Trotsky wrote a few years after the Chinese revolution:

> While at the bottom, in the agrarian bases of the Chinese economy, the bourgeoisie is organically and unbreakably linked with feudal forms of exploitation, at the top it is just as organically and unbreakably linked with world finance capital. The Chinese bourgeoisie cannot on its own break free either from agrarian feudalism or from foreign imperialism.[18]

Stalin and Bukharin argued that the revolution which had begun in China, being a bourgeois revolution, could not set itself socialist tasks; that the bourgeoisie supporting the Kuomintang was playing a revolutionary role, and therefore it was the duty of the CCP to maintain unity with it. In seeking support for this strategy from Lenin's concept of the 'Democratic Dictatorship of Workers and Peasants' they completely distorted Lenin's position. In 1905 Lenin did not seek an alliance with the liberal bourgeoisie against Tsarism; on the contrary he argued very strongly that the bourgeois revolution could conquer in Russia only under the leadership of the working class, in an inevitable clash with the liberal bourgeoisie.

When Lenin argued that the coming revolution would be bourgeois democratic, he meant that this revolution resulted from a conflict between the productive forces of capitalism on the one hand and Tsarism, landlordism and other relics of feudalism on the other. The task of the democratic dictatorship was not to create a socialist society but to get rid of the dead wood of medievalism.

Lenin and the Bolsheviks claimed for the proletariat the role of leader in the democratic revolution. The Mensheviks reduced its role to that of an 'extreme opposition'. They interpreted the bourgeois revolution in a way in which the role of the proletariat would be subordinate to and dependent upon the bourgeoisie.[19] Lenin wrote:

> Social Democrats... rely wholly and exclusively on the activity, the class-consciousness and the organisation of the proletariat, on its influence among the labouring and exploited masses.[20]

From the independence and hegemony of the proletariat in the bourgeois revolution it is only one step to Lenin's position that in the process of the revolution the proletariat may *overstep* bourgeois democratic limitations.

> ...from the democratic revolution we shall at once and precisely in accordance with the measure of our strength, the strength of the class conscious and organised proletariat, begin to pass to the socialist revolution. We stand for uninterrupted revolution. We shall not stop half-way.[21]

> Ours is a bourgeois revolution, *therefore*, the workers must support the bourgeoisie, say the Potresoves, Gvozdyovs and Chkheidzes...
> Ours is a bourgeois revolution, we Marxists say, *therefore* the workers must open the eyes of the people to the deception practised by the bourgeois politicians, teach them to put no faith in words, to depend entirely on their *own* strength, their *own* organisation, their *own* unity and their *own* weapons.[22]

Even the Mensheviks, who did seek an alliance with the bourgeoisie, did not dream of accepting the discipline of a party dominated by the bourgeoisie. Stalin's and Bukharin's policy, as Trotsky pointed out, was a caricature not of Bolshevism, but even of 1905 Menshevism.

Finally, about the class nature of the KMT: it did not matter how many petty bourgeois, or workers or peasants were in the KMT, it was still fundamentally a party of the bourgeoisie led by representatives of that class.

The course of the Chinese revolution of 1925-27 completely disproved the stand of Stalin and Bukharin while confirming to the hilt the analysis of Trotsky.

The coup of 20 March 1926

A few weeks after the Kuomintang was admitted into the Comintern as an associate party and Chiang Kai-shek became an honorary member of the ECCI (Trotsky was the only member of the Politburo who voted against this)—he showed his gratitude by carrying out his first anti-Communist coup.

Several hours before dawn, on the morning of 20 March 1926, Chiang Kai-shek's troops arrested all political commissars attached to the army, who were mostly members of the CCP. Other prominent Communists, including the members of the Hong Kong strike committee, were also arrested. All Soviet advisers in the city were placed under house arrest. Teng Yen-ta, a Communist sympathiser who was political director of the Whampoa Military Academy, was also detained.

What was the reaction of Stepanov, the leading Soviet adviser to Chiang Kai-shek, to the coup of 20 March? He argued that the Communists had committed errors, using,

> inappropriate radical propaganda in the Army on the problems of imperialism, the peasantry, and communism and thus antagonising the KMT leadership.
> The above points naturally and unavoidably caused unpleasant feelings among high-ranking military officers...
> [The Communists] only try as their primary policy openly to expand the Chinese Communist Party and to grab complete control over everything everywhere. Thus, they have alienated the KMT and have aroused jealousy on the part of KMT members.[23]

Everything should be done, Stepanov argued, to keep on good terms with Chiang Kai-shek.

> The possible future appointment of Chiang to the post of Commander-in-Chief should sufficiently satisfy his lust for position and power...
> It would naturally be unfortunate both for the revolution and for himself if Chiang wants further to attack the Left. Yet Chiang can never destroy the Left for, warmly received everywhere, the Left has substantial force. For Chiang to fight such force is to seek self-extermination.

Chiang, a man of intelligence and ambition, will surely not resort to such a course. He claims he has learned an invaluable lesson from the incident of March Twentieth. His action was not influenced by the Left but was instigated by counter-revolutionaries of the Right. If we could inject into him a small dose of revolutionary ideology and surround him with the brave influence of the Left, we would ensure against repetition of the March Twentieth Incident. We are now creating conditions unfavourable to the occurrence of another such incident. We are trying to make Chiang cooperate with us again by satisfying his desire for glory and enabling him to achieve greater power and strength than he now enjoys.[24]

Another Soviet adviser, Nilov, said a little later, on 10 April:

Under no circumstances should communism be stressed; this might arouse fear among the people.

On the surface, we should take an interest in and not assume the attitude of neglecting Sun Yat-senism...

In principle, the CCP should be entirely open in the Army and therefore it is proposed that complete lists of Communist members be handed over to the respective commanders...[25]

And a further Soviet adviser stated: Chiang Kai-shek,

is a very clever statesman. I believe that when the [KMT] Central Executive Committee plenary session meets, all traces of the March 20th incident will be wiped out and Chiang can be persuaded to lean to the Left.[26]

And Stepanov again. Chiang Kai-shek,

is filled with revolutionary ideas far superior to the other militarists. I believe that trivial details of his behaviour are but signs of his weakness for self-aggrandisement and self-glorification. They may be overlooked.

The incident of March Twentieth is perhaps not entirely without benefit. I agree with Hei-hsing. The incident is like cancer, for which it is wise to have an operation. Sores remain, however, and we should by all means see that they are cured.

No one can guarantee at present that Chiang will always be one of us, but we must utilise him for the cause of the National Revolution.[27]

Following the coup a meeting of the Central Executive Committee of the KMT was called for 15 May. Isaacs records its response to events:

At the opening session Chiang introduced and hammered through a special resolution 'for the readjustment of Party affairs'. It was framed to limit and define within the closest possible bounds the organisational activity of the Communist members of the Kuomintang. Communists were required 'not to entertain any doubt on or criticise Dr. Sun or his principles'. The Communist Party was required to hand over to the Standing Committee of the Kuomintang Executive a list of its membership inside the Kuomintang. Communist members of municipal, provincial, and central party committees were limited to one-third of the committee membership. Communists were banned from serving as heads of any Party or Government department. Kuomintang members, on the other hand, were enjoined 'not to engage in any other political organisation or activity.' That is, Communists could join the Kuomintang, but members of the Kuomintang could not join the Communist Party without forfeiting their Kuomintang cards. All instructions henceforth issued by the Communist Central Committee to its own members were to be submitted first to a special joint committee of the two parties for approval...

Chiang was formally put at the head of the Party. Plans for launching a northern military expedition were also approved and Chiang Kai-shek was appointed Commander-in-Chief of all the expeditionary armies. Subsequently a set of special decrees conferred emergency power upon Chiang for the duration of the campaign. All Government and Party offices were subordinated to the headquarters of the Commander-in-Chief. The Military Council originally conceived as a civilian check on militarist ambitions, passed entirely into Chiang's hands. He became arbiter of the Government's finances. He controlled the political department, the arsenals, the general staff, the military and naval schools. The Canton Government was transformed into a military dictatorship. Chiang's victory was complete.[28]

On 29 July

> Chiang Kai-shek's headquarters proclaimed martial law. Public organisations, assemblies, the press, workers' and peasants' voluntary corps, strikes, all came within the orbit of military authority. Three days later an order was issued 'forbidding all labour disturbances for the duration of the Northern expedition.'
> ...On 9 August the authorities stepped in with regulations for the compulsory arbitration of all labour disputes under Government auspices. Workers were forbidden to bear arms of any description, to assemble, or to parade.[29]

On 12-18 July the Central Committee of the CCP adopted a comprehensive set of resolutions on the peasant movement aimed at mollifying the KMT leadership. The resolutions argued that the peasant movement had developed the disease of ultra-leftism, of extremism. It was important to fight against the idea of expropriating the landlords. Instead,

> Rent ceilings to be fixed by the government. Peasants to receive at least 50 per cent of the crops.
> ...In case of conflict between landlords and poor peasants, we should find means to utilise the old peasant organisations as the mediating party.
> ...Our policy toward landlords is to unite the self-cultivating peasants, hired farm labourers, tenant farmers, and middle and small landlords in a united front. Those big landlords who do not actively engage in oppressive activities are to be neutralised. Attacks should be concentrated on the most reactionary big landlords. In case of big landlords who are members of the bad gentry or local bullies, we should not simply propose the slogan, 'Down with the landlords'...[30]

The CCP was told to attack only the *bad* landlords. Instead of Lenin's alliance of the proletariat with the poor peasantry while neutralising the middle peasants, and fighting against the landlords and the kulaks, we have here an alliance of workers, poor peasants, middle peasants, kulaks and 'good landlords'.

Stalin's and Bukharin's reaction to the March Twentieth Coup

Stalin and Bukharin concealed the fact of the coup from the ranks of the International. Isaacs writes:

> They suppressed all news of its occurrence. The facts were kept not only from the Russian workers and the other sections of the Comintern, but from its Executive Committee and even from the other members of the Executive Committee's presidium... When news of the coup appeared in the imperialist press in China and abroad... the centrally-geared machinery of the Comintern press started turning our vehement denials.
>
> 'Reuter's Telegraphic Agency... recently issued the statement that in Canton, Chiang Kai-shek, the supreme commander of the revolutionary troops... had carried out a coup-d'état. But this *lying report* (emphasis in original) had soon to be denied. The Kuomintang is not a tiny group with a few members, but is a mass party in the true sense of the word and revolutionary Canton and the revolutionary Canton Government are founded on this basis. It is, of course, impossible there to carry out a coup-d'état overnight', wrote the central organ of the Comintern on April 8, 1926. (**International Press Correspondence**, 8 April 1926).
>
> Far from being converted into an instrument of bourgeois policy, the Canton government was more than ever 'aiming at the world revolution' and extending its power into the neighbouring provinces as a 'Soviet government'.
>
> 'The perspectives for the People's Government in Canton were never so favourable as they are now...' the same Comintern report continued. 'The province of Kwangsi will shortly form a Soviet Government... *the power of the generals, as a result of the national revolutionary movement, is beginning to disappear.* (Emphasis in original). The Kuomin Government is now proceeding to organise all district and town administrations within the province of Kwantung according to the Soviet system.'
>
> 'The reactionary British Press at Hong Kong and in London have spread sensational stories of disruption within the Nationalist Government in an effort to further their

imperialist propaganda,' said a Moscow dispatch to the **New York Daily Worker** on April 21, 1926. 'These reports have no real basis. They are nothing but provocative manoeuvres of British imperialism. There has been no insurrection in Canton. The basis of the reports seems to be certain differences (!) between a general of the Canton Army, Chiang Kai-shek and the Canton Government. These differences were not concerned with matters of principle and had no connection with an armed struggle for power. The differences have since been abolished and Canton remained the stronghold of the movement for the emancipation of the Chinese people. The attempt of British imperialism to utilise the unimportant differences in Canton in its own interests has failed...'[31]

But the coup of March Twentieth could not be hidden from the Chinese Communists. Isaacs writes:

> This cringing policy did not go unchallenged in the ranks of the Communist Party. In Shanghai a group of comrades raised the demand for the immediate withdrawal of the Party from the Kuomintang, declaring it was impossible for the Communists to work effectively under the conditions laid down by the May 15 Kuomintang plenary session. Both the Central Committee in Shanghai and the Kwangtung Party organisation vigorously opposed this instinctively correct proletarian demand...
>
> The voices that called for resumption of independence made themselves heard to such an extent that even Chen Tu-hsiu wrote to the Comintern proposing substitution of a two-Party bloc outside the Kuomintang instead of work within the Kuomintang. A decision to this effect was actually adopted by the Communist Central Commitee at its plenary session in June, 1926. It was immediately and drastically condemned by the Comintern.[32]

And what conclusion did Mikhail Borodin, the representative of the Politburo of the CPSU to the KMT, draw from the coup? The Communists should be more submissive: 'The present period is one in which the Communists should do coolie service for the Kuomintang,' he declared.[33]

The massacre of the workers of Shanghai

After concentrating political and military control over Canton in his hands at the time of the coup, Chiang Kai-shek took to the field in July 1926 for the conquest of Central and North China, aided by Russian arms, a staff of Russian military advisers and a vast propaganda machine lubricated and propelled by the CCP.

The Northern March coincided with the rise of a vast mass movement in the provinces of Kiangsi, Hunan and Hupeh, drawing fresh millions into the struggle and before long engulfing Wuhan and Shanghai.

> In the actual fighting peasant detachments were found wherever the clash was fiercest. Railway and telegraph workers paralysed the enemy's communications. Peasant intelligence made all the enemy staff secrets almost instantly available to the advancing Nationalists.[34]

The growth of the peasant movement was spectacular.

> By the end of November there were in Hunan fifty-four organised *hsien* with a total registered membership in the peasant associations of 1,071,137. By January 1927 this number had passed 2,000,000. The peasants first demanded rent reduction, abolition of the miscellaneous tax burdens, and arms to fight the village gentry. Village authority fell largely to the peasant associations and in Hunan the step from refusal to pay all rent to the outright seizure of the land was quickly taken.[35]

What was Moscow's attitude to this rising mass movement? It was so eager not to antagonise the KMT that on 29 October 1926 the Politburo sent a telegram to Voitinsky, the Comintern representative in Shanghai, urging the CCP to keep the rebellious peasant movement in check.[36] Despite the situation in Canton since the coup of 20 March, Stalin had the audacity to say: the advance of the Canton troops meant 'freedom of assembly, freedom to strike, freedom to organise for all the revolutionary elements in China in general and for the workers in particular.'[37] In December 1926 the ECCI passed a resolution stating:

> The machinery of the national-revolutionary Government provides an extremely effective channel for approaching the

peasantry, and the Communist Party must make use of it. In the recently liberated provinces a State apparatus of the Canton type will be established. The task of communists and their revolutionary allies is to permeate the new government apparatus; in order to give practical expression to the agrarian programme of the national revolution...

In order to intensify their activities in the ranks of the Kuomintang with the object of influencing the further development of the revolutionary movement, communists must enter the Canton Government... The extension of the Canton Government's power to large areas gives this question of communist participation in the National Government greater urgency than ever.

The Communist Party of China should seek to make the Kuomintang a genuinely national party, a firm revolutionary bloc of the proletariat, the peasantry, the urban petty bourgeoisie, and other oppressed strata who are waging an energetic struggle against imperialism and its agents...

The Canton Government, despite its bourgeois democratic character, basically and objectively contains within itself the germ of a revolutionary petty-bourgeois State of the democratic dictatorship of the revolutionary bloc of proletariat, peasantry and urban petty bourgeoisie. The petty bourgeois democratic movement is becoming revolutionary in China because it is an anti-imperialist movement. The Canton Government is a revolutionary one primarily in virtue of its anti-imperialist character.[38]

It seemed the coup of 20 March had never happened. The Northern March proceeded.

In Shanghai the workers had responded to the victorious advance of the Northern Expedition with a strike wave of unexampled depth and militancy.[39]

The Nationalist troops occupied Hangchow on 17 February and next day advanced to Kashing, less than fifty miles from Shanghai. The vanguard moved up the railway as far as Sungkiang, only twenty-five miles away. In Shanghai all grew taut. The General Labour Union issued orders for a general strike effective the morning of the 19th in expectation of a further Nationalist advance. The workers answered the call with machine-like precision.

...The strike was complete. Practically every worker in Shanghai came out onto the streets. Their ranks were swelled when they were joined by shop employees and the hordes of the city poor. Between 500,000 and 800,000 people were directly involved.[40]

On 21 March the CCP led the Shanghai workers in an armed insurrection which succeeded in destroying the control of the Northern warlords; the armed workers now maintained order throughout Shanghai (except for the foreign concessions). Armed workers took control of the police stations and local military posts, the telephone and telegraph offices.[41]

On the eve of Chiang Kai-shek's entering Shanghai, Chen Tu-hsiu again appealed to the leadership of the Comintern to allow the CCP to leave the KMT. Again he was pressed to reaffirm allegiance to the KMT and grant control of Shanghai to Chiang Kai-shek. The Chinese Communists were very disciplined and abided by the Comintern instruction. The central slogan of the victorious insurrection in Shanghai was 'Hail the national revolutionary army! Welcome to Chiang Kai-shek!'

On 26 March Chiang Kai-shek entered Shanghai. How did the Communist leaders react to this event?

A big meeting called by the French Communists in Paris on March 23, 1927, at which the leaders of the Communist Party of France, Semard, Monmousseau, Cachin and others appeared, sent the following telegram to the Kuo Min Tang: 'The workers of Paris greet the entry of the revolutionary Chinese army into Shanghai. Fifty-six years after the Paris Commune and ten years after the Russian, the Chinese Commune marks a new stage in the development of the world revolution.

The organ of the German Communists, **Die Rote Fahne** prints a picture of Chiang Kai-shek on March 17 1927, and presents him as the leader of the revolutionary workers of China...[42]

Pravda of 22 March exclaimed: 'The keys to Shanghai were handed over by the victorious workers to the Canton army. In this fact is expressed the great heroic act of the Shanghai proletariat!'[43]

On 5 April Stalin spoke to a large meeting of 3,000 officers in the Hall of Columns in Moscow answering the warning of Trotsky and the Opposition:

> Chiang Kai-shek is submitting to discipline... The Kuomintang is a bloc, a sort of revolutionary parliament, with the Right, the Left, and the Communists. Why make a coup d'état? Why drive away the Right when we have the majority and when the Right listens to us? The peasant needs an old, worn-out jade as long as she is necessary. He does not drive her away. So it is with us. When the Right is of no more use to us, we will drive it away. At present we need the Right. It has capable people, who still direct the army and lead it against the imperialists. Chiang Kai-shek has perhaps no sympathy for the revolution, but he is leading the army and cannot do otherwise than lead it against the imperialists. Besides this, the people of the Right have relations with the generals of Chang Tso-lin and understand very well how to demoralise them and induce them to pass over to the side of the revolution, bag and baggage, without striking a blow. Also, they have connections with the rich merchants and can raise money from them. So they have to be utilised to the end, squeezed out like a lemon, and then flung away.[44]

Compare this with Trotsky's stand as expressed in a memorandum sent to the Politburo on 31 March. Trotsky emphasised the rising strength of the insurgent workers and peasants who, if organised in Soviets, could save the revolution from a military coup.

> The officer cadre, as far as one can tell from the available materials, is characterised by bourgeois and landlord origins and by sympathies tending to favour those same classes. Apprehensions regarding a Chinese variant of Bonapartism are apparently rather strong among revolutionary circles in China, nor can one say by any means that these fears are unfounded. Under existing conditions it would seem there is no more effective measure for countering such dangers than

the establishment of soldiers' sections of soviets, beginning with *the garrisons in the major proletarian centres*.[45]

Three days later Trotsky submitted a very strong article to **Pravda** that did not get published. He reiterated and emphasised that Chiang Kai-shek was preparing a coup.

It was quite symptomatic that on 18 April—six days after Chiang Kai-shek's massacre of Shanghai workers—the Comintern Secretariat sent Trotsky a routine circular inviting him to autograph, as other Soviet leaders did, a picture of Chiang Kai-shek as a token of friendship. Trotsky later published his outraged reply.[46] It did not take long for Chiang Kai-shek to show how 'revolutionary' he was.

> At four o'clock on the morning of 12 April a bugle blast sounded from Chiang Kai-shek's headquarters... A Chinese gunboat at anchor off Nantao answered with a toot on its siren. 'Simultaneously the machine guns broke loose in a steady roll'. The attack was launched in Chapei, Nantao, the Western District, in Woosung, Pootung, and Jessfield. It came as no surprise to anyone except the workers because all the authorities concerned, Chinese and foreign, after midnight were secretly made cognisant of the events which were to take place in the morning.
>
> Mobilised for action at all points, the gangsters, dressed in blue denim uniform; and wearing white arm-bands bearing the Chinese character *kung* (labour), 'had feverishly worked through the night organising secret parties to appear at dawn as though from nowhere...'[47]

> Every worker who resisted was shot down in his tracks. The remainder were lashed together and marched out to be executed either in the streets or at Lunghua headquarters...
> Foreign forces co-operated in the reign of terror now instituted throughout the city...
> Everywhere rigid house-to-house searches were conducted and wholesale arrests made. Prisoners were handed over in batches to the military headquarters at Lunghua.[48]

Tens of thousands of Communists and workers who had followed them were slaughtered.

Bedfellows of Wang Ching-wei

Chiang Kai-shek's Shanghai coup d'état dealt a staggering blow to the revolution [wrote Isaacs], but it need not have been mortal. Immense reserves still existed in Hunan and Hupeh where the revolutionary tide was just sweeping in, where the peasants were rising to seize the land and the workers in organisation and power were already capable of becoming the leaders of the agrarian revolt and the guardians of its conquests. There was still time to mobilise and weld these forces for a new offensive, to crush the reaction which ruled in the east with Shanghai as its centre.[49]

A counter-offensive against Chiang Kai-shek would have demanded a radical change in the policy of the Comintern. Instead Stalin and Bukharin repeated the same line as hitherto, now orienting themselves on the 'Left Kuomintang' government of Wuhan headed by Wang Ching-wei. The Left Kuomintang was temporarily in conflict with Chiang Kai-shek and was anxious to benefit from Communist support.

On 21 April Stalin wrote the following:

Chiang Kai-shek's coup means that from now on there will be in South China two camps, two governments, two armies, two centres, *the centre of revolution in Wuhan*, and the centre of counter-revolution in Nanking.

This means that the revolutionary Kuomintang in Wuhan, by a determined fight against militarism and imperialism, will in fact be converted into an organ of the revolutionary-democratic dictatorship of the proletariat and the peasantry...[We must adopt] *the policy of concentrating the whole power in the country in the hands of the revolutionary Kuomintang... It further follows that the policy of close co-operation between the Lefts and the Communists within the Kuomintang in this stage acquires special force and special significance... and that without such co-operation the victory of the revolution is impossible.*[50]

On 30 May at the Eighth Plenum of the ECCI Bukharin moved a resolution on the Chinese question:

The ECCI observes that the course of the Chinese revolution

has confirmed the evaluation of its moving forces given at the last (seventh) enlarged plenum ...

Despite partial defeat and the counter-revolution of Chiang Kai-shek and Co. the revolution has moved to a higher stage; the bloc of bourgeoisie, petty bourgeoisie, peasantry, and proletariat has broken down and has begun to change into a bloc of proletariat, peasantry, and petty bourgeoisie, in which the leading role of the proletariat is steadily growing...The ECCI believes that the tactics of a bloc with the national bourgeoisie in the period of the revolution that has now closed were completely correct...

The Wuhan Government and the left Kuomintang express in their basic tendencies the revolutionary bloc of the urban and rural petty bourgeois masses with the proletariat...

The ECCI believes that the Chinese CP should apply all its efforts, jointly with the left Kuomintang, to a vigorous campaign for the mobilisation and organisation of the masses. The most energetic recruiting of workers into the party, the most energetic recruiting, in town and village, of the labouring masses into the Kuomintang, which it is necessary to change as quickly as possible into the broadest mass organisation—that is the chief task of the Chinese CP at the present moment...[51]

The ECCI 'decisively rejects the demand [of the Opposition] to leave the KMT'.

The Kuomintang in China is the specific Chinese form of the organisation in which the proletariat works together with the petty bourgeoisie and the peasantry.[52]

Regarding the Wuhan government the resolution stated:

The ECCI considers incorrect the view which underestimates the Wuhan Government and in practice denies its powerful revolutionary role. The Wuhan Government and the leaders of the left Kuomintang by their class composition represent not only the peasants, workers and artisans, but also a part of the middle bourgeoisie...

The ECCI believes that the Chinese CP should take a most energetic part in the work of the Wuhan 'provisional revolutionary Government'...[53]

To 'strengthen the centre of the revolution in Wuhan' two CCP members joined the KMT Government: T'an P'ing-shan as Miniser of Agriculture, and Su Chao-cheng as Minister of Labour, 'the classic posts of hostages', to use Trotsky's phrase. In fact their role turned out to be to restrain the peasants and workers.

Trotsky's speech to the Eighth Plenum of the ECCI sharply attacked the Stalin-Bukharin policy.

> The workers of Shanghai and Hankow will surely be surprised when they read that the April events developed in complete harmony with the historical line of march that Comrade Bukharin had previously outlined for the Chinese revolution.
>
> ...We do not want to assume even a shadow of responsibility for the policy of the Wuhan government and the leadership of the Kuomintang, and we urgently advise the Comintern to reject this responsibility. We say directly to the Chinese peasants: the leaders of the left Kuomintang of the type of Wang Ching-wei and Company will inevitably betray you if you follow the Wuhan heads instead of forming your own independent soviets. The agrarian revolution is a serious thing. Politicians of the Wang Ching-wei type, under difficult conditions, will unite ten times with Chiang Kai-shek against the workers and peasants. Under such conditions, two Communists in a bourgeois government become impotent hostages, if not a direct mask for the preparation of a new blow against the working masses. We say to the workers of China: the peasants will not carry out the agrarian revolution to the end if they let themselves be led by petty bourgeois radicals instead of by you, the revolutionary proletariat. Therefore, build up your workers' soviets, ally them with the peasant soviets, arm yourselves through the soviets, draw soldiers' representatives into the soviets, shoot the generals who do not recognise the soviets, shoot the bureaucrats and bourgeois liberals who will organise uprisings against the soviets. Only through peasants' and soldiers' soviets will you win over the majority of Chiang Kai-shek's soldiers to your side.[54]

Isaacs writes the following on the activities of the Communist Minister of Agriculture in the Wuhan Government:

After assuming his post, T'an P'ing-shan immediately issued instructions to the peasants forbidding 'rash acts' against the Tuhao and gentry, threatening 'severe punishment'...

The Government therefore announces its policy that all irresponsible acts and illegal deeds of the peasants be nipped in the bud... peace must reign in the villages. It must not be annihilated by the peasants' excessive demands.[55]

Similar language was used by the Communist Minister of Labour who, in a circular issued a few days after he took office, complained of the 'infantile activity on the part of the newly liberated sections of labour and the peasantry.'[56]On 1 June Stalin sent a telegram to the Comintern delegates in China urging them to keep the agrarian revolution within the limits necessary to preserve the alliance with the KMT.[57]

A few days after the Eighth Plenum of the ECCI praised the revolutionary character of the Wuhan Government, the left KMT general Hsü k'e-hsiang began a massacre of Communists and trade unionists in Changsha, the capital of Hunan province. Following this the CCP was suppressed by the Wuhan Government and the two Communist members resigned. On 15 July the KMT Political Council expelled the Communists from the KMT and in the next few days many Communists were arrested and executed.

It took some three years to expose the Stalin-Bukharin policy of reliance on Chiang Kai-shek. It took a couple of months to do the same for the policy of reliance on Wang Ching-wei.

The Canton Putsch

To cover up the crimes committed towards the Chinese revolution by the policy of tail-ending the KMT, Stalin and Bukharin now swung into an adventure, which again was paid for by the blood of thousands of Chinese workers.

After opposing the slogan of the soviet while the revolution was rising, now, after its shattering defeat, Stalin and Bukharin became enthusiastic about it. **Pravda** declared: 'The crisis of the KMT places the question of soviets on the order of the day. The slogan of soviets is correct now...'[58]

Trotsky, who had argued for the slogan of soviets up to now ridiculed this new late turn of Stalin and Bukharin: 'To use the slogan of soviets in a period of bourgeois reaction is to trifle, ie, to make a mockery of soviets.'[59]

At the Fifteenth Congress of the CPSU Stalin completed his conquest of the Opposition and got through the wholesale expulsion of its members from the party. 'By accident' a Communist insurrection in Canton was made to coincide with this Congress.

On 11 December 1927 the insurrection began. To lead it a soviet was *appointed*:

> Four days before the insurrection fifteen men were selected at a secret meeting, nine of them representing the tiny groups of workers under Communist leadership or influence, three of them representing the cadets' regiment, and three who were supposed to represent the peasants of Kwangtung. These fifteen men constituted nothing less than the Canton Council of Workers', Peasants' and Soldiers' Deputies![60]

What a fraudulent soviet! The whole essence of the soviet is that it is democratically elected, rooted in the working class, and workers identify with it.

The workers were hardly involved in the Canton insurrection. As Isaacs writes:

> The great majority of the workers and artisans of Canton stood apart from the struggle. No general strike call was issued. Only a few handfuls of chauffeurs, printers, ricksha coolies and some others quit work eagerly to grasp rifles. Railway workers and river sailors continued at their jobs. They transported troops rushing to crush the uprising. They helped Kuomintang officials flee the city.[61]

The insurgents held their ground for some fifty hours.

> By the afternoon of 13 December the last of the defenders of the Canton Commune had been wiped out... The final toll of the counted dead was 5,700.[62]

Trotsky wrote that the Canton insurrection was timed to give the Stalinist majority a 'victory' in China 'to cover up the physical extermination of the Russian Opposition.'[63]

After the massacre of Shanghai, wrote Trotsky,

> Every mistake of the leadership is made 'good', so to speak,

through measures against the Opposition. The day the dispatch on Chiang Kai-shek's coup was made known in Moscow we said to each other: The Opposition will have to pay dearly for this...[64]

Now, after the debacle of the 'Canton Commune' the price the Opposition had to pay was even stiffer.

The development of Trotsky's stand in the Chinese Revolution

The most complete collection of Trotsky's articles, speeches and notes on China, many never published previously, is taken from the Trotsky archives in Harvard and put together in the book **Leon Trotsky on China**.

A number of aspects of the collection strike the reader forcibly. First of all, prior to 4 March 1927, ie, five weeks before the Shanghai massacre, there are only four entries.

The first is a very short and quite light article, written for the Soviet press in response to the May Thirteenth Incident of 1925.

The second is entitled 'Problems of our Policy with respect to China and Japan'. This was the report of a special Politburo Commission charged with preparing recommendations for Soviet foreign policy in the Far East. Trotsky chaired the commission, whose other members were Chicherin, Dzerzhinsky and Voroshilov, all supporters of Stalin and Bukharin. The Commission made its recommendations in strictly diplomatic terms, without any reference to the objectives and policies of the CCP; it contained no sustained analysis of developments in China. The report was approved by the Politburo.

The third item is a letter to Radek of 30 August 1926. This was the first systematic presentation of Trotsky's views regarding the problems of the Chinese revolution.

As against these three articles written up to the end of August 1926—ie, during the fifteen months since the beginning of the Chinese revolution—there are 30 articles, notes and speeches delivered in the next fourteen months. Completely missing from these is any consideration of the foundation of the CCP in 1921, its joining of the KMT in 1923-4, the mass awakening of the Chinese proletariat demonstrated in the over a year-long general strike in Hong Kong-Canton, or Chiang Kai-shek's coup of 20 March 1926.

This lacuna has to be explained.

The first element in any explanation is Trotsky's complete resignation from active politics between the end of the 'literary debate' at the end of of 1924 and the formation of the United Opposition in June 1926.

As early as 1923 Trotsky opposed the CCP's entering the KMT, and in the following two years he restated his view on a few occasions at meetings of the Politburo. But being completely isolated in the Politburo he did not repeat his position before the wider forum of the Central Committee. Nor did he once speak about China at meetings of the ECCI. Not once did he allow himself to express any differences with the Politburo on the question of China.

When the United Opposition was formed Trotsky's writing on China suffered from the necessity of compromise with Zinoviev, who as President of the Comintern until May 1926 had a large responsibility for the policy of the Comintern on China. In his own faction too Trotsky had a number of individuals who advocated the adherence of the CCP to the KMT, including Ioffe, Radek, Preobrazhensky and Smilga.

Ioffe signed the agreement with Sun Yat-sen on 26 January 1923 which included the statement that 'it is not possible to carry out either communism or even the Soviet system in China'. (See p. 189) (It is significant that Maring-Sneevliet, who played a crucial role in pushing the CCP to join the KMT, later became a prominent member of the Trotskyist Opposition).

As regards Radek, we have already referred to his attack on the CCP leadership at the Fourth Congress of the Comintern for opposing entry into the KMT; they needed to grasp the fact that 'neither the question of Socialism, nor that of the Soviet republic are now on the order of the day'.[65]

Radek was in a very exposed position: since May 1925 he had headed the Sun Yat-sen University in Moscow, and had to explain Comintern policy to its Chinese students. As late as 3 March 1927 we find a letter from Radek to Trotsky arguing for the continuing adherence of the CCP to the KMT.[66]

Besides the inter-factional calculations leading Trotsky to fudge his differences with Zinoviev, Radek and Co., there could have been another, related factor. Trotsky wanted to avoid allowing past policy differences to impinge upon the dispute with Stalin and Bukharin on current policy. This short-termism encouraged a 'rotten compromise' (to use Lenin's description of such arrangements).

It is not clear from Trotsky's writings and speeches when he became convinced that the theory of permanent revolution applied not only to Russia but had wider, international significance and so applied also to China. It is difficult to be clear on this point, because again and again Trotsky declared the theory irrelevant to China, but obviously under pressure from the Zinovievites and Radek.

In his letter to the CC resigning from the post of People's Commissar of War (15 January 1925) Trotsky wrote:

> I absolutely deny that the formula 'permanent revolution', which applies wholly to the past, in any way caused me to adopt a careless attitude toward the peasantry in the conditions of the Soviet revolution. If at any time after October I had occasion, for private reasons, to revert to the formula 'permanent revolution', it was only a reference to party history, ie, to the past, and had no reference to the question of present-day political tasks.[67]

In a speech to the Fifteenth Conference of the CPSU on 1 November 1926 Trotsky said:

> I have no intention, comrades, of raising the question of the theory of permanent revolution. This theory—in respect both to what has been right in it and to what has been incomplete and wrong—has nothing whatever to do with our present contentions. In any case, this theory of permanent revolution, to which so much attention has been devoted recently, is not the responsibility in the slightest of either the Opposition of 1925 or the Opposition of 1923, and even I myself regard it as a question which has long been consigned to the archives.[68]

In a speech to the Seventh Enlarged Plenum of the ECCI on 9 December 1926 Trotsky said:

> The theory which is now dragged into discussion (quite

artificially and not in the interests of the cause)—the theory of permanent revolution—I have never considered (even at the time when I did not see the inadequacies of this theory)—never considered it to be a universal doctrine applicable generally to all revolutions... The concept of permanent revolution was applied by me to a definite stage of development in the historical evolution of Russia.[69]

On 14 December 1926 a letter to the Presidium of the ECCI signed by Trotsky, Zinoviev and Kamenev, stated:

It is not true that we defend 'Trotskyism'. Trotsky has stated to the International that on all the fundamental questions over which he had differences with Lenin, Lenin was right—in particular on the questions of permanent revolution and the peasantry.[70]

It would be a mistake to assume that Trotsky was always absolutely clear about the role of the theory of permanent revolution in analysing the prospects of the Chinese revolution, and his formulations contradicting the theory appear long before the bloc with the Zinovievists. Thus, for instance, in a speech to the Communist University of the Toilers of the East, entitled 'Prospects and Tasks in the East', on 2 April 1924, Trotsky said:

There is no doubt whatever that if the Kuomintang Party in China succeeds in uniting China under a national-democratic regime, the capitalist development of China will make enormous strides forward. And all this leads to the mobilisation of countless proletarian masses which will immediately emerge from a prehistoric, semi-barbarian state and will be thrust into the whirlpool of industrialism.[71]

This is far from permanent revolution.

It is only in September 1927, in his 'New Opportunities for the Chinese Revolution, New Tasks, and New Mistakes' that Trotsky for the first time *clearly and openly* uses the theory of permanent revolution for analysing the perspectives of the Chinese revolution.

...the retreat from the revolution by the bourgeoisie—the big bourgeoisie and the middle and upper petty bourgeoisie in the city and the countryside, and the intelligentsia as well, is an accomplished fact. Under these conditions, the call for a democratic dictatorship of the proletariat and peasantry— given a new revolutionary upsurge—will prove to be vague and amorphous. And any vague and amorphous slogan in a revolution becomes dangerous for the revolutionary party and the oppressed masses...

The Chinese revolution at its new stage will win as a dictatorship of the proletariat or it will not win at all.[72]

Trotsky repeats the same argument in his 'The Chinese Question after the Sixth Congress' (4 October 1928):

The solution of fundamental bourgeois and democratic problems in China ends entirely in the dictatorship of the proletariat. To oppose to it the democratic dictatorship of the proletariat and peasantry is to devote oneself to a reactionary attempt that seeks to drag the revolution back to stages already traversed by the coalition of the Kuomintang.[73]

Again, on the question of the CCP being inside the KMT Trotsky over time expressed very conflicting views.

Although he was against the CCP being in the KMT since 1923[74] not only were the mass of the workers or the rank and file of the party not cognisant of Trotsky's real position, but even the leading bodies of the party and the Comintern—the Central Committee and the ECCI—knew nothing about it. Trotsky's *public* statements contradicted his real position. Thus, on 25 March 1926 Trotsky wrote:

With regard to the people's armies it is necessary to conduct comprehensive political, educational, and organisational work (in the Kuomintang and Communist Party) in order to convert them into an effective stronghold of the popular revolutionary movement independent of personal influence. ...The Canton government should concentrate all its efforts on strengthening the republic internally by means of agrarian, financial, administrative, and political reforms; by drawing the broad popular masses into the political life of the South Chinese Republic, and by strengthening the latter's internal defensive capacity.[75]

In his article, 'The Chinese Revolution and the Theses of

Comrade Stalin' (7 May 1927) Trotsky wrote:

> A revolutionary Kuomintang has yet to be formed. We are in favour of the Communists working inside the Kuomintang and patiently drawing the workers and peasants over to their side.

But Trotsky makes it clear that politically the CCP should preserve its independence.

> The Communist Party can gain a petty bourgeois ally not by prostrating itself before the Kuomintang at every one of its vacillations, but only if it appeals to the workers openly and directly in its own name, under its own banner, organises them around it...[76]

Trotsky goes on to spell out what is involved in the political independence of the CCP from the KMT.

> For this it is necessary:
> ...to reject categorically such forms of the bloc which directly or indirectly hinder the independence of our own party and subordinate it to the control of other classes;...
> to reject categorically such forms of the bloc in which the Communist Party holds down its banner and sacrifices the growth of its own influence and its own authority in the interests of its allies;...
> to establish the conditions and limits of the bloc with thorough precision and let them be known to all;...
> for the Communist Party to retain full freedom of criticism and to watch over its allies with no less vigilance than over an enemy without forgetting for a moment that an ally who bases himself upon other classes or depends upon other classes is only a temporary confederate who can be transformed by the force of circumstances into an opponent and an enemy;...
> finally, to rely only upon ourselves, upon our own organisation, arms, and power.[77]

For the first time Trotsky argues openly in writing for the CCP to leave the KMT in a document entitled 'The Communist Party and the Kuomintang' (10 May 1927).

This document appears to have been written for circulation

to the Trotskyist Oppositionists or perhaps to the United Opposition as a whole.

> By remaining in the same organisation with the Wang Ching-weis, we are sharing the responsibility for their wavering and betrayals.
>
> It is necessary to formulate the reasons we have remained in the Kuomintang up to the present. At the present time—and this is most important of all—it is necessary to formulate with just as much clarity and accuracy the reasons we must now leave the Kuomintang. The reasons for leaving it multiply by the day...[78]

In public Trotsky was still not as clearly for the break of the CCP from the KMT. Thus in his speech to the Eighth Plenum of the ECCI (May 1927) Trotsky, as spokesman of the United Opposition, said:

> I can accept remaining within the really revolutionary Kuomintang only on the condition of complete political and organisational freedom of action of the Communist Party with a guaranteed, common basis for actions of the Kuomintang together with the Communist Party...
>
> The alliance between the Communist Party and the real revolutionary Kuomintang must not only be maintained but must be extended and deepened on the basis of mass soviets.[79]

In private correspondence Trotsky was far more critical of the CCP's remaining in the KMT. Thus in a letter to Radek on 4 March 1927 he writes:

> When should the communists have withdrawn from the Kuomintang? My memory of the history of the Chinese revolution in recent years is not concrete enough and I do not have the materials at hand; therefore, I will not venture to say whether it was necessary to pose this question point-blank as early as 1923, 1924, or 1925... we are dreadfully late. We have turned the Chinese Communist Party into a variety of Menshevism...
>
> We must recognise that for the Communist Party to remain in the Kuomintang any longer threatens to have dire

consequences for the proletariat and for the revolution; and above all, it threatens the Chinese Communist Party itself with a total degeneration into Menshevism.[80]

Typically Zinoviev argued for the CCP to remain inside the 'Left KMT' even after the Shanghai massacre. His ideas were extremely muddled, as can be seen from a comparison of two quotations from one and the same 'Theses on the Chinese Revolution' delivered to the Politburo on 15 April 1927. First,

> The Chinese revolution will be victorious under the leadership of the working class or not at all. Otherwise, the bourgeoisie will take the whole affair in its hands, in one way or another it will come to an agreement with foreign imperialism...

The second quote:

> In the present military and political situation the Communist Party of China can and must remain in the Kuomintang, but only in order to gather its forces, to begin immediately to rally the masses under its banner, to conduct a relentless struggle against the Right Kuomintang and to strive for their expulsion and destruction. Our slogan under the present circumstances is not withdrawal from the Kuomintang, but the *immediate announcement and realisation of the complete and unconditional and organisational independence of the Communist Party of China from the Kuomintang, that is, the complete political and organisational autonomy of the Communist Party of China.*

And to cap it all Zinoviev called for the immediate establishment of Soviets.[81]

Zinoviev, Kamenev, and even Radek, Preobrazhensky and possibly also Rakovsky, still rejected the theory of permanent revolution and stuck to the formula of the 'democratic dictatorship'.

For Trotsky, the hesitation, the hedging about, must have gone against the grain, as a main characteristic of his thinking was sharpness, decisiveness. Tragically, he was completely unaware of Chen Tu-hsiu's appeal to the Comintern leadership for the CCP to split from the KMT. Stalin and Bukharin kept this secret. It is ignorance of this fact that explains Trotsky's writing to Radek as late as 4 March 1927: 'If...the Chinese Communist Party does not want to leave the KMT under present conditions of large-scale class struggle... then we have before us a Martinovite party'.[82] Trotsky was not acquainted at all with the confidential communications that passed between Moscow and Wuhan. Not only did he not know about the stand of the CCP leadership, but none of the Chinese leaders knew of Trotsky's position, as was made clear many years later by Peng Shu-tse, a member of the Central Committee of the CCP and a future Trotskyist.[83] This lack of knowledge must have had a very damaging effect on Trotsky's grasp of the situation in China and of his ability to adopt a clear stand.

On 23 June 1927 Trotsky sent a circular to members of the United Opposition entitled 'Why Have We Not Called for Withdrawal from the Kuomintang until Now?' In this document he is brutally clear:

> The reasons we have not called for withdrawal from the Kuomintang until now (a serious blunder) can be correctly formulated in only one way that will account for both past and present. That is approximately as follows:
> We have proceeded from the fact that the Communist Party has spent too much time in the Kuomintang and that our party and the Comintern have been overly occupied with this question, but that openly calling for immediate withdrawal from the Kuomintang would even further sharpen the contradictions within our own party. We formulated the kind of conditions for the Chinese Communist Party's remaining in the Kuomintang, which—in practice, if not on paper— essentially excluded the possibility that the Chinese Communist Party would remain within the Kuomintang organisation for a long period. We tried in this way to devise a *transitional* formula that could become a bridge our Central Committee could use to retreat from its erroneous course to a correct one. We posed the question *pedagogically* and not *politically*. As always in such cases this turned out to be mistake. While we were busy trying to enlighten a mistaken leadership, we were sacrificing political clarity with respect to the ranks. Because of this, the very way in which the

question was raised was distorted. The Central Committee did not use our bridge, crying that the Opposition was in fact *in favour* of withdrawal from the Kuomintang. We were compelled to 'justify' ourselves and argue that we were not in favour of withdrawal...

Our mistake was in pedagogical watering down, softening and blunting our position on the basic question. It has yielded nothing but minuses for us: vagueness of position, defensive protestation, and lagging behind the events. We are putting an end to this error by openly calling for immediate withdrawal from the Kuomintang![84]

In the document entitled 'New Opportunities for the Chinese Revolution, New Tasks and New Mistakes' (September 1927) Trotsky comes out openly for withdrawal of the CCP from the KMT:

We must openly announce a break of the Communist Party with the Kuomintang, openly declare the Kuomintang an instrument of bourgeois reaction, and expel it in disgrace from the ranks of the Comintern.[85]

For a long time the Opposition was willing to attack the policy of Stalin and Bukharin which subordinated the CCP to the Kuomintang and led to the smashing of workers' strikes and peasant risings, but it still held that the Communists should remain in the KMT. This was a contradictory and self-defeating attitude. For if it was considered that the Communists should stay in the KMT, then it was inevitable that they would have to abide by KMT policy.

Trotsky explained the long delay in coming out openly for the CCP to leave the Kuomintang in a letter to Max Shachtman of 10 December 1930:

You are quite right when you point out that the Russian Opposition, as late as the first half of 1927, did not demand openly the withdrawal from the Kuomintang. I believe, however, that I have already commented on this fact publicly somewhere. I personally was from the very beginning, that is, from 1923, resolutely opposed to the Communist Party joining the Kuomintang, as well as against the acceptance of the Kuomintang into the 'Kuomintern'. Radek was always with Zinoviev against me. The younger members of the Opposition of 1923 were with me, almost to a man. Up to 1926, I always voted independently in the Political Bureau on this question, against all the others...

In 1926 and 1927, I had uninterrupted conflicts with the Zinovievists on this question. Two or three times the matter stood at the breaking point. Our centre consisted of approximately equal numbers from both of the allied tendencies, for it was after all only a bloc. At the voting, the position of the 1923 Opposition was betrayed by Radek, out of principle, and by Piatakov, out of unprincipledness. Our faction (1923) was furious about it, demanded that Radek and Piatakov be recalled from the centre. But since it was a question of splitting with the Zinovievists, it was the general decision that I must submit publicly in this question and acquaint the Opposition in writing with my standpoint.[86]

Trotsky made concessions to the Zinovievites, and to Radek, Preobrazhensky, Piatakov and Smilga—and thus indirectly to Stalin and Bukharin—by not openly promoting the theory of permanent revolution as it applied to China. While avoiding the term, he nevertheless used the theory in all his analysis of events and the main proposals for action. He demonstrated a genius of insight, a sound grasp of events, a faultless prognosis, and his warnings against the crimes of Stalin and Bukharin were clear clarion calls. The theory of permanent revolution dominated his thinking even when he gave lip service to the 'rotten compromise' with Zinoviev and Co.

Sadly, the compromise with the Zinovievites and Radek did nothing but muddy the water. In the end it did not consolidate the United Opposition around Trotsky. In a letter of 8 January 1931 'To the Chinese Left Opposition' he wrote:

It is worthy of note that all the Russian Oppositionists who adopted the Zinovievist or a conciliatory position... subsequently capitulated. On the other hand, all the comrades who are today in gaols or in exile were from the very beginning opponents of the entry of the Communist Party into the Kuomintang. This shows the power of a principled position![87]

The path of conciliation and compromise taken by Trotsky was particularly sad because the Chinese revolution pre-eminently exposes the bankruptcy of the Stalin-Bukharin policy in the Comintern and confirms the theory of permanent revolution.

In retrospect it is very clear that while the theory of permanent revolution had been *positively* confirmed in the Russian revolution of 1917, it was confirmed again—in a *negative* sense—in the Chinese revolution of 1925-27.

While the rise of the Chinese revolution gave a strong fillip to the Opposition in Russia, the defeat of this revolution dealt it a massive blow. Many members of the Opposition, on seeing the bankruptcy of the Stalin-Bukharin policy on China, thought this would lead to success for the Opposition. Trotsky was never of this view. In his autobiography he wrote:

> Many younger comrades thought the patent bankruptcy of Stalin's policy [in China] was bound to bring the triumph of the opposition nearer. During the first days after the *coup d'état* by Chiang Kai-shek, I was obliged to pour many a bucket of cold water over the hot heads of my young friends—and over some not so young. I tried to show them that the opposition could not rise on the defeat of the Chinese revolution. The fact that our forecast had proved correct might attract one thousand, five thousand, or even ten thousand new supporters to us. But for the millions the significant thing was not our forecast but the fact of the crushing of the Chinese proletariat. After the defeat of the German revolution in 1923, after the break-down of the English general strike in 1926, the new disaster in China would only intensify the disappointment of the masses in the international revolution. And it was this same disappointment that served as the chief psychological source for Stalin's policy of national-reformism.[88]

Chapter ten

The penultimate episode
of the United Opposition

THE CHINESE events gave a fillip to the United Opposition. After the Opposition's winter hibernation of 1926-7, Chiang Kai-shek's massacre of the Shanghai workers gave it a nasty jolt.

Shortly after the massacre a statement was issued called the 'Declaration of the Eighty Four'. It was signed by 84 leading members of the Opposition and circulated on the eve of the Eighth Enlarged Plenum of the ECCI which opened on 18 May 1927. The Declaration was open for further signatures throughout the summer. According to an Opposition letter to the Politburo of 18 October 1927, 863 additional signatures were obtained. Kamenev at the Fifteenth Party Congress (December 1927) claimed 'about 3,000 signatures'. The idea of collecting signatures widely for the Declaration, Trotsky explained in a letter of 12 July 1927, came from one of the leaders of the Opposition who held an ambassadorial post abroad (either Krestinsky or Antonov-Ovseenko) and was proposed as a measure of self-protection.[1]

Until the 'Declaration of the Eighty Four' the Opposition failed to get a hearing for its criticism of the Stalin-Bukharin policy in China—none of its statements or protests were published,* and

---

*See Trotsky's letter of 18 April 1927 to the Politburo complaining that he had been refused the record of the session of the Central Committee of July 1926 and the record of Stalin's speech on China delivered to the Moscow organisation on 5 April 1927.[2] See also Trotsky's letter of protest to the Politburo and Presidium of the Central Control Commission of 16 May 1927 on the decision of the Politburo of 12 May not to publish articles submitted by him on the Chinese situation to **Pravda** and **Bolshevik**.[3] Even Trotsky's speech of May 1927 to the ECCI on the Chinese question was excluded from the published record of the session.[4]

the Politburo and Central Committee had refused to convene a special meeting to discuss the question.

The Declaration marked a change from the Opposition's October 1926 renunciation of factional activity and marked a new effort to win influence in the rank and file of the party.

The Declaration sharply criticised not only the Stalin-Bukharin policy in China but also the Anglo-Russian Committee. The issue of this Committee had become intertwined with the question of the Chinese revolution when the General Council of the TUC supported the British navy's bombardment of Nanking in March 1927. Despite this, the Soviet leaders refused to withdraw from the Anglo-Russian Committee. In April representatives of the Soviet trade unions, in a meeting with representatives of the British trade unions in Berlin, reiterated their support of the Anglo-Russian Committee even though the British unions refused to back the CP call for a 'Hands Off China' campaign. On 12 May British police raided the Soviet trade mission in London and launched an anti-Communist witch hunt.

The 'Declaration of the Eighty Four' connected the wrong policies of the Stalin-Bukharin leadership in China and Britain with the internal policies of the same leadership in Russia in the fields of peasant policy, industrialisation, wages policy, housing, employment etc.

To overcome the wrong policies of the leadership it was crucial to achieve democracy in the party, the Declaration stated:

> The fundamental prerequisites for solving the problems facing the party at present...*is the revival of democracy within the party and reinforcement of the real, living, and effective links between the party and the working class.*[5]

On 24 May Trotsky addressed the ECCI. He had to begin with a protest against the Executive's treatment of Zinoviev, its former President; now he was not even admitted to the session. Trotsky spoke of the 'intellectual weakness, the lack of certainty in their own position', which led Stalin and Bukharin to conceal from the International the thesis of the Opposition on China.

> Here in Moscow every expression of opinion, oral or written, in favour of the Opposition on the basic problems of the Chinese revolution is treated as a crime against the party.

The ECCI should publish its own proceedings: 'The problems of the Chinese revolution cannot be stuck into a bottle and sealed up.' The bureaucratic regime that suppressed democracy in the Russian party also,

> weighs heavily on the International. One does not trust himself to speak a word of criticism openly, on the false pretence of not wanting to harm the Soviet Union. But that is exactly how the greatest harm is done.[6]

The Chinese experience proved this. Bukharin and Stalin were concerned only with self-justification, covering up their disastrous mistakes. On 5 April, ie, a week before Chiang Kai-shek's coup in Shanghai, Stalin boasted at a party meeting in Moscow that 'we will use the Chinese bourgeoisie and then toss it away like a squeezed-out lemon'. Trotsky commented: 'The stenogram of this speech by Stalin was never made public, because a few days later the squeezed-out lemon seized power and the army.'

Soviet advisers and Comintern envoys, especially Borodin, behaved as if they represented some sort of,

> Kuomintern; they hindered the independent policy of the proletariat, its independent organisation, and especially its armament... Heaven forbid, with arms in hand the proletariat would frighten the great spectre of the national revolution, hovering over all the classes... The Communist Party of China has been a shackled party in the past period. It did not have so much as its own newspaper. Imagine what this means in general and especially in revolution! Why has it not had, and has not yet to this day, its own daily paper? Because the Kuomintang does not want it... This means to disarm the proletariat politically.[7]

Chiang Kai-shek's coup in Shanghai spurred the Opposition into action. Trotsky writes in his autobiography: 'A wave of excitement swept over the party. The Opposition raised its head'.[8] Many in the Opposition were under the illusion that the events in China would bring the Opposition to power in the Russian Communist Party. Trotsky, cool-headed and realistic, had to disabuse them, as we have shown.

Stalin uses war scare against the Opposition

While the ECCI was in session the tension between Britain and the Soviet Union reached a critical point, and the British Government broke off relations with Russia. Stalin said to the ECCI:

> I must state, comrades, that Trotsky has chosen for his attacks...an all too inopportune moment. I have just received the news that the English Conservative government has resolved to break off relations with the USSR. There is no need to prove that what is intended is a wholesale crusade against communism. The crusade has already started. Some threaten the party with war and intervention; others with a split. There comes into being something like a united front from Chamberlain to Trotsky... You need not doubt that we shall be able to break up this new front.[9]

The war scare served to justify further repression of the Opposition. Krupskaya's reasoning was typical. In the previous years she had supported the Opposition in its effort to draw attention to certain dangers. Now she dissociated herself from it: 'The Soviet Union is menaced by armed aggression, and in these conditions...it is essential that our Party be a united whole, and that the masses which surround it also close their ranks.'[10]

Intensifying his attack, Stalin sent many Opposition leaders abroad, on the pretext that they were needed for various diplomatic missions.

Krestinsky was in Berlin; Rakovsky was sent to Paris as Soviet ambassador to France, where Piatakov, Preobrazhensky and Vladimir Kossior were also posted as trade representatives; Kamenev was made an ambassador to Italy for a time, and with him was the Oppositionist Avilov-Glebov; Antonov-Ovseenko and Kanatchikov were the Soviet representatives in Prague; Ufimtsev and Semashko in Vienna; Kopp in Stockholm; Mdivani in Tehran; Ausen in Constantinople and Kraevsky in Latin America.[11] Practically all the other signatories to the 'Declaration of the Eighty Four' were demoted, and on the pretext of administrative appointments, moved to remote provinces.

It was such an administrative transfer that caused a

significant incident. On 9 June Ivar Smilga was ordered to leave Moscow and to take up a post at Khabarovsk on the Manchurian frontier. The leader of the Baltic fleet in the October revolution, a distinguished political commissar in the civil war and an economist, Smilga was one of the most respected and popular leaders of the Zinovievite faction.

Smilga was seen off at the Yaroslav station in Moscow by thousands of Oppositionists. Both Trotsky and Zinoviev made speeches. This was the first public manifestation the Opposition made against Stalin. Arising out of it, the ruling group charged Trotsky and Zinoviev with carrying inner-party issues outside the party.

Many hundreds of Oppositionists who were present at the Yaroslav station were expelled from the party. The ruling group connected this expulsion with the threat of foreign war facing the Soviet Union. The excitement around the demonstration at the Yaroslav station lasted throughout the summer.

Trotsky and Zinoviev were brought before the Presidium of the Central Control Commission on two charges: (1) making a factional speech at the Plenum of the ECCI; (2) participating in the farewell demonstration over Smilga at Yaroslav station.

Defendant Trotsky turns prosecutor

Trotsky appeared before the Presidium of the Central Control Commission on 24 July. Here he gave one of his most brilliant speeches.[12] He replied briefly to the two formal charges laid against him. He denied the right of the Central Control Commission to sit in judgment over him for a speech he had delivered before the Executive of the International. He would similarly deny 'a District Control Commission the right to sit in judgment upon me for any speech I may have made as a member of the Central Committee of the party'.

As to the second charge, the farewell demonstration for Smilga, the ruling group denied that it had intended to penalise Smilga by sending him to Khabarovsk:

If Smilga was sent, as a matter of normal procedure, to work in Khabarovsk, then you cannot dare claim that our collective farewell was a demonstration against the Central Committee.

However, if this is an administrative exile of a comrade, who is at the present moment needed at responsible posts, that is, at fighting Soviet posts, then you are duping the party.

The accusations were mere pretexts. The ruling group was determined 'to hound the Opposition and to prepare for its physical annihilation'. The war scare was produced in order to intimidate and silence critics.

We declare that we shall continue to criticise the Stalinist regime so long as you do not physically seal our lips. Until you clamp a gag on our mouths we shall continue to criticise this Stalinist regime which will otherwise undermine all the conquests of the October revolution... We will continue to criticise the Stalinist regime as a worthless regime, a regime of backsliding, an ideologically emasculated, narrow-minded and short-sighted regime.

The Opposition had nothing in common with those old-time patriots for whom Tsar and Fatherland were one. They were accused of aiding the British Tories. In fact it was Stalin and Bukharin with their Anglo-Russian Committee policy who aided Chamberlain's foreign policy, including the rupturing of relations with the Soviet Union.

You have told the workers of the world, and above all our Moscow workers, that in the event of war the Anglo-Russian Committee would be the organising centre of the struggle against imperialism. But we have said and still say that in the event of war the Anglo-Russian Committee will be a ready-made trench for all the turn-coats of the breed of the false, half-way friends of the Soviet Union, and for all the deserters to the camp of the enemies of the Soviet Union. Thomas gives open support to Chamberlain. But Purcell supports Thomas, and that is the main thing. Thomas maintains himself upon the support of the Capitalists. Purcell maintains himself by deceiving the masses and lends Thomas his support. And you are lending support to Purcell. You accuse us of giving support to Chamberlain. No! It is you yourselves who are linked up with Chamberlain through your Right wing. It is you who stand in a common front with

Purcell who supports Thomas and, together with the latter, Chamberlain. That is the verdict of a political analysis and not a charge based on calumny.

At party cells official agitators asked suggestive questions 'worthy of the Black Hundreds' about the sources from which the Opposition obtained means for carrying on with its activity.

If you were really a Central Control Commission, you would be duty-bound to put an end to this dirty, abominable, contemptible and purely Stalinist campaign against the Opposition.

If the ruling group genuinely cared for the security of the country they would not have dismissed the best military workers, Smilga, Mrachkovsky, Lashevich, Bakaev and Muralov, only because they belonged to the Opposition.

Trotsky went on to assault the 'theory of socialism in one country' which reflected the rising bureaucracy which in its turn reflected the strengthening of the power of the kulaks and NEPmen and the decline in social weight of the proletariat.

Trotsky ended his speech with a recollection of the experience of the French revolution and the Thermidorean reaction to it.

He started by referring to a conversation between Soltz, an old and respected Bolshevik chairing the meeting, and one of the adherents of the Opposition.

'What does the Declaration of 84 mean?' said Soltz. 'What does it lead to? You know the history of the French Revolution—and to what this led: to arrests and to the guillotine.' Comrade Vorobiev, with whom comrade Soltz was talking, asked him, 'So then, is it your intention to guillotine us?' To which Soltz replied by going into a lengthy explanation, 'In your opinion, wasn't Robespierre sorry for Danton when sending him to the guillotine? And then Robespierre had to go himself... Do you think he was not sorry? Sure he was, but he had to do it...'

Trotsky goes on:

During the Great French Revolution, many were guillotined. We, too, had many people brought before the firing squad.

But in the Great French Revolution there were two great chapters, of which one went like this [*points upward*] and the other like that [*points downward*]. When the chapter headed like this [*upwards*] the French Jacobins, the Bolsheviks of that time, guillotined the Royalists and the Girondists. We, too, have had a similar great chapter when we, the Oppositionists, together with you, shot the White Guards and exiled the Girondists. And then there began another chapter in France, when... the Thermidorians and the Bonapartists from among the Right wing Jacobins—began exiling and shooting the Left Jacobins—the Bolsheviks of that time. I should like comrade Soltz to think his analogy through to the end and, first of all, to give himself an answer to the following question: In accordance with which chapter is Soltz preparing to have us shot? [*Commotion in the hall.*] This is no jesting matter; revolution is a serious business. None of us is scared by firing squads. We are all old revolutionists. But the thing is to know *whom to shoot, and in accordance with which chapter*. When we did the shooting we were firm in our knowledge as to the chapter. But, comrade Soltz, do you clearly understand in accordance with which chapter you are now preparing to shoot? I fear, comrade Soltz, that you are about to shoot us in accordance with the...Thermidorian chapter.

Trotsky went on to explain that his adversaries were mistaken in implying that he was calling them by abusive names.

It is thought that the Thermidorians were arrant counter-revolutionists, conscious supporters of the monarchic rule, and so on. Nothing of the kind! The Thermidorians were Jacobins, with this difference, that they had moved to the Right... Do you think on the very next day after the 9th of Thermidor they said to themselves: We have now transferred power into the hands of the bourgeoisie? Nothing of the kind! Refer to all the newspapers of that time. They said: We have destroyed a handful of people who disrupted peace in the party, but now, after their destruction, the revolution will triumph completely. If comrade Soltz has any doubts about it...

SOLTZ: You are practically repeating my own words.

TROTSKY: So much the better...

I shall read you what was said by Brival, who was a Right Jacobin, one of the Thermidorians, when he reported about the session of the Convention during which Robespierre and the other Jacobins were handed over to the Revolutionary Tribunal: 'Intriguers and counter-revolutionists covering themselves with the toga of patriotism sought the destruction of liberty; the Convention decreed to place them under arrest. These representatives were: Robespierre, Couthon, Saint-Just, Lebas and Robespierre the Younger. The chairman asked what my opinion was. I replied: Those who had always voted in accordance with the spirit of the principles of the Mountain...voted for the arrest. I did even more than that, for I am one of those who proposed this measure. Moreover, as secretary, I made haste to sign and to transmit this decree of the Convention.' That is how the report was made by a Soltz...of that time. Robespierre and his associates—those were the counter-revolutionists. 'Those who had always voted in accordance with the spirit of the principles of the Mountain' signified in the language of that time, 'those who had always been Bolsheviks.' Brival considered himself an old Bolshevik. 'As secretary, *I made haste* to sign and to transmit this decree of the Convention.' Today, too, there are secretaries who make haste 'to sign and to transmit.' Today, too, there are such secretaries...

The Thermidorians too, Trotsky went on, had attacked the Left Jacobins amid cries of *la patrie en danger*! They were convinced that Robespierre and his friends were only 'isolated individuals.' They branded them as 'aristocrats' and agents of Pitt, just as the Stalinists had denounced the Opposition as the agents of Chamberlain, 'that modern pocket edition of Pitt.'

The odour of the 'second chapter' assails one's nostrils...the party regime stifles everyone who struggles against Thermidor. In the party the mass worker has been stifled. The rank and file worker is silent...

An anonymous regime of terror was instituted, for silence was made compulsory, 100% votes and abstention from all criticism were demanded, thinking in accordance with orders from above was made obligatory, and men were compelled to unlearn to think that the party is a living, independent organism and not a self-sufficing machine of power...

Similarly,

The Jacobin clubs, the crucibles of revolution, became the nurseries of future functionaries of Napoleon. We should learn from the French Revolution. But is it really necessary to repeat it? [*Shouts*]

Despite great differences between the Opposition and the ruling group in the party, a split could be avoided.

...we possess gigantic ideological wealth of accumulated experience in the works of Lenin, in the program of the party, in the traditions of the party. You have squandered a great deal of this capital, you have substituted for a lot, the cheap surrogates... But a good deal of pure gold still remains. In the second place, we have the present historical period of abrupt turns, gigantic events, colossal lessons from which one can and must learn. There are stupendous facts, which provide the test for the two lines. But you must not dare hide these facts. Sooner or later they will become known anyway. You cannot hide the victories and defeats of the proletariat.

What was needed for the party to overcome the crisis?

...a more healthy and flexible regime in the party so as to enable the gigantic events to provide the text for the antagonistic lines without any convulsions. It is necessary to secure for the party the possibility of ideological self-criticism on the basis of the great events. If this is done, I am certain that, in a year or two, the course of the party will be rectified. There is no need to rush, there is no necessity for adopting such decisions as cannot be later remedied. Beware lest you are compelled to say: We parted company with those whom we should have preserved, while preserving those from whom we should have parted.

Stalin presses on with the assault on the Opposition

The final collapse of the Chinese revolution and the dissolution of the Anglo-Russian Committee demonstrated the complete bankruptcy of the Stalin-Bukharin policies abroad; this made Stalin intent on achieving the complete suppression of the Opposition at home.

At the same time, internal developments in Russia pushed Stalin and Bukharin in the same direction. The economy of the country went into a deep crisis as a result of their policies. E.H. Carr writes:

> In May-June 1927 serious signs of strain began to appear. In the Volga and North Caucasian regions, and in Kazakhstan, free market prices for grain moved sharply ahead of the official prices. About the same time symptoms of a general scarcity made themselves felt, after a long interval, in the food shops of Moscow and other large cities. By the autumn of 1927 shortages in the cities had become widespread and chronic. A writer in the Vesenkha newspaper, referring primarily to textiles and other manufactured goods, described how groups gathered in shops discussing the shortages and recalling the famine years, and went from shop to shop in search of scarce goods, aggravating the impression of a crisis. In Moscow, butter, cheese and milk were no longer to be had—or not at prices which most people could afford; and supplies of bread were irregular.[13]

And the historian Michel Reiman writes:

> With increasing frequency, the authorities took measures that cut the real wages and social gains of the labouring sectors of the population. Social and political ferment intensified, becoming an important part of the general crisis.[14]

Thus far Stalin had managed to suppress all Trotsky's criticisms. Almost any one of Trotsky's recent speeches and writings would have exploded the authority of Stalin and Bukharin. But Trotsky's voice was not heard by the mass of the people. The approach of the Fifteenth Party Congress offered Trotsky and Zinoviev an opportunity to state their views. So Stalin hastened to ban the Opposition once and for all.

On 27 June Trotsky wrote a letter to the Central Committee entitled 'The Party Crisis Deepens'.

...the party finds itself in the worst crisis it has experienced since the revolution. And now, more than ever, it must be resolved.

In direct conjunction with the recent setbacks in China, which were brought about to a significant extent by incorrect leadership of the Chinese revolution, the international situation has abruptly worsened. The danger of war and intervention is unquestionable...

The party crisis must be resolved.

The Central Committee is trying to resolve it by the mechanical suppression of the Opposition... Party opinion is being openly prepared for the expulsion of the Opposition from the party.

...To surgically remove, behind the backs of the party ranks, the Opposition section of the party, which includes hundreds and thousands of comrades who have passed through the fires of three revolutions, fought on the fronts of the civil war, led the revolutionary struggle of the proletariat and stood at the head of the proletarian dictatorship at the most difficult moments—that is not the way out of the situation. Only by the Leninist road can we restore to the party *genuine unity, which means above all maximum active participation by the entire mass of the party* and its readiness to accept all sacrifices for the sake of the victory of the proletarian revolution and socialism.

[The CC] should bring to the knowledge of the party ranks all the documents, including ours, with which the party ranks can orient themselves in the present complex situation. It should print these documents and send them to all party organisations as material for the Fifteenth Congress (with only about four months remaining until the opening of the congress).[15]

The day after writing this letter Trotsky wrote to Ordzhonikidze, the Chairman of the Central Control Commission, protesting against rumours spread by some party bureaucrats of an intention to expel Trotsky and twenty of his supporters from the party.[16]

Now the press began to report resolutions of local party organisations demanding the expulsion of Trotsky and Zinoviev.

Stalin's most effective argument against the Opposition was that it was weakening the Soviet Union in the face of a hostile capitalist world. Trotsky, in his letter to Ordzhonikidze of 11 July, attempted to counter this argument by invoking a famous precedent to support his claim that in a period of war danger criticism of the ruling group could serve the needs of defence.

The French bourgeoisie at the outset of the imperialist war had at its head a government without rudder or sails. The Clemenceau group was in opposition to that government. In spite of the war and the military censorship, in spite even of the fact that the Germans were within eighty kilometres of Paris (Clemenceau said 'precisely because of that') Clemenceau conducted a furious struggle against the weak-kneed and wavering petty bourgeois policies, and for imperialist ferocity and ruthlessness. Clemenceau did not betray his class, the bourgeoisie; on the contrary, he served it more faithfully, more firmly, decisively, and wisely, than did Viviani, Painlev... and Company. This was shown by the subsequent course of events. The Clemenceau group came to power, and by a more consistent, a more predatory imperialist policy, it secured the victory of the French bourgeoisie. Were there any commentators in France who put the label of 'defeatists' on the Clemenceau group? No doubt there were: fools and gossips will be found among the camp followers of all classes. But they are not always given the opportunity to play an equally important part.[17]

The reaction of the Stalinists and Bukharinists was immediate. Trotsky was threatening to stage a coup in the middle of the war, while the enemy army might be standing 80 kilometres from Moscow—no other proof of his being a counter-revolutionary was needed. From then until the end of the year, until Trotsky's banishment, the hue and cry about the Clemenceau statement went on unabated.

Stalin and Bukharin could easily distort the meaning of the Clemenceau statement, not only because they had the monopoly of the propaganda machine, but also because very few people knew the story of Clemenceau.

On 1 August a joint Plenum of the Central Committee and Central Control Commission again considered the motion to expel

Trotsky. Now the Clemenceau statement provided the central item in the indictment of the Opposition leaders: that they would not be loyal in war, and would not contribute to the defence of the Soviet Union.

Trotsky appeared before the Plenum, not as a humble defendant, but as the courageous prosecutor. He recalled the high responsibility he had borne for many years for Soviet defence policy and for formulating the Comintern's views on war and peace.

He attacked Stalin's and Bukharin's reliance for defence on 'rotten ropes'—the Anglo-Russian Committee they had hailed as a bulwark against war.

> Your present policy is a policy of rotten props on an international scale. You successively clutched at Chiang Kai-shek, Feng Yu-hsiang, Tang Chen-chih, Wang Ching-wei, Purcell, Hicks and Cook. Each of these ropes broke at the moment when it was most sorely needed... In the event of war you will have to stumble time and again over 'surprises'. The rotten ropes will fall apart in your hands.

That is why the Opposition had to criticise the Stalinist leadership.

> But does not the criticism of the Opposition reflect upon the authority of the U.S.S.R. in the international labour movement?
> We would never think of even posing such a question. This very posing of the question of authority is worthy of the papal church, or feudal generals. The Catholic Church demands an unquestioning recognition of its authority on the part of the faithful. The revolutionist gives his support, while criticizing, and the more undeniable is his right to criticize, all the greater is his devotion in struggling for the creation and strengthening of that in which he is a direct participant...
> What we need is not a hypocritical 'Union sacre' but honest revolutionary unity....
> The Opposition is for the victory of the U.S.S.R.; it has proved this and will continue to prove this in action, in a manner inferior to none. But Stalin is not concerned with that. Stalin has essentially a different question in mind, which he does

not dare express, namely 'Does the Opposition really think that the leadership of Stalin is incapable of assuring victory to the U.S.S.R.?'

And Trotsky ended his speech for the prosecution thus:

> Every Oppositionist, if he is a genuine Oppositionist and not a fraud, will assume in the event of war whatever post, at the front or behind the lines, that the party will intrust to him, and carry out his duty to the end. But not a single Oppositionist will renounce his right and his duty, on the eve of war, or during the war, to fight for the correction of the party's course—as has always been the case in our party—because therein lies the most important condition for victory. To sum up. For the socialist fatherland? Yes! For the Stalinist course? No![18]

Stalin's assault on Trotsky

On 9 August, at the joint Plenum of the Central Committee and the Central Control Commission, Stalin made a vicious assault on Trotsky's Clemenceau thesis.[19] On the same day the Plenum passed a resolution 'On the Violation of Party Discipline by Zinoviev and Trotsky'. It rehearsed in detail the crimes of the Opposition since 1923, and especially since 16 October 1926, when the United Opposition announced its giving up of all factional activities and then broke its promise. The Plenum called on the Opposition to abandon the 'semi-defencist' attitudes implicit in the Clemenceau thesis and the slander about a Thermidorian degeneration of party and state, to desist from attempts to split the Russian party and the Comintern. The CC decided to remove from the agenda the expulsion of Zinoviev and Trotsky from the Central Committee, hoping that they would stop their factionalism. Instead a 'severe reprimand and warning' was delivered to them. The resolution went on to warn of the consequences of any future violation of discipline.[20]

The pressure of the Stalinist machine succeeded in creating some fissures in the Opposition leadership. The unstable, wobbly Zinoviev welcomed the resolution, seeing in it a step towards peace in the party: 'The Bolshevik Party can resolve serious differences without shake-up, on the path of genuine Leninist unity.'[21] At the same time Ioffe wrote to Trotsky protesting against the vacillation of the Opposition, against its compromising stance toward Stalin and his accomplices. Ioffe condemned the wording the Opposition used at the Plenum, namely, 'We will carry out all the decisions of the CPSU and its Central Committee'; 'We are prepared to do everything possible to destroy all factional elements which have formed themselves as a consequence of the fact that, because of the inner regime of the party, we were compelled to inform the party of our opinions that had been falsely reported in the press of the whole country.'[22]

On 15 August a letter from the Zinovievists contained a thinly veiled warning against 'light-headed and adventurist tactics' which might lead to the ultimate disaster of the 'exclusion of the Opposition from the party.' These were warning signals that the bloc between Trotsky and Zinoviev was in danger.

The Platform of the United Opposition

In preparation for the Fifteenth Congress of the party the leaders of the United Opposition in September 1927 prepared the Platform of the Opposition, a full and systematic statement of its policy.

Victor Serge describes the way the platform was drafted:

Zinoviev undertook to work out the chapters on agriculture and International in collaboration with Kamenev; the chapter on industrialisation was assigned to Trotsky; Smilga and Piatakov, helped by some young comrades, also worked on the draft, which was submitted, as each section came out, to our meetings and, wherever possible, to groups of workers. For the last time (but we had no suspicion that this was so) the Party returned to its tradition of collective thinking, with its concern to consult the man in the workshop.[23]

Trotsky wrote that 200 party members contributed to the Platform.[24]

The Platform developed further the policies that Trotsky had put forward as early as 1922 regarding the industrialisation of the country. As we have seen[25], in November 1922 Trotsky argued for economic planning. He made it clear that this would not mean getting rid of the market at a stroke, nor did it mean the end of the NEP. Again at the Twelfth Party Congress (April 1923) he developed the same ideas further.[26] From 1922 onwards he was arguing for a comprehensive economic plan. He was concerned that while NEP had succeeded in restoring agriculture—and that had been its main intent—it was unable to solve the fundamental problems of the Russian economy, particularly the problem of industrialisation. The lag of industry behind restored agriculture led to a conflict between industry and agriculture, as was demonstrated in what Trotsky termed the 'scissors crisis': the rise in industrial prices and the decline in agricultural ones threatened to undermine agricultural production. Politically, the crisis threatened to undermine the worker-peasant alliance and to arouse the peasantry against the regime. In the Platform Trotsky develops the same arguments further.

Many passages in the Platform are devoted to showing the growth of the kulak danger, and the increasing exploitation of the poor and middle peasants.

The Soviet government should orientate itself on the agricultural workers, the poor peasants and the middle peasants.

> *In the class struggle now going on in the countryside the party must stand, not only in words but in deeds, at the head of the farmhands, the poor peasants, and the basic mass of the middle peasants, and organise them against the exploitative aims of the kulak.*

While collectivisation of agriculture was to be encouraged, this should be gradual: private farming would continue to be the dominant form in the countryside for a long time to come. Not only did the workers and poor peasants need to be aided, but also the middle peasants.

> *The growth of individual farming must be offset by more rapid development of collective farming.* It is necessary to appropriate funds systematically year after year to assist the poor peasants who have organised in collectives.
> At the same time, we must give more systematic help to poor peasants who are not in the collectives, by freeing them entirely from taxation by assigning them suitable plots of land and providing credit for agricultural implements and by bringing them into the agricultural cooperatives.

The agricultural cooperatives and collectives must be

voluntary organisations without coercion or the dead hand of bureaucracy.

> A successful cooperative structure is conceivable only if the participants enjoy a maximum of independent initiatives. Proper relations by the cooperatives with large-scale industry and the proletarian state presuppose a normal regime in the cooperative organisations, excluding bureaucratic methods of regulation.[27]

The peasants who do not join the collective farms should not be neglected either.

> The party ought to promote by all means the economic advancement of the *middle peasants*—by a wise policy of prices for grain, by the organisation of credits and cooperatives accessible to them, and by the systematic and gradual introduction of this most numerous peasant group to the benefit of large-scale, mechanised, collective agriculture.

What about the kulaks? They will continue to exist but the expansion of their wealth and power should be restricted.

> The task of the party in relation to the growing kulak strata ought to consist in the all-sided limitation of their efforts at exploitation... The following measures are necessary: a steeply progressive tax system; legislative measures to protect hired labour and regulate the wages of agricultural workers; a correct class policy in regard to land division and utilisation; the same thing in regard to supplying tractors and other instruments of production to the villages...
>
> The existing system of a single agricultural tax ought to be changed in the direction of freeing the 40 to 50 per cent of poorer and poorest peasant families from all taxation, without any additional tax being imposed upon the bulk of the middle peasants. The dates of tax collection should be accommodated to the interests of the lower groups of tax payers.[28]

The Platform envisaged the continuation of NEP, and therefore, although it was intended to exercise greater control over the kulaks and NEPmen, to tax them more heavily and to promote collectivisation in the countryside, the liquidation of the kulaks and of the private sector or duress against the peasants, was out of the question. How radically different this agricultural policy was from Stalin's future forced collectivisation!

Finally, Trotsky saw the collectivisation of agriculture as following the industrialisation of Russia and not as Stalin saw it, as a prerequisite for industrialisation. The Platform wrote:

> The inadequate tempo of industrial development leads... to a retardation of the growth of agriculture... only a powerful socialist industry can help the peasants transform agriculture along collective lines.

The balanced growth of industry and agriculture, where industry was the motor of advance, was crucial.

> The chronic lagging of industry, as well as transport, electrification, and construction, behind the demands and needs of the population, the economy, and the social system as a whole, hold all economic circulation in the country in a terrible vice. It reduces the sale and export of the marketable part of our agricultural production. It restricts imports to extremely narrow limits, drives up prices and production costs, causes the instability of the *chervonets*, and retards the development of the productive forces. It delays all improvement in the material condition of the proletarian and peasant masses, causes the dangerous growth of unemployment and the deterioration of housing conditions. It undermines the bond between industry and agriculture and weakens the country's defence capability.
> The inadequate tempo of industrial development leads in turn to a retardation of the growth of agriculture.[29]

Where were the sources for investment in industry to be found?

The Platform speaks of 500 to 1,000 million roubles per annum to be granted to industry by 1931. The bourgeoisie and the kulaks were to pay higher taxes, in the region of 150-200 million. In addition, 10 per cent of the more prosperous peasants were to contribute to a compulsory loan of 150 million puds of grain. It was estimated that this stratum possessed some 8,000-9,000 million puds in reserve.[30] The Platform's investment targets were extremely modest compared with those Stalin imposed in the Five Year Plans. Thus the Plenum of the Central Committee of December 1930 fixed the target for investment in industry at 7,470 million roubles.[31]

Industrialisation should not be at the cost of agriculture, the Platform said. On the contrary, 'no industrialisation is possible without decisively raising the level of the productive forces in agriculture.' [32]

Industrialisation should also not be accompanied by a decline in workers' standards of living, but on the contrary, these should rise.

> The material positions of the proletariat within the country must be strengthened both absolutely and relatively (growth in the number of employed workers, reduction in the number of unemployed, improvement in the material level of the working class...)[33]

A whole chapter of the Platform is devoted to the condition of the workers, which had seen a serious deterioration in recent years.

> The decisive factor in appraising the progress of our country along the road of socialist construction must be the growth of our productive forces and the dominance of the socialist elements over the capitalist—*together with improvement in all the living conditions of the working class...*
>
> The attempt to push the vital interests of the worker into the background and, under the contemptuous epithet of 'narrow craft professionalism' to counterpose them to the general historical interests of the working class is theoretically wrong and politically dangerous.

Workers' conditions had sharply deteriorated in the recent period.

> The numerical growth of the working class and the improvement of its situation has almost stopped, while the growth of its enemies continues, and continues at an accelerated pace. This inevitably leads not only to a worsening of conditions in the factories but also to a lowering of the relative weight of the proletariat in Soviet society...
>
> Thus real wages for the present year have stood still,

approximately at the level of the autumn of 1925...
Moreover, all the data indicate that the growth of wages is lagging behind the growth of labour productivity. The intensity of labour is increasing—the bad conditions of labour remain the same.

Elsewhere V.M. Smirnov, a close ally of Trotsky, noted that between October 1924 and October 1926, while workers' output rose by 47.5 per cent, workers' wages rose by only 15 per cent, and purchasing power still remained below pre-war levels.[34]
The rationalisation of production, so loudly praised by the authorities, actually damaged workers' conditions.

In practice, 'rationalisation' often comes down to 'throwing out' some workers and lowering the material conditions of others. This inevitably fills the masses of workers with a distrust of rationalisation itself.[35]

The weakest—women and youth—suffer most.

When labour's living standards are under pressure, it is always the weakest groups that suffer most: unskilled workers, seasonal workers, women and adolescents.
In 1926 there was an obvious lowering of the wages of women as compared with those of men in almost all branches of industry...
The average earnings of adolescents, in comparison with the earnings of workers as a whole, are steadily declining. In 1923 they were 47.1 per cent, in 1924 45 per cent, in 1925 43.⁴ per cent, in 1926 40.5 per cent, in 1927 39.5 per cent...

If the conditions of the urban workers were bad, those of agricultural workers were even worse.

Of the approximately 3,500,000 wage workers in the country, 1,600,000 are farmhands, men and women. Only 20 per cent of these farmhands are organised in unions... Real wages on the average are not over 63 per cent of their pre-war level. The working day is rarely less than ten hours. In the majority of cases it is, as a matter of fact, unlimited. Wages are paid irregularly and after intolerable delays.

Added to this is the scourge of unemployment.

The official number of registered unemployed in April 1927 was 1,478,000... The actual number of unemployed is about 2,000,000. The number of unemployed is growing incomparably faster than the total number of employed workers. The number of unemployed industrial workers is growing especially rapidly... The consequences of this state of affairs will be an increase in the number of homeless children, beggars, and prostitutes. The small unemployment insurance paid to those who are out of work is causing justifiable resentment.[36]

Factory management is more and more autocratic.

The regime within the factories has deteriorated. The factory administrative bodies are striving more and more to establish their unlimited authority. The hiring and discharge of workers is actually in the hands of the administration alone. Pre-revolutionary relations between supervisors and workers are frequently found.[37]

The workers were further and further alienated from the trade unions.

In the staff of the elected executive bodies of ten industrial unions, the percentage of workers from the bench and non-Party militant workers is extremely small (12-13 per cent). The immense majority of delegates to the trade union conferences are people entirely dissociated from industry... The independent initiative of the mass of workers organised in the trade unions is being replaced by agreements between the secretary of the party group, the factory director, and the chairman of the factory committee... The attitude of the workers to the factory and shop committees is one of distrust. Attendance at the general meetings is low.

The dissatisfaction of the worker, finding no outlet in the trade union, is driven inwards. 'We mustn't be too active—if you want a bite of bread, don't talk so much.'[38]

A number of practical proposals were put forward to improve workers' conditions:

The most immediate task is to raise wages at least to correspond to the achieved increase in the productivity of labour. The future course should be a systematic elevation of real wages to correspond to every rise in labour productivity. It is necessary to achieve an increasing equalisation in the wages of different groups of workers, by way of a systematic raising of the lower-paid groups; in no case by a lowering of the higher paid.

For women workers, 'equal pay for equal work'. Provision to be made for women workers to learn skilled trades...

At every trade union congress (including the all-union congress) and in all the elected bodies of the trade unions (including the All-Union Central Council of Trade Unions) there must be a majority of workers directly engaged in industry.[39]

The raising of the social weight of the proletariat by increasing its size and improving its material conditions must be accompanied by the strengthening of proletarian democracy, increasing the power of the Soviets.

It is necessary:

1. To adopt a firm policy of struggle against *chinovnichestvo* [the virulent old Russian form of bureaucratism]—to wage this struggle as Lenin would, on the basis of a real fight to check the exploitative influence of the new bourgeoisie and the kulaks by way of a consistent development of workers' democracy in the party, the trade unions, and the soviets.

2. To make it our watchword to draw the state nearer to the worker, the farmhand, the poor peasant, and the middle peasant—against the kulak—unconditionally subordinating the state apparatus to the essential interests of the toiling masses.

3. As the basis for reviving the soviets, to increase the class activity of the workers, farmhands, and poor and middle peasants.

4. To convert the urban soviets into real institutions of proletarian power and instruments for drawing the broad mass of the working people into the task of administering socialist construction—to realise, not in words but in deeds, control by the urban soviets over the work of the regional executive committees and the bodies subject to those committees.

5. To put a complete stop to the removal of elected soviet officials, except in case of real and absolute necessity, in which cases the causes should be made clear to the electors.
6. We must see that the most backward unskilled worker and the most ignorant peasant woman become convinced by experience that in any state institution whatsoever they will find attention, counsel, and all possible support.[40]

The party had also to change. The social composition of the party had to be improved.

The number of factory workers in the leading bodies of the party is next to nothing. In the regional committees, it is 13.2 per cent; in the county committees, from 9.8 to 16.1 per cent...
It is necessary to adopt immediately a series of measures for the improvement of the social composition of the party and of its leading bodies.[41]

It was necessary to restore inner-party democracy.

Bureaucratism is growing in all spheres, but its growth is especially ruinous in the party...
The last few years have seen a systematic abolition of inner-party democracy...
Not only have careerism, bureaucratism, and inequality grown in the party in recent years, but muddy streams from alien and hostile class sources are flowing into it—for example, anti-Semitism. The very self-preservation of the party demands a merciless struggle against such defilement.[42]

The Platform, however, maintained some serious defects. While, as we have seen, it devoted great attention to the living standards of the working class, it paid little attention to the question of the relations of production in the factories—only one paragraph in which it was noted that 'the regime in the factories has deteriorated' and that 'pre-revolutionary relations between foremen and workmen are frequently found.' It made no specific proposals and raised no demands with regard to increasing or re-establishing workers' control of industry.
It also suffered from the inheritance of the exceptional

conditions of the civil war, when the one-party system was transformed from a necessity into a virtue. The Platform states:

> The dictatorship of the proletariat imperiously demands a single and united proletarian party as the leader of the working masses and the poor peasantry. Such unity, unweakened by factional strife, is unconditionally necessary to the proletariat in the fulfilment of its historic mission.[43]

Finally, the weakest section of the Platform was that dealing with the Comintern which was written by Zinoviev. It deals with the Anglo-Russian Committee and with the Stalin-Bukharin policy in China. Among other things the section includes a statement that Trotsky renounced the theory of permanent revolution.

Trotsky, in **The Third International After Lenin**, admits that the Platform dealt with the Chinese revolution very inadequately and in part positively falsely.[44]

The Preobrazhensky whip

The Opposition was slandered profusely. As it pointed to the enormous growth of the kulaks and the threat they represented to the regime, Stalin and Bukharin accused the Opposition of wishing to 'rob the peasants'.[45] When the Opposition pointed to the lag of industry behind the needs of the national economy, and the inevitable consequences thereof—the price 'scissors', the goods famine, the rupture of the *smychka* between proletariat and peasantry—Stalin and Bukharin called the Opposition 'super industrialisers'. When the Opposition pointed to the incorrect prices policy, which did not reduce the high cost of living but aided the profiteers, Stalin and Bukharin accused the Opposition of advocating a policy of raising prices. To support these distortions, Stalin and Bukharin—above all the latter—unscrupulously used the words of Preobrazhensky.

Evgeny A. Preobrazhensky was the chief economist of the Trotskyists. His book, **Novaia Ekonomika** came out in 1926. The main chapter first appeared in late 1924.

Preobrazhensky posed the crucial question facing a backward economy: where to find capital resources for industrial development. His reply was: largely among the peasants; the socialist or state sector was too small and undeveloped to provide enough capital from within itself. Industry by itself could not produce the resources needed for rapid industrialisation. Its profits or surplus could make up only a small part of the required accumulation fund. The rest had to be obtained from the incomes earned in the private sector of the economy.

The formation period of capitalism was called by Marx the epoch of 'primitive capitalist accumulation'. Preobrazhensky argued that the Soviet Union had to find its counterpart in 'primitive socialist accumulation' which was to create the future socialist society. (The originator of this term was not Preobrazhensky but V.M. Smirnov).

Marx explained that before the process of automatic accumulation under capitalism could be set in motion, it was necessary at a preceding stage to go through a period of forced accumulation of capital: this was the stage of the enclosures which created workers out of peasants by 'the separation of the producers from the means of production', this was also the stage in which the robbing of colonies and the slave trade facilitated the creation of capitalism. Preobrazhensky argued that similarly 'in order that the complex of the state economy may be able to develop all its economic advantages and establish for itself a new technical base' socialism must pass through a preliminary stage of 'primitive accumulation'.

The means by which the resources of the private sector were to be transferred to the socialist sector were analysed in detail by Preobrazhensky, and cover taxation, the acquisition of incomes from the monopoly of foreign trade, credits, loans, etc. The most important source was to be that of 'non-equivalent exchanges', which would result from the manipulation of the prices of industrial goods.

On 12 December 1924 **Pravda** published a long article by Bukharin viciously attacking Preobrazhensky. The distortion of Preobrazhensky's position was quite astonishing. Bukharin declared categorically: 'There can be no doubt that comrade Preobrazhensky sees the workers' state as possessing colonies', and the exploitation of the peasants is a form of 'internal colonialism'. This statement by Bukharin flew in the face of Preobrazhensky's words:

> As regards colonial plundering, a socialist state, carrying out a policy of equality between nationalities and voluntary entry

by them into one kind or another of union of nations, repudiates on principle all the forcible methods of capital in this sphere. This source of primitive accumulation is closed to it from the very start and forever.[46]

After this scandalous distortion of Preobrazhensky's position regarding colonies, Bukharin goes on to claim that he was for the exploitation of the peasantry by the proletariat, for the 'devouring of peasant economy by the state economy', for raising the price of industrial goods so as to bleed the peasants, and so on. Preobrazhensky is also accused of calling for the exploitation of the proletariat by the state.

Preobrazhensky rejected these accusations of Bukharin with complete disdain. He explained that the term 'exploitation' used in his book was transformed by Bukharin from relations between economic systems to relations between classes.

> The task of the socialist state consists here not in taking from the petty bourgeois producers less than capitalism took, but in taking more *from the still larger income* which will be ensured to the petty producers by the rationalisation of everything, including the country's petty production.[47]

What about Bukharin's accusation that Preobrazhensky saw 'the socialisation of peasant economy as lying through the devouring of this economy by the state economy'? Preobrazhensky argues exactly the opposite: it is only after a great advance of industry that aid could be given to the peasantry to socialise agriculture. The development of industry would not be based on robbing agriculture, but on the contrary, the socialisation of agriculture would depend on the pouring of resources into agriculture from industry.

> Without a rapid development of the State economy there cannot be a sufficiently rapid development of peasant co-operation... And any rapid development of State industry is impossible without a sufficiently rapid accumulation in our State industry.[48]

The socialisation of agriculture would be gradual and would take a very long historical period.

Furthermore, Bukharin distorted Preobrazhensky's position

regarding prices policy. He summed up Preobrazhensky's attitude in two words: 'Raise them!' Preobrazhensky's reaction was sharp:

> To put it mildly, this is a scandalous falsehood. I nowhere in my work say anything about raising prices. I specially pointed out that a policy of accumulation is not only possible for us but also will in fact take place with falling or stable prices.[49]

Preobrazhensky did not advocate the impoverishment of the peasants. His aims would be realised if industrial costs were reduced and agricultural productivity increased, thus leading to a rise in the peasants' income.

Bukharin accused Preobrazhensky of saying the state economy should 'devour' the peasant economy, thus killing 'the goose that lays the golden eggs for our state industry, that is that he proposes to hinder the development of peasant economy'. In fact Preobrazhensky argues exactly the opposite: for the encouragement of the peasant economy as a necessary condition for industrialisation.

What about Bukharin's accusation that Preobrazhensky stood for the increased exploitation of the workers in the process of primitive socialist accumulation, similar to that which happened to workers during the period of primitive capitalist accumulation? This again is a scandalous distortion. This is what Preobrazhensky actually wrote on the subject:

> We said... that it is characteristic of capitalism, especially in the period of primitive accumulation, to take a ruthless, barbarous, spendthrift attitude to labour power, which it attempts to treat like any other purchased commodity which forms one of the elements of production. The limits of exploitation and oppression in this sphere are the purely physiological limits (the worker has to sleep and eat), or else the resistance of the working class. Later the relation of forces between workers and capitalists in the economic struggle is a very important factor restricting the tempo and amount of capitalist accumulation on the basis of production. As against this, from the moment of its victory the working class... cannot have the same attitude to its own labour power, health, work and conditions as the capitalist has. This constitutes a definite barrier to the tempo of socialist

accumulation, a barrier which capitalist industry did not know in its first period of development.

Insistence on the eight-hour day was a case in point.[50]

> Our labour protection is, on the one hand, a policy of preserving and qualitatively improving the most important productive force, the most important factor in socialist accumulation, namely, the labour-power of the proletariat, and, on the other hand, in its extension to private economy, it imposes a restriction on the rate and amount of capitalist accumulation.[51]

Preobrazhensky's project of primitive socialist accumulation had nothing in common with the future Stalinist policy starting in 1928 of forced expropriation of the peasantry and their inclusion in collective farms, compulsory deliveries of agricultural products at low prices while the prices of industrial consumer goods increased significantly, thus robbing the peasantry. It had nothing to do with Stalin's forced industrialisation at breakneck speed with the emphasis on heavy industry.

The distortion of the meaning of Preobrazhensky's 'primitive accumulation' by Stalin and Bukharin was used as justification to accuse Trotsky of neglecting the peasants, and opposing Lenin's formula of the *smychka* between the proletariat and the peasantry.

Trotsky used the phrase 'primitive socialist accumulation' in his speech to the Twelfth Party Congress (April 1923). And throughout the years 1923-1927 he looked upon Preobrazhensky as the chief economist of the Trotskyist Opposition. However, there was a deep difference between Trotsky and Preobrazhensky. Preobrazhensky, although referring again and again to the international revolution, still constructed his theory in such a way as to imply that primitive socialist accumulation might be carried out by the Soviet Union in isolation. This prospect appeared unreal to Trotsky, who did not see how the Soviet Union in isolation could raise itself to the industrial levels of the West. It was his politics of economic isolation (together with a rejection of the theory of permanent revolution) that opened the door for Preobrazhensky's reconciliation with 'socialism in one country'. *(see over)

It should also be said that given a prolonged delay in the arrival of the international revolution (virtually inevitable after the defeat in China), and given the general poverty of Russia, in particular the low productivity of labour in Russian industry, any attempt to apply Preobrazhensky's programme of 'primitive socialist accumulation' was likely in *practice* to lead to some variant of Stalinist, ie, state capitalist, industrialisation regardless of Preobrazhensky's intentions.

The fundamental and intractable problem was that on the basis of poverty it was impossible to levy the surplus necessary for rapid and sustained industrialisation, either from the peasants or the workers, other than by forcible exploitation. Exploitation, however, has its own social logic—it requires a privileged social class, raised above the workers, to manage and enforce it. In Russia at the end of the 1920s, this social class could only be the state bureaucracy, with or without Stalin as an individual. Salvation lay only along the road of spreading the revolution. Marx foresaw the essence of the problem eighty years earlier when he wrote in **The German Ideology**, 'this development of productive forces...is an absolutely necessary practical premise because without it want is merely made general, and with destitution the struggle for necessities and all the old filthy business would necessarily be reproduced.'[53]

Preobrazhensky was exiled in 1927, readmitted into the party in 1929, expelled again in 1931, and then again readmitted. His

---

*Trotsky made it clear, as early as 2 May 1926, that Preobrazhensky's formulation contained a serious danger of leading to conclusions compatible with the doctrine of 'socialism in one country'. Trotsky wrote:

'In the analysis of our economy from the point of view of internal dynamics (struggle and co-operation) the laws of value and socialist accumulation are in principle fruitful in the highest degree. It is true to say that they alone are correct. The investigation necessarily must begin within the framework of a closed Soviet economy. But there now arises the danger that this methodological approach will be turned into the formalistic economic perspective of "the development of socialism in one country". It should be expected, for the danger is there, that the supporters of this philosophy...will now attempt to transform Preobrazhensky's analysis, converting methodological approach into a general quasi-autonomous process. Come what may, it is necessary to avoid such plagiarism and such falsification. The internal dynamics of the law of value and socialist accumulation have to be posed in the context of the world economy.'[52]

last public appearance was at the Seventeenth Party Congress in 1934, in which he denounced Trotskyism and praised Stalin to the skies:

> I was considered one of the theoreticians of Trotskyism. You know that my theoretical works, including **The New Economics**, were used as weapons in the struggle against the party. You know that my important error consisted in mechanically comparing our economy with capitalism and erecting a law of 'primitive socialist accumulation.' I brought into this theoretical construction the lack of faith in the peasantry and contempt for the peasants which were characteristic of Trotskyism... I though that by exploiting the peasants, by concentrating the resources of the peasant economy in the hands of the state, it would be possible to build industry and develop industrialisation. This is a crude analogy with primitive capitalist accumulation... I parted company with Leninism. Events wholly disproved what I had asserted, and Lenin's forecasts were later triumphantly made into reality under Stalin's leadership. Collectivisation, that is the essential point. Did I foresee collectivisation? I did not... As you know, neither Marx nor Engels, who wrote a great deal about the problems of socialism in the village, visualised just how village life would be revolutionised. You know that Engels tended to the view that it would be a rather long evolutionary process. What was needed was Stalin's remarkable far-sightedness, his great courage in facing the problems, the greatest hardness in applying policies.[54]

Chapter eleven

The United Opposition is smashed

The Wrangel amalgam

THE WRITING of the Platform and the efforts of the Opposition to publish it and get it into the hands of the party rank and file brought the conflict with the Stalinist machine to a head.

The Opposition failed to collect the number of signatures for the Platform it expected. Serge writes:

> ...we collected signatures to the Platform. 'If we get 30,000 of them', said Zinoviev, 'they won't be able to stop us speaking at the Fifteenth Congress...' We managed, with considerable difficulty to gather five or six thousand. Since the situation was taking a rapid turn for the worse, only a few hundred, the names of the men of the Bolshevik Guard, were sent to the Central Committee. Events were speeding to a conclusion which would make all this petitioning appear in its true light: as mere child's play.[1]

The Platform was submitted to a joint meeting of the Politburo and the Central Control Commission on 8 September at which Stalin delivered a long speech, and the Opposition was denied the right to reply. The Central Committee did not publish the Platform as part of the pre-Congress discussion material. Moreover, it forbade the Opposition to circulate the document by its own means.

The Opposition was not ready to give up its right to argue its case. An underground printing plant—made up of an ancient hectograph and three or four typewriters—under the direction of Mrachkovsky, was set in motion to reproduce the Platform. On the night of 12-13 September the GPU raided the printing shop, and arrested several men engaged in producing the Platform. The GPU's report on the raid alleged that a former officer of Wrangel's White Guard had been involved in setting up the printing shop. On the day of the raid Trotsky had left for the Caucasus. Several leaders of the Opposition—Preobrazhensky, Mrachkovsky and Serebriakov—declared that they assumed full responsibility for the publication of the Platform. All three were immediately expelled from the party, and one—Mrachkovsky—was imprisoned.

The charge that the Opposition had ties with White Guards was trumpeted. On 22 September a communication relating to the discovery of the printshop was issued in the name of the Politburo and the Presidium of the Central Control Commission, and transmitted to all party organisations. This stated that 'a number of the arrested non-party people were found to be actually involved with certain individuals from military circles who were planning a military coup in the USSR modelled on Pilsudski's coup'.[2] It was in fact found that the 'Wrangel officer' was a GPU *agent provocateur*. Nevertheless, the objective of further discrediting the Opposition had been accomplished. 'The myth about the "Wrangel officer" is being broadcast through the land, poisoning the minds of a million party members and tens of millions of non party men', reported the Opposition leaders. They charged Stalin with a deliberate fraud—'Without his consent, approval, and encouragement, no one would have ever dared to throw into the party ranks fraudulent accusations about the participation of Opposition Communists in a counter revolutionary organisation.'[3]

This amalgam was a precursor to future ones culminating in the Moscow Trials of the 1930.

At the Plenum of the Central Committee and the Central Control Commission of 21-23 October Stalin moved the expulsion of Trotsky and Zinoviev from the Central Committee. Trotsky, seeing his last opportunity to speak his views slipping away, took this occasion to attack Stalin, for the first time in public, on the basis of Lenin's Testament, only to be rebuffed by the General Secretary who quoted back to him Trotsky's own article of 1925 in which he denied the existence of any such document when Eastman published it in the **New York Times**.[4] Ordzhonikidze and Bukharin were said to have shouted: 'Trotsky's place is in the inner prisons of the GPU'.[5] And Stalin made an ominous remark:

> It is said that disorganisers who have been expelled from the Party and conduct anti-Soviet activities are being arrested. Yes, we arrest them and we shall do so in future if they do not stop undermining the Party and the Soviet regime. (*Voices*: 'Quite right! Quite right!') [6]

On 23 October the Central Committee expelled Zinoviev and Trotsky from its ranks.[7]

Opposition leaders' direct appeal to workers

The next stage of the struggle was the Opposition's attempt at a direct appeal to the masses. Many small meetings were held in workers' flats. Trotsky in his autobiography writes:

> Secret meetings were held in various parts of Moscow and Leningrad, attended by workers and students of both sexes, who gathered in groups of from twenty to one hundred and two hundred to hear some representative of the opposition. In one day I would visit two, three, and sometimes four of such meetings. They were usually held in some worker's apartment. Two small rooms would be packed with people, and the speaker would stand at the door between the two rooms. Sometimes everyone would sit on the floor; more often the discussion had to be carried on standing for lack of space. Occasionally representatives of the Control Commission would appear at such meetings and demand that everyone leaves. They were invited to take part in the discussion. If they caused any disturbance they were put out. In all, about 20,000 people attended such meetings in Moscow and Leningrad. The number was growing. The opposition cleverly prepared a huge meeting in the hall of the High Technical School which had been occupied from within. The hall was crammed with two thousand people, while a huge crowd remained outside in the street. The attempts of the administration to stop the meeting proved ineffectual. Kamenev and I spoke for about two hours. Finally the Central Committee issued an appeal to the workers to break up the meetings of the Opposition by force. This appeal was merely

a screen for carefully prepared attacks on the Opposition by military units under the guidance of the GPU. Stalin wanted a bloody settlement of the conflict. We gave the signal for a temporary discontinuance of the large meetings. But this was not until after the demonstration of November 7.[8]

The greatest demonstration in support of the Opposition leaders took place in October. The Central Executive Committee of the Soviets held its session in Leningrad. In honour of the occasion the authorities staged a mass demonstration. Trotsky remembers:

> When the masses learned that we [Trotsky and Zinoviev] were on the last platform, the character of the demonstration changed instantly. The people began to pass by the first trucks indifferently, without even answering the greetings from them, and hurried on to our platform. Soon a bank of thousands of people had been formed around our truck. Workers and soldiers halted, looked up, shouted their greetings, and then were obliged to move on because of the impatient pressure of those behind them. A platoon of police which was sent to our truck to restore order was itself caught up by the general mood and took no action. Hundreds of trusted agents of the apparatus were despatched into the thick of the crowd. They tried to whistle us down, but their isolated whistles were quite drowned by the shouts of sympathy. The longer this continued, the more intolerable the situation became for the official leaders of the demonstration. In the end, the chairman of the Central Executive Committee and a few of its most prominent members came down from the first platform around which there was nothing but a vast gulf of emptiness and climbed onto ours, which stood at the very end and was intended for the least important guests. But even this bold step failed to save the situation, for the people kept shouting names—and the names were not those of the official masters of the situation.[9]

Serge gives a somewhat different description of the demonstration:

> ...the demonstrators made a silent gesture by lingering on

the spot, and thousands of hands were outstretched, waving handkerchiefs or caps. It was a dumb acclamation, futile but still overwhelming.

Zinoviev and Trotsky received the greeting in a spirit of happy determination, imagining that they were witnessing a show of force. 'The masses are with us', they kept saying that night. Yet what possibilities were there in masses who were so submissive that they contained their emotions like this? As a matter of fact everybody in that crowd knew that the slightest gesture endangered his own and his family's livelihood.[10]

Zinoviev and Trotsky drew very different conclusions from the demonstration. As Trotsky remembers:

Zinoviev was instantly optimistic, and expected momentous consequences from this manifestation of sentiment. I did not share his impulsive estimate. The working masses of Leningrad demonstrated their dissatisfaction in the form of platonic sympathy for the leaders of the opposition, but they were still unable to prevent the apparatus from making short work of us. On this score I had no illusions. On the other hand, the demonstration was bound to suggest to the ruling faction the necessity of speeding up the destruction of the opposition, so that the masses might be confronted with an accomplished fact.[11]

A further opportunity for the Opposition leaders to test their popularity was a celebration of the tenth anniversary of the October revolution. They decided to march in separate contingents carrying their own banners, 'Strike against the Kulak, the NEPman and the Bureaucrat!' 'Against Opportunism, Against a Split—For the Unity of Lenin's Party!' 'Let us Carry Out Lenin's Testament!' The Stalinists were determined to suppress such independent demonstrations. Trotsky describes the events in Moscow:

On November 7, the placards of the opposition were snatched from their hands and torn to pieces, while their bearers were mauled by specially organised units. The official leaders had learned their lesson in the Leningrad demonstration, and this time their preparations were much more efficient... As volunteers in the fight against the 'Trotskyists' notoriously non-revolutionary and sometimes sheer Fascist elements in the streets of Moscow were now coming to the aid of the apparatus. A policeman, pretending to be giving a warning, shot openly at my automobile.[12]

Victor Serge gives a vivid description of the day in Leningrad:

In Leningrad, adroit marshals allowed the Oppositionists to march past the official dais under the windows of the Winter Palace, before cramming them away between the caryatid statues of the Hermitage Museum and the Archives building. I ran foul of several barriers and was unable to join the procession. I stopped for a moment to survey the multitude of poor folk carrying the red flags. From time to time an organiser turned back to his group and raised a hurrah which found a half-hearted chorus in echo. I went a few paces nearer the procession and shouted likewise—alone with a woman and a child a few steps behind me. I had flung out the names of Trotsky and Zinoviev; they were received by an astonished silence.

The few hundred Oppositionists found themselves quite isolated.

Several hundred Oppositionists were there engaged in fraternal battle against the militia. The horses' breasts were constantly pushing back the crowd, but the same human wave returned to meet them, led by a tall, beardless, open-faced soldier, Bakaev, the former head of our Cheka. I also saw Lashevich, big and thick-set, who had commanded armies, throwing himself, together with several workers, on a militiaman, dragging him from the saddle, knocking him down, and then helping him to his feet while addressing him in his commander's voice: 'How is it that you are not ashamed to charge at the workers of Leningrad?' Around him billowed his soldier's cloak, bare of insignia. His rough face, like that of some drinker painted by Franz Hals, was crimson red. The brawl went on for a long time. Around the tumultuous group, of which I was part, a stupefied silence reigned.[13]

The events of 7 November, which demonstrated the passivity of the mass of the workers, their lack of will to fight for the

Opposition, caused a crack in the Opposition leadership. Zinoviev as usual flip-flopped from euphoria to deep depression. On 7 November he wrote to Trotsky: 'All the information at hand indicates that this outrage will greatly benefit our cause. We are worried to know what happened with you. Contacts [that is, secret discussions with the workers] are proceeding very well here. The change in our favour is great. For the time being we do not propose to leave.' Trotsky's comment was: 'This was the last flash of energy from the opposition of Zinoviev. A day later he was in Moscow insisting on the necessity of surrender'.[14]

The events showed that a minority of party members supported the Opposition, and at the other extreme another minority supported Stalin and Bukharin. On the face of it there was symmetry between the Left and Right. Actually there was *asymmetry*. For the ruling group to win it needed the passivity of the mass of the workers, while the Opposition needed the activity and consciousness of the masses for success.

On 14 November the Central Committee and Central Control Commission, convened for an extraordinary session, expelled Trotsky and Zinoviev from the party as guilty of incitement to counter-revolutionary demonstrations. The Oppositionists Kamenev, Smilga, Evdokimov, Rakovsky, Avdeev were expelled from the Central Committee; and Muralov, Bakaev, Shklovsky, Peterson, Soloviev and Lizdin were expelled from the Central Control Commission.[15]

Ioffe's suicide

On 16 November Adolf Abramovich Ioffe committed suicide. Ioffe had been a friend of Trotsky since before 1910 when he helped Trotsky to edit the Viennese **Pravda**. With Trotsky he joined the Bolshevik Party in July 1917 and was a member of its Central Committee during the October revolution. In a note he wrote to Trotsky just before his death he described his suicide as a protest against the expulsion of Trotsky and Zinoviev from the party, and he expressed his horror at the indifference with which the party had received it. Ioffe wrote to Trotsky:

> You and I, dear Lev Davidovich, are bound to each other by decades of joint work, and, I make bold to hope, of personal friendship. This gives me the right to tell you in parting what

I think you are mistaken in. I have never doubted the rightness of the road you pointed out, and as you know I have gone with you for more than twenty years, since the days of 'permanent revolution'. But I have always believed that you lacked Lenin's *unbending will,* his *unwillingness to yield,* his readiness even to remain alone on the path that he thought right in anticipation of a future majority, of a future recognition by everyone of the rightness of his path. *Politically, you were always right,* beginning with 1905, and I told you repeatedly that with my own ears I had heard Lenin admit that even in 1905, *you, and not he,* were right. One does not lie before his death, and now I repeat this again to you... But you have often *abandoned your rightness* for the sake of an overvalued agreement, or compromise. This is a mistake... the guarantee of the victory of your rightness lies in nothing but the extreme unwillingness to yield, the strictest straightforwardness, the absolute rejection of all compromise; in this very thing lay the secret of Lenin's victories.[16]

Trotsky writes:

Ioffe's funeral was set for a working day at an hour that would prevent the Moscow workers from taking part in it. But in spite of this it attracted no less than ten thousand people and turned into an imposing oppositionist demonstration.[17]

This was the Opposition's last public meeting and demonstration.

How Strong was the Opposition?

The crisis of the policies of Stalin and Bukharin on the international front—above all China—and on the home front—the worsening economic situation—gave the Opposition a great fillip in 1927.

The historian Michel Reiman, in his important book **The Birth of Stalinism**, tries to give a picture of the strength of the Opposition, relying largely on top-secret directives, Central Committee and government protocols and reports, and letters from officials in Moscow to Soviet representatives in Berlin—all preserved in the political archives of the German Foreign Ministry. Reiman writes:

> The importance of the left opposition is often underestimated in the literature. It is considered an important current in Soviet ideological and political life, a kind of 'revolt of the Leaders' in the context of the power struggle with Stalin...

But this evaluation is wrong. It was not only made up of chiefs without Indians.

> ...many authors doubt that the opposition had any substantial influence on the mass of party members and even less on broader sections of the population. One can hardly agree with such views: they seem paradoxical indeed in light of the mountain of ammunition expended on the opposition by the party leadership in those years—the multitude of official declarations, reports, pamphlets, and books, not to mention the mass political campaigns that penetrated even the remotest parts of the USSR.

And Reiman goes on to write:

> In the spring of 1926 the United Opposition, based on a cadre of old and experienced party leaders, conquered some fairly significant positions. It consolidated its influence in Leningrad, the Ukraine, Transcaucasia, and the Urals region; in the universities; in some of the central government offices; in a number of factories of Moscow and the central industrial region; and among a section of the command staff of the army and navy, which had passed through the difficult years of the civil war under Trotsky's leadership. Repression by the party leadership prevented the opposition from growing, but its influence was still much greater than indicated by the various votes taken in the party cells.[18]

A year later, in June and July 1927,

> ...opposition activity was spreading like a river in flood. The opposition organised mass meetings of industrial workers in Ivanovo-Voznesensk, Leningrad, and Moscow; at a chemical plant in Moscow shouts were heard: 'Down with Stalin's dictatorship! Down with the Politburo!'[19]

The Opposition had quite an influence among Red Army personnel.

Many tried and tested officers belonged to the opposition, and they would be sorely missed in the event of a military conflict.

Qualitatively supporters of the Opposition were superior to Stalin's supporters.

In the eyes of contemporaries, the energy, commitment, and enthusiasm of the oppositionists contrasted favourably with the bureaucratic sluggishness of their adversaries.[20]

The activity of the Opposition was very impressive indeed. Reiman writes:

...the small amount of existing material gives an impressive picture. Even after the plenum [of the Central Committee and Central Control Commission banning the opposition] the party organisations continued to be flooded—especially in the large urban centres and the two capitals—with opposition literature and leaflets. [GPU] reports of heightened opposition activity came one after the other from various cities and from entire provinces—Leningrad, the Ukraine, Transcaucasia, Siberia, the Urals, and of course, Moscow, where the greater number of opposition political leaders were working. There was a steadily growing number of illegal and semi-legal meetings attended by industrial workers and young people. The influence of the opposition in a number of large party units became quite substantial. It hampered the former free functioning of the Stalinist party apparatus. The army was also strongly affected by opposition activity. Reports on a significant rise in the authority of the opposition came from the Leningrad military district and the garrison in Leningrad, from Kronstadt, and from troop units in the Ukraine and Byelorussia.[21]

What was the size of the Opposition?

Victor Serge described the two wings of the United Opposition—the Trotskyists and Zinovievists—at the time of its formation in the middle of 1926.

Zinoviev had several thousand adherents in Leningrad, bound together by the ties of old comradeship and the strength of the local Party machine... the left wing of the movement, of which Trotsky was the most authoritative spokesman, lacked a proper organisation of its own. In Moscow, it had some 600 members, in Leningrad about 50, and in Kharkov several hundred...[22]

In 1927 the Opposition's size and influence increased greatly. Stalin, in a speech delivered at the Plenum of the Central Committee on 19 November 1928, had to admit that about 10,000 party members voted with the Opposition on the eve of the Fifteenth Party Congress, while another 20,000 party members sympathised with the Opposition without voting for it.[23] These figures contradict the figures Stalin gave in his report to the Fifteenth Party Congress: '...a little over 4,000 voted for the opposition'.[24] One pointer to the size of the Opposition's support was the turnout of 10,000 people to Ioffe's funeral that, as we have mentioned, took place during a working day at a time that would have prevented many Moscow workers from participating.

The Stalinist machine did not deal with the Opposition with kid gloves. In party meetings, when Oppositionists spoke, ruffians were sent to break the meetings up. Trotsky, in a speech of 23 October 1927, said:

Fascist gangs of whistlers, using their fists, throwing books or stones, the prison bars—here for a minute the Stalinist path had paused. But this path is predestined... Stalinism finds in this act its most unrestrained expression, reaching open hooliganism... the goal is to cut off the Opposition and physically destroy it. One can hear already voices: 'We will expel a thousand, we'll shoot a hundred—and have peace in the party'.[25]

Party secretaries threatened to have anyone who voted for an Opposition resolution—voting was open—expelled from the party.[26] The party bureaucracy descended into the gutter, using even the weapon of anti-Semitism (the three leaders of the Opposition—Trotsky, Zinoviev and Kamenev—were Jewish). Trotsky quoted a letter he received from a worker describing how a secretary of a party cell spoke and the reaction:

'The Yids on the Politburo are kicking up a fuss'... No-one dared report this to any quarter—for the very same openly-stated reason: they will kick us out of the factory...

In other words: *members of the Communist Party are afraid to report to the party institutions about Black Hundred agitation, thinking that it is they who will be kicked out, not the Black Hundred gangster.*[27]

A 1926 report from Smolensk quotes a peasant saying:

'Our good master, Vladimir Ilich had only just passed away when our Commissars began to fight among themselves, and all this is due to the fact that the Jews became very numerous, and our Russians do not let them have their way, but there is nobody to suppress them, and each one considers himself more intelligent than the others.' The GPU reported that some 'unconscious' workers in Bryansk were saying that Trotsky, Zinoviev, Kamenev, and others were Jewish by origin and that when Lenin died, Trotsky wanted to lead the state, that is, to take Lenin's place and put Jews in all the responsible positions, but Trotsky and his opposition were unable to do this, and that is why they were fighting against the Central Committee of the Party.[28]

The Sekhondo Chitinskogo provincial committee reported a speaker saying: 'Trotsky a long time ago began on a splitting policy. Trotsky cannot be a Communist. His very nationality shows that he must favour speculation... They [Trotsky and Zinoviev] have made a mistake about the Russian spirit. The Russian worker and peasant will not follow these NEPmen'.[29]

Stalin's comment on the issue of anti-Semitism was calculated to encourage it. He told his supporters: 'We are fighting Trotsky, Zinoviev and Kamenev not because they are Jews, but because they are Oppositionists.'[30]

To return to the question of the size of the Opposition: even if we accept the highest estimate—10,000 who voted for the Opposition and 20,000 who were sympathetic—it was still a tiny proportion of all party members. In 1927 the party had 724,000 members. However, among the Old Bolsheviks support for the Opposition was quite significant. In 1922 there were only 10,431 party members who had joined before the February revolution;

in 1925 the surviving number was 8,249; and in 1927 not more than 5,000.[31]

The great majority of party members were lethargic and passive. If not for this they would not have tolerated the hooligans who shouted down Opposition speakers and broke up their meetings. An active audience would have ejected the hooligans. Again and again we read reports about party meetings in which the Opposition got derisory support. This could not have happened had the members been more active. In a large meeting in Moscow in August 1927, where Rykov spoke, his resolution for the expulsion of Trotsky and Zinoviev was voted for unanimously. Similarly in Leningrad, where Bukharin spoke, the resolution was passed by 3,500 to 6.[32] When Bukharin reported on the decision of the Central Committee to expel Trotsky and Zinoviev to a meeting of six thousand party members in Leningrad, Evdokimov and Bakaev spoke on behalf of the Opposition but registered only two dissentient votes.[33]

The Fifteenth Congress and the break-up of the United Opposition

On the eve of the Fifteenth Congress—2-19 December 1927—the bloc of Trotskyists and Zinovievists was disintegrating. Trotsky called: 'Everyone remains at his post! Let nobody leave!' But Zinoviev and Kamenev were looking for capitulation. Victor Serge writes:

> The Leningrad tendency, Zinoviev, Kamenev, Yevdokimov, and Bakaev, favoured capitulation. 'They want to hound us from the Party; we have to stay in it at all costs. Expulsion means political death, deportation, the impossibility of intervening when the coming crisis of the regime begins... Nothing can be done outside the Party. Humiliations are of small account to us.'...
>
> The Oppositional Centre sat in ceaseless debate throughout the Congress. Our Leningrad allies finally proposed: 'Let us throw ourselves on their mercy and drink the cup of humiliation.' The following exchange of replies took place between Zinoviev and Trotsky, on slips of paper passed from hand to hand. Zinoviev: 'Leon Davidovich, the hour has come when we should have the courage to capitulate...' Trotsky:

'If that kind of courage were enough, the revolution would have been won all over the world by now.'[34]

On 14 November 31 Oppositionists issued a statement addressed to the Central Control Commission against the expulsion of Trotsky, Zinoviev and other leading members of the Opposition, reaffirming their loyalty to the party and emphasizing their opposition to factionalism and the creation of a new party. The Opposition stated that it was discontinuing the unofficial meetings they had been holding. Without these meetings, and with the press closed to them, the Opposition accepted complete gagging. On 17-20 November Trotsky wrote a statement endeavouring to explain that this was not a capitulation by the Opposition: abiding by the decision to discontinue factional work does not mean giving up the struggle for the views of the Opposition. There is not going to be 'abandonment of its platform and views, or of the propagation and defence of these views in the party... repressive measures will not frighten the opposition'.[35]

But the Opposition statement of 14 November was in fact a big step backward that paved the way for even further retreats.

In speech to the Sixteenth Moscow Regional Party Conference on 23 November Stalin referred to the declaration of the 31 Oppositionists as 'hypocritical'.

The opposition has twice deceived the Party. Now it wants to deceive the Party a third time. No, comrades, we have had enough of deception, enough of games. (*Applause*.)

...What next? The limit has been reached, comrades, for the opposition has exceeded all bounds of what is permissible in the Party. It cannot go on swinging from side to side in two parties at once, in the old, Leninist Party, the one and only Party, and in the new, Trotskyist party. It must choose between these two parties.[36]

When the Fifteenth Party Congress opened, it was revealed that there was not a single Oppositionist among the 1,600 delegates. On the second day of the Congress—3 December—the Opposition issued a new statement: 'The Statement of the 121', which was a compromise between the Trotskyists and Zinovievites, the former wanting to continue the struggle, the latter to capitulate. 'The Statement of the 121' said:

The unity of the Communist Party is the highest principle in the epoch of the proletarian dictatorship... we have taken the path of factionalism, which at times took extremely sharp forms; and on several occasions we resorted to methods which go against party discipline...There are no programmatic differences between us and the party. We have pointed out the presence and the growth of Thermidorian dangers in the country, and the insufficient measures being taken to guard against them; but we never thought and do not now think that our party or its CC have become Thermidorian, or that our state has ceased to be a workers' state. We stated this categorically in our Platform. We still maintain, and shall continue to maintain, that our party has been and is the embodiment of the proletarian vanguard, and that the Soviet state is the embodiment of the proletarian dictatorship...

We cannot renounce views which we are convinced are correct, and which we have submitted to the party in our Platform and our theses; but to preserve the unity of the party, to safeguard its full fighting capacity as the leader of the state and the world proletarian movement, we declare to the congress that we will cease all factional work, dissolve all factional organisations, and call upon all those sharing our way of thinking in the party and the Comintern to do the same...

We shall continue to work for our party and shall defend our views only within the limits imposed by the party rules and the formal decisions of the party. That is the right of every Bolshevik, as laid down in many basic congress decisions in Lenin's lifetime and since. This declaration is the expression of our firm determination.

We are convinced that we express the views of all those who share our ways of thinking who have been expelled from the party, and that, on the basis of this declaration, the party should take the first step toward restoring a normal party life, by readmitting those who have been expelled, releasing from prison those who have been arrested for Oppositional activities, and giving each of us the opportunity to demonstrate the firmness of our resolve by our work in the party.

The Declaration ended with these words:

At the congress and during the party discussions before the congress we defended our views with firmness and determination. Now that we have decided to submit to the congress, we shall carry out this resolve with equal firmness and determination, as true soldiers of the Bolshevik proletarian army.[37]

So the Opposition reaffirmed that they had no 'programmatic differences' with the ruling group, undertook to end factional activities, pleaded for the reinstatement of those expelled, and gave advance assurance of submission to decisions of the Congress!

This crawling did not save the Opposition. On the same day that the 'Declaration of the 121' was issued, Stalin viciously assaulted the Opposition leaders at the Congress: they repudiated the possibility of 'the victorious building of socialism in one country'; they accused the party of 'Thermidorian degeneration'. Stalin ended his speech with an uncompromising demand that the Opposition,

renounce its anti-Leninist views openly and honestly before the whole Party. The Party has called upon the opposition to admit its mistakes and denounce them in order to free itself of them once and for all. The Party has called upon the opposition completely to disarm, both ideologically and organisationally...

If the opposition disarms—well and good. If it refuses—we shall disarm it ourselves.[38]

Kamenev tried to plead with the Congress, giving a pathetic description of the Opposition's plight:

We have to choose one of two roads. One of these roads is that of a second party. That road, under the conditions of the dictatorship of the proletariat, is ruinous for the revolution. It is the road of political and class degeneration. This road is closed to us, forbidden by the whole system of our views, by all the teachings of Lenin on the dictatorship of the proletariat. There remains, therefore, the second road. This road is...to submit completely and fully to the party. We choose this road, for we are profoundly convinced that a correct Leninist policy can triumph only in our party and through it, not outside the party and against it.[39]

The resolution of the Congress to expel the Opposition broke the will of the Zinovievites and fatally undermined the bloc. On 10 December both sections of the Opposition submitted statements to the Congress: the Zinovievites put forward a document of surrender, the Trotskyists a recapitulation of their principled stand.

The Zinovievite statement, signed by Kamenev, Bakaev, Avdeev and Evdokimov, stated:

> The resolution of the Congress on the report of the Central Committee declares that belonging to the Trotskyist Opposition and propagating its views are incompatible with continued membership of the Bolshevik Party. The Fifteenth Congress, in this way, not only rejected our views, but banned its propaganda... We consider it obligatory to abide by the decision of the Congress...
> In view of this, and in abiding by the resolution of the Congress, we state the following:
> 1. That the Opposition faction should cease to exist, and 2. that decisions of the Congress to ban the propagating of its views is accepted for implementation by all of us.

The Trotskyist statement, signed by Muralov, Rakovsky and Radek, stated:

> Abiding by the decisions of the Congress, we will discontinue all factional work, dissolve all factional organisations, and call upon our co-thinkers to do the same...
> At the same time we believe that our views, as set forth in our Platform and theses, can be defended by every one of us within the limits of the party rules. To renounce the defence of our views within the party would be politically the same as to renounce those views themselves.[40]

Although both declarations accepted the abandonment of factional activity, the Trotskyist one asserted the right of individual members to defend their views. Both ate humble pie. But while the Zinovievites made it clear they were ready to give up the struggle, the Trotskyists insisted on fighting for their views.

All the crawling of the Zinovievites did not save them from expulsion from the party.

On 19 December, the last day of the Congress, Kamenev brought to Rykov a declaration signed by 23 expelled members of the Zinovievite wing of the Opposition, which he asked leave to read to the Congress. Kamenev was refused admission, but the Declaration was read by Rykov from the chair. It included a recantation of the 'anti-Leninist views' of the Opposition, recognised as 'errors' the setting up of the secret printing press, the 7 November demonstration and the links with the dissident Maslow-Fischer group in Germany, and asked once more for forgiveness. 'Harsh as may be for us the demand of the Congress...we...bow our will and our ideas to the will and ideas of the party...the sole supreme judge of what is useful or harmful to the victorious progress of the revolution.'

This abject surrender made no impact. Rykov, in the name of the Presidium of the Congress, proposed not to examine the declaration, but to instruct the Party Central Committee and Central Control Commission to receive only individual applications for reinstatement of former members of the Opposition, and to postpone consideration of them until six months had elapsed after their receipt. The Congress adopted a resolution in this sense. Zinoviev and Kamenev had been ignominiously told to wait.[41]

Trotsky was contemptuous toward the capitulators Zinoviev and Kamenev. Shortly after the end of the Fifteenth Congress he wrote:

> The renegacy of Zinoviev and Kamenev was fed by the false belief that one can get oneself out of any historical situation by a cunning manoeuvre instead of by maintaining a principled political line... All double-dealing and careerist elements concerned with saving their own skins thus seem to gain ideological justification. Abandoning the defence of one's views means in particular justifying that broad layer of corrupted philistines in the party who sympathise with the Opposition but vote with the majority.[42]

The Fifteenth Congress expelled 75 Oppositionists, including Kamenev, Piatakov, Radek, Rakovsky and Smilga. Immediately after the congress 1,500 Oppositionists were expelled and 2,500 signed statements of recantation—these were practically all Zinovievites.[43]

The zigzags of fighting Stalin, then stopping the fight in order to avoid a fresh outbreak of inner-party struggle, could not but weaken and disorientate Trotsky's own supporters. One cannot hold cadres if they have to abstain from action. Trotsky himself could keep his own spirit alive however hard the going: throughout the years 1923-27 he did not stop criticising official policies and the regime, even if he had to use hints and allusions, quite unintelligible to many. Rank and file oppositionists cannot survive politically without a fight in the here and now.

Months later, on 23 May 1928, Trotsky admitted that far too many concessions had been made toward Zinoviev and Company,

> yielding to weakness of character, indecisiveness, left-centrism, and demands for protective coloration... On the eve and during the Fifteenth Congress the urge for protective coloration totally overran us, on our right flank. This found expression in a number of declarations which were meaningless or actually wrong. We corrected this distortion with difficulty and with damage to the party.[44]

The bloc with Zinoviev led to the distancing of some of Trotsky's supporters from him.

In December 1928 Trotsky explained: 'For the sake of the bloc [with the Zinovievites] we made isolated, partial concessions. Most often these were concessions to some of our closest co-thinkers who gravitated towards the Zinovievists.'[45]

But still Trotsky was convinced that a bloc with Zinoviev was useful. He wrote: '...the bloc was necessary and a step forward.'[46]

First of all, 'in coming to us [Zinoviev] dealt an irreparable blow to the legend of Trotskyism.'[47] Also, 'hundreds of Petrograd workers did not follow [Zinoviev when he capitulated to Stalin], but remained with us.'[48]

Unfortunately the first gain, the 'blow to the legend of Trotskyism' that Zinoviev delivered when he formed the bloc was largely undone when he capitulated to Stalin and then vehemently denounced Trotskyism. The second, the gain of 'hundreds of

Petrograd workers' needs to be taken with reservation. First, many of Trotsky's own supporters were damaged by the concessions made for Zinoviev in order to preserve the bloc. After all, workers appreciate more than anything boldness, firmness, intransigence of leadership. Very few of the Zinovievites survived the Stalinist persecution to fight on in the years following the collapse of the bloc.

The experience of the period 1923-27, when Trotsky made many compromises and concessions (to members of his own faction—above all Radek and Piatakov), to Zinoviev and Kamenev, and finally to Stalin and Bukharin, led to the comments that Ioffe made in his letter to Trotsky before he committed suicide.

After 1927, when Trotsky grasped the enormity of Stalin's crimes, and called him 'the gravedigger of the revolution', when the bloc with Zinoviev and Kamenev fell apart—from then onwards Trotsky became completely uncompromising.

Trotsky banished to Alma-Ata

The Politburo decided to deport Trotsky from Moscow. To avoid the scandal of forced deportation, Stalin wanted Trotsky to leave 'of his own free will' for Astrakhan, on the Caspian Sea. Trotsky refused. On 12 January 1928 the GPU informed him that under Article 58 of the Criminal Code, ie, under the charge of counter-revolutionary activity, he would be deported to Alma-Ata, the capital of Kazakhstan, near the Chinese frontier. Natalia Sedova writes:

> Leon Davidovich's forced departure for Alma-Ata was originally fixed for January 16, 1928. But on that day thousands of citizens invaded the railway station and a large crowd of factory workers blocked the line while other workers searched the entire train for Trotsky. The militia was afraid to intervene. A telephone call postponed our departure for two days.
>
> Early next morning the GPU turned up. Our departure had been brought forward by 24 hours and now there were no longer any pretences... We refused to leave. Trotsky had no intention of giving even the slightest impression that he was acquiescing or passively submitting to so odious and arbitrary

a measure. Together with our son Lyova, Ioffe's widow and the wife of Beloborodov (who had recently been ousted from his post of People's Commissar for the Interior and was also about to be deported), we locked ourselves in a room. One of the officers, a man called Kishkin, who had more than once accompanied Leon Davidovich to the front, set about breaking down the door. At the same time, he shouted, 'Shoot me, Comrade Trotsky!' He was ashamed of what he was doing, but felt compelled to obey orders. A bullet would have put him out of his misery. His shouts later cost him his life. What better evidence could there have been of his subconscious Trotskyism. When the door was eventually forced, Trotsky refused to leave and soldiers had to carry him out.

Alma-Ata is four thousand kilometres from Moscow and 250 kilometres from a railway.

Three of Trotsky's secretaries had decided to join him in exile: in theory there was nothing to stop them settling in Alma-Ata and working for a deportee. One of them, Sermuks, had the audacity to demand a room in our hotel. I used to catch sight of his tall figure, his fine fair head and his friendly face in the corridor. We managed to speak to him only once... He was arrested and spent the rest of his life in jail or exile. Poznansky suffered the same fate. Georgy Butov, the third of Leon Davidovich's secretaries fared even worse.[49]

Butov was arrested, pressed to give false evidence, and went on a hunger strike for fifty days that ended in his death in a prison hospital.[50] Two days after Trotsky was banished from Moscow,

an official *communique* announced that thirty active members of the opposition, including Trotsky, Radek, Smilga and I. Smirnov, had been expelled from Moscow. Rakovsky was sent to Astrakhan; Radek to Tomsk and then to Tobolsk; most of the other leading Trotskyists were scattered over Siberia. The equivocations of Zinoviev and Kamenev won for them the mild sentence of banishment to Kaluga, a provincial capital some 800 miles south-west of Moscow; and even this sentence does not seem to have been strictly enforced.[51]

In Conclusion

In answering the question: why in the battles between them did Trotsky lose and Stalin win, many writers look to the psychological traits of the contenders, Stalin being more cunning and a better organiser than Trotsky. This explanation is curious. Trotsky, the organiser of the October revolution and of the Red Army inferior to Stalin?! Such an explanation, even if it describes Stalin's nasty character, gives him far too much honour as the demiurge of history.

It was the objective conditions that determined how successful the Opposition could be. As Trotsky wrote in 1940 in his book **Stalin**:

> The Left Opposition could not achieve power and did not hope even to do so—certainly not its most thoughtful leaders. A struggle for power by the Left Opposition, by a revolutionary Marxist organisation, was conceivable only under the conditions of a revolutionary upsurge. Under such conditions the strategy is based on aggression, on direct appeal to the masses, on frontal attack against the government. Quite a few members of the Left Opposition had played no minor part in such a struggle and had first-hand knowledge of how to wage it. But during the early twenties and later, there was no revolutionary upsurge in Russia, quite the contrary. Under such circumstances it was out of the question to launch a struggle for power.[52]

Understanding the limits that objective conditions imposed on the Opposition could have led it to simple passivity. But Trotsky had throughout his political life been an enemy of mechanical materialism, of fatalism. To Trotsky, as to Marx, 'men make their own history, though not in circumstances of their own choosing.' Therefore, in the period of reaction the revolutionary should take into account the low level of activity and consciousness of the masses without simply reflecting it.

> ...the conditions of Soviet reaction were immeasurably more difficult for the Opposition than the conditions of the Tsarist reaction had been for the Bolsheviks. But, basically, the task remained the same—the preservation of revolutionary traditions, the maintenance of contact among the advanced

elements within the Party, the analysis of the developing events of the Thermidor, the preparation for the future revolutionary upsurge on the world arena as well as in the USSR. One danger was that the Opposition might under-estimate its forces and prematurely abandon the prosecution of this task after a few tentative sallies in which the advance guard necessarily crashed not only against the resistance of the bureaucracy but against the indifference of the masses as well. The other danger was that, having become convinced of the impossibility of open association with the masses, even with their vanguard, the Opposition would give up the struggle and lie low until better times.[53]

If there was a serious weakness in the Opposition stand, it was its acceptance of the one-party system and the ban on factions in the party—a ban imposed under the extraordinary circum-stances of economic and social collapse of exhausted Russia at the end of the civil war. This largely explains the continuous zigzags of the Opposition: in fighting the Stalinist ruling group, then retreating, giving up practical activity; again, spurred on by events at home and abroad, starting the fight again, then stopping in the middle of the struggle.

One should have a sense of proportion about the strengths and weaknesses of Trotsky's stand in the years 1923-27. While his *strategic* direction was correct, he made a number of serious *tactical* blunders and compromises. The point is not that had he been firmer he would have been able to beat Stalin, but that he would have laid firmer bases for the growth of the Opposition, not allowing the 1923 Opposition to wither on the vine, not disorienting his followers in the foreign Communist Parties (this being especially important in view of what was to come), and so on.

One should be clear about the relation between Trotsky's errors and their consequences. The disproportion between the two was a result of the reactionary character of the historical stage. Not a few mistakes were committed by the Bolshevik leaders during 1917 and the period of the civil war. But the sweep of the revolution repaired the errors. Now the march of reaction exacerbated the impact of every error committed by Trotsky.

Russia's economic backwardness, the weakness of the

proletariat, the rise of the kulak, NEPman and bureaucrat, and above all the defeat of the international revolution, underlined the massive cleft between Trotsky's great aims and the puny means at his disposal. This chasm between means and ends could have led Trotsky either to strive for the final goal while overlooking the lack of means—an ultra-left stand—or to the opposite: to capitulate to the prevailing circumstances, and give up the final aim. Trotsky chose a third option: to fight for the final aim while flexibly veering in the face of the massive pressure of reactionary forces. In this principled but flexible stand of Trotsky lies the heroism and tragedy of his life at that time.

Notes

INTRODUCTION

1. N.N. Sukhanov, **The Russian Revolution 1917. A Personal Record**, London 1955, p. 230
2. K. Marx, **The Class Struggle in France**, in K. Marx and F. Engels, **Collected Works**, Vol.10, p. 99
3. See T. Cliff, **Trotsky** Vol.2, London 1990, p. 277
4. L. Trotsky, **Permanent Revolution and Results and Prospects**, London 1971, p. 49
5. Trotsky, **The Challenge of the Left Opposition (1928-29)**, hereafter referred to as **Challenge (1928-29)**, New York 1981, p. 147
6. Trotsky, **Writings (1930-31)**, New York 1973, p. 225
7. Trotsky, **Writings (1933-34)**, New York 1972, pp. 117-8
8. Trotsky, **Writings (1929)**, New York 1975, p. 60
9. Trotsky, **The Challenge of the Left Opposition (1923-25)**, hereafter referred to as **Challenge (1923-25)**, New York 1980, p. 78
10. Trotsky, **The Challenge of the Left Opposition (1926-27)**, hereafter referred to as **Challenge (1926-27)**, New York 1980, p. 394
11. Trotsky, **The Revolution Betrayed**, London 1987, p. 98
12. Trotsky, **My Life**, New York 1960, p. 537

Chapter 1: THE NEW COURSE CONTROVERSY

1. Trotsky, **My Life**, p. 482
2. See Cliff, **Trotsky** Vol. 2, pp. 263-9
3. **Dvenadtsatii sezd RKP(b)**, Moscow 1923, p. 320
4. M. Dobb, **Soviet Economic Development since 1917**, London 1948, p. 42

5. Ibid, pp. 46-7
6. Ibid., p. 93
7. E. H. Carr, **The Interregnum, 1923-1924**, hereafter referred to as **The Interregnum**, London 1954, p.75
8. Ibid., pp 77-8
9. Ibid., p. 123
10. Ibid., p. 85
11. W. Duranty, **I write as I please**, New York 1925, p. 138
12. J.B. Hatch, **Labor and Politics in NEP Russia: Workers, Trade Unions, and the Communist Party in Moscow, 1921-26**, Ph.D Thesis, University of California, Irvine 1985, p. 195
13. Ibid., p. 109-110
14. V. Sorinn, **Rabochaia Gruppa**, Moscow 1924, pp. 97-112
15. Hatch, pp 220-1
16. Trotsky, **Challenge (1923-25)**, pp. 55-6
17. Ibid., p. 58
18. Carr, **The Interregnum**, pp. 368-70
19. Trotsky, **My Life**, pp. 498-9
20. Trotsky, **Stalin**, London 1947 p. 381
21. **Trinadtsataia Konferentsiia RKP(b)**, Moscow 1924, pp. 106-7
22. **KPSS v rezoliutsiiakh i resheniiakh sezdov, konferentsii i plenumov TsK**, hereafter refered to as **KPSS v rez.**, Moscow 1953, Vol. 1, pp. 767-8
23. Trotsky, **Challenge (1923-25)**, p. 408
24. Trotsky, 'The New Course', **Challenge (1923-25)**, p. 67
25. **Trinadtsatii sezd RKP(b)**, Moscow 1924, p. 154
26. Trotsky, **Challenge (1923-25)**, pp. 123-4
27. Ibid., pp. 125-6
28. Ibid., pp. 91-2
29. Ibid., p. 92
30. Ibid.
31. Ibid., p. 75
32. Ibid., pp. 119-20
33. Ibid., p. 140
34. Ibid., p. 72
35. Ibid., p. 69
36. Ibid., pp. 78-9
37. Ibid., pp. 80-1, 86
38. **Izvestiia TsK RKP(b)**, June 1923
39. Cliff, **Trotsky**, Vol. 2, p. 260
40. **Desiatii sezd RKP(b)**, Moscow 1921, pp. 350-1
41. See Cliff, **Trotsky**, Vol. 2, p. 277
42. **Pravda**, 19 Jan. 1924, quoted in Carr, **The Interregnum**, p. 125
43. L. Trotsky, **Nashi Politicheskye Zadachi**, Geneva, 1904, p. 105, quoted in Cliff, **Trotsky**, Vol. 1, London 1989, p. 63

Chapter 2: THE CAMPAIGN AGAINST TROTSKY

1. J. V. Stalin, **Works**, Moscow 1949, Vol. 5, pp. 394-5
2. Carr, **The Interregnum**, pp. 319, 322-3
3. M. Eastman, **Since Lenin Died**, London 1925, p. 53
4. I. Deutscher, **The Prophet Unarmed**, London 1959, p.126
5. Quoted by Trotsky at Thirteenth Party Congress, May 1924,
   Challenge (1923-25), p. 149
6. **Trinadtsaia konferentsiia RKP(b)**, p. 218
7. Ibid., p. 108
8. Ibid., p. 126
9. Hatch, pp. 406-412
10. **Trinadtsaia konferentsiia RKP(b)**, Moscow 1963, pp. 131-3
11. **Pravda**, 18 December 1923
12. T. E. Nisonger, **The Leningrad Opposition of 1925-26 in the
    Communist Party of the Soviet Union**, PhD Thesis, Columbia
    University, 1976, p. 111
13. **Trinadtsaia konferentsiia RKP(b)**, pp. 124, 133
14. G. Zinoviev, **Chetirenadtsatii sezd VKP(b)**, Moscow 1926, p. 459
15. Eastman, p. 82
16. Trotsky, **Stalin**, p. 387
17. Stalin, **Works**, Vol. 6, pp. 24-5
18. **KPSS v rez.**, Vol.1, p. 784-5
19. Trotsky, **My Life**, p. 508
20. Ibid., p. 511
21. Stalin, **Works**, Vol. 6, pp. 47-53
22. Trotsky, **My Life**, p. 514
23. **Pravda**, 30 January 1924, quoted in Carr, **The Interregnum**, p. 349
24. Trotsky, **My Life**, p. 514
25. Ibid., p. 515
26. **Leon Trotsky Speaks**, New York 1972, p. 196
27. Trotsky, **The Revolution Betrayed**, pp. 97-8
28. The fullest report of this meeting is in B. Bazhanov, **Stalin**, Paris
    1931, pp. 32-4; quoted in Carr, **The Interregnum**, pp. 360-1
29. Stalin, **Works**, Vol. 10, p. 181
30. **Trinadtsatii sezd RKP(b)**, p. 115
31. Trotsky **Challenge (1923-25)**, p. 158
32. Ibid., p. 160
33. Stalin, **Works**, Vol. 6, p. 267
34. Ibid., pp. 153-4
35. Ibid., p. 161
36. Ibid., p. 162
37. Stalin, **Works**. Vol. 6, pp. 238-9
38. **Trinadtsatii sezd RKP(b)**, p. 261

39. **KPSS v rez.**, Vol. 1, pp. 819-21
40. Trotsky, **My Life**, pp. 499-500
41. **Biulleten Oppozitsii**, No. 75-76, March-April 1939, p. 32

Chapter 3: THE GERMAN REVOLUTION OF 1923

1. R. Fischer, **Stalin and German Communism**, London 1948, p. 312
2. W. D. Angress, **Stillborn Revolution: the Communist Bid for Power in Germany, 1921-23**, Princeton 1963, pp. 396-7
3. Ibid., pp. 285, 350
4. E. Anderson, **Hammer or Anvil**, London 1945, p. 91
5. P. Broué, **Révolution en Allegmagne 1917-1923**, Paris 1971, p. 679
6. Ibid., pp. 698-700
7. A. Rosenberg, **A History of the German Republic**, London 1936, p. 194
8. Fischer, pp. 291-2
9. Broué, p. 710
10. Anderson, pp. 92-3
11. Angress, p. 302
12. Broué, p. 554
13. Ibid., p. 706
14. Carr, **The Interregnum**, p. 187
15. Trotsky, **Stalin**, pp. 368-9
16. I. Deutscher, 'Record of a Discussion with Heinrich Brandler', **New Left Review**, September-October 1977, p. 76
17. Trotsky, **The First Five Years of the Communist International**, New York 1953, Vol. 2, pp. 347, 349-50
18. Deutscher, Op cit, pp. 51-2, 76
19. Trotsky, **How the Revolution Armed**, London 1981, Vol 5, pp. 202-3
20. Lenin, **Works**, Vol. 25, pp. 285-6
21. Carr, **The Interregnum**, p. 221
22. C. Harman, **The Lost Revolution, Germany 1918 to 1923**, London 1982, p. 289
23. Trotsky, **Challenge (1923-25)**, p. 95
24. Trotsky, **The Third International After Lenin**, New York 1936, p. 95
25. Trotsky, **Challenge (1928-29)**, p. 259

Chapter 4: THE LESSONS OF OCTOBER

1. **Protokoll: Fünfter Kongresses der Kommunistischen Internationale** (n.d.), Vol. 2, pp. 583, 619
2. Trotsky, **Challenge (1923-25)**, p. 200
3. Ibid., p. 212
4. Ibid., pp. 213-4
5. Ibid., p. 211
6. Ibid., p. 216
7. Ibid., p. 235
8. Ibid., p. 220
9. Ibid., pp. 251-2
10. L.B. Kamenev, 'The Party and Trotskyism' in **Za Leninizm**, Moscow 1925, p. 70
11. Zinoviev, 'Bolshevism or Trotskyism', ibid., p. 132
12. Ibid., pp. 126-9
13. Ibid., p. 151
14. Stalin, **Works**, Vol. 6, p. 341
15. Ibid., p. 342
16. Ibid., pp. 342-3
17. Ibid., p. 344
18. Ibid., pp. 350-1
19. Ibid., pp. 365-6
20. Ibid., p. 373
21. N.I. Bukharin, 'The Theory of Permanent Revolution', **Za Leninizm** pp. 367, 372
22. N. Krupskaya, 'To the Question of the Lessons of October', ibid., pp. 152-6
23. **Moskovskie bolsheviki v borbe s pravym i 'levym' opportunizmom 1921-29**, Moscow 1969, pp. 108-9
24. Ibid., pp. 100-1, 106
25. **Partiia v borbe za vosstanovlenie narodnogo khoziaistva 1921- 25** gg. Moscow 1961, pp. 536-7
26. Eastman, p. 123
27. Trotsky, **My Life**, p. 516
28. **Dvenadtsatii sezd RKP(b)**, p. 134
29. Trotsky, **Challenge (1923-25)**, pp. 267-8
30. Ibid., p. 300
31. Ibid., p. 301
32. Ibid., p. 261
33. **Pravda**, 13 December 1924, quoted in E.H. Carr, **Socialism in One Country**, Vol. 2, London 1964, p. 29
34. Trotsky, **The Stalin school of Falsification**, New York 1962, pp. 89-99
35. Trotsky, **My Life**, p. 517

36. Ibid., p. 491
37. Stalin, **Works**, Vol. 6, pp. 378-97
38. V. I. Lenin, **Sochineniia**, Vol. 27, p. 387
39. Ibid., Third edition, Vol. 25, pp. 473-4
40. See Lenin, **Sochineniia**, Vol. 31, p. 370
41. Stalin, **The Theory and Practice of Leninism**, Communist Party of Great Britain, 1925, pp. 455-6
42. Stalin, **Sochineniia**, Vol. 6, pp. 107-8
43. K. Marx and F. Engels, **Manifesto of the Communist Party**, in K. Marx and F. Engels, **Collected Works**, Vol. 6 p. 486
44. Trotsky, **The Permanent Revolution and Results and Prospects**, p. 156
45. See N. Bukharin, **Tekushchii Moment i Osnovy Nashei Politiki**, Moscow 1925
46. **KPSS v rez**. Vol. 2, p. 77
47. **Challenge (1926-27)**, p. 384
48. Trotsky, **The Revolution Betrayed**, p. 292
49. Trotsky, **Challenge (1928-29)**, p. 216
50. Trotsky, **Challenge (1923-25)**, p. 306
51. Ibid., pp. 304-5
52. Ibid., p. 305
53. Stalin, **Works**, Vol. 7, p. 390
54. N. Popov, **Outline History of the CPSU**, London n.d., Vol 2, p. 216; **KPSS v rez.**, Vol 1, pp. 913-21
55. V. Serge, **Memoirs of a Revolutionary**, London 1984, p. 209
56. Deutscher, **The Prophet Unarmed**, pp. 249-50
57. Trotsky, **Challenge (1923-25)**, p. 312
58. Ibid., p. 315
59. Trotsky, **Challenge (1928-29)**, p. 223
60. **Sunday Worker**, 2 August 1925

Chapter 5: TROTSKY ON CULTURE

1. Trotsky, **Problems of Everyday Life**, New York, 1973, p. 53
2. Quoted in C. Rosenberg, **Education and Society**, London, n.d.p., p. 23
3. Trotsky, **Problems of Everyday Life**, pp. 50-1
4. Ibid, p. 171
5. Ibid.
6. Ibid., p. 71
7. Ibid., p. 61
8. Ibid., p. 71
9. Ibid., p. 59, my emphasis
10. Ibid., p. 50
11. Ibid., p. 51

12. Ibid., p. 52
13. Ibid., p. 143
14. Ibid., pp. 146-7
15. Ibid., p. 149
16. Ibid., p. 153
17. Ibid., p. 154
18. Ibid., p. 157
19. Ibid., p. 131
20. Ibid., p. 53
21. Trotsky, **Women and the Family**, New York, 1970, pp. 45, 42
22. Trotsky, **Problems of Everyday Life**, p. 65
23. Trotsky, **Women and the Family**, pp. 43, 48, 45
24. Trotsky, **Problems of Everyday Life**, p. 79
25. Trotsky, **Women and the Family**, pp. 29-30
26. Ibid., p. 28
27. Trotsky, **Problems of Everyday Life**, p. 70
28. Ibid., p. 132
29. Ibid., p. 173
30. Trotsky, **Literature and Revolution**, Ann Arbor 1971, p. 60
31. Ibid., pp. 9-10
32. Ibid., p. 77
33. Ibid., p. 24
34. E.H. Carr, **Socialism in One Country**, Vol. 1, London 1958, p. 80
35. Cliff, **Trotsky**,Vol. 2, p. 234
36. C. Claudin-Urondo, **Lenin and the Cultural Revolution**, Hassocks 1977, p. 56n
37. Lenin, **Sochineniia**, xxiv, p. 305, Quoted in Carr, **Socialism in One Country**, Vol. 1, p. 50
38. Lenin, **Sochineniia**, xxv, pp. 409, 636, 637, quoted in Carr, **Socialism in One Country**, Vol. 1, p. 51
39. Trotsky, **Literature and Revolution**, p. 19
40. Lenin, **Sochineniia**, xxvii, p. 51; quoted in Carr, **Socialism in One Country**, Vol. 1, p. 50
41. Trotsky, **Literature and Revolution**, p. 14
42. Deutscher, **The Prophet Unarmed**, p. 198
43. Carr, **Socialism in One Country**, Vol.2, p. 87
44. **Leon Trotsky on Literature and Art**, New York 1970, p. 119
45. Ibid., p. 121
46. Trotsky, **Problems of Everyday Life**, p. 210
47. Ibid., p. 200
48. Ibid., p. 211
49. Ibid., p. 221
50. Ibid., p. 214
51. Ibid., p. 201
52. Deutscher, **The Prophet Unarmed**, p. 198
53. Trotsky, **Literature and Revolution**, p. 230

Chapter 6: SPLIT IN THE TROIKA

1. Carr, **Socialism in One Country**, Vol. 1, pp. 190-1
2. Ibid., pp. 192-4
3. Ibid., pp. 224-5
4. Ibid., p. 226
5. Ibid., p. 228
6. Ibid., p. 230
7. Ibid., pp. 231-2
8. Ibid., p. 253
9. Ibid., p. 254
10. Ibid., p. 257
11. Ibid., pp. 247-8
12. Ibid., pp. 254-5
13. **Bolshevik**, 30 April 1925, quoted in Carr, **Socialism in One Country**, Vol. 1, p. 260
14. Ibid., p. 262
15. Ibid., p. 268
16. Ibid., p. 270
17. Ibid., p. 285
18. Serge, p. 177
19. Trotsky, **Challenge (1928-29)**, pp. 62-3
20. Carr, **Socialism in One Country**, Vol. 1, pp. 286-7
21. G. Zinoviev, **Leninizm**, Leningrad 1925, p. 281
22. Ibid., p. 302
23. Ibid., pp. 302-7
24. Ibid., p. 318
25. Ibid., p. 377
26. Carr, **Socialism in One Country**, Vol. 1, p. 291-3
27. Ibid., p. 295
28. **Chetirnadtsatii sezd VKP(b)**, Moscow 1926, pp. 158-66
29. Ibid., pp. 274-5
30. Stalin, **Works**, Vol. 7, p. 402
31. Ibid., p. 390
32. Ibid., p. 398
33. **Chetirnadtsatii sezd VKP(b)** pp. 504-5
34. Ibid, p. 524
35. **KPSS v rez.** Vol. 2, pp. 90-2
36. Nisonger, p. 39
37. Serge, p. 211
38. Nisonger, p. 64
39. Ibid., pp. 66-7
40. Ibid., p. 95
41. Ibid., p. 131
42. Ibid., pp. 302, 310

43. Ibid., pp. 132-4
44. Ibid., p. 411
45. Ibid., pp. 412-3
46. **The Case of Leon Trotsky**, London, 1937, pp. 322-3
47. Trotsky, **Challenge (1923-25)**, p. 395
48. Deutscher, **The Prophet Unarmed**, p. 249
49. Trotsky, **Challenge (1923-25)**, pp. 385-6
50. Ibid., pp. 393-4
51. Ibid., p. 395
52. Trotsky, **My Life**, pp. 521-2
53. **Biulleten Oppozitsii**, Nos. 29-30, September 1930, p. 34
54. Quoted in Stalin, **Works**, Vol. 8, p. 247

Chapter 7: THE UNITED OPPOSITION

1. Trotsky, in **Biulletin Oppozitsii**, Nos. 54-55, March 1937, pp. 11-12
2. Serge, pp. 212-3
3. Trotsky, **My Life**, p. 521
4. Serge, p. 220
5. Trotsky, **The Stalin School of Falsification**, New York 1962, p. 91
6. Quoted in Stalin, **Works**, Vol. 8, pp. 248-9
7. Trotsky, **Challenge (1926-27)**, p. 74
8. Ibid., p. 84
9. Ibid., pp. 78-9
10. Ibid., p. 80
11. **KPSS v rez.** Vol. 2, pp. 160-66
12. E.H. Carr, **Foundations of a Planned Economy**, London 1971, Vol. 2, p. 14
13. Deutscher, **The Prophet Unarmed**, p. 281
14. **Writings of Leon Trotsky, (1939-40)**, New York 1973, p. 175
15. Stalin, **Works**, Vol. 8, pp. 221-3
16. Trotsky, **Challenge (1926-27)**, pp. 127-9
17. **Leon Trotsky on France**, New York 1979, pp. 230-1
18. A. Ciliga, **The Russian Enigma**, London 1979, p. 8
19. V. Serge and N. Sedova, **The Life and Death of Leon Trotsky**, London 1975, p. 149
20. Stalin, **Works**, Vol. 8, p. 300
21. Trotsky, **Challenge (1926-27)**, p. 134
22. Ibid., p. 144
23. Ibid., pp. 158-9
24. Ibid., p. 145
25. **Piatnadtsataia konferentsiia VKP(b)**, Moscow 1927, pp. 698-707
26. Deutscher, **The Prophet Unarmed**, pp. 304-5

27. J. Degras, ed., **The Communist International, 1919-1943. Documents**, London 1971, Vol. 2, pp. 330-5
28. Trotsky, **Challenge (1926-27)**, pp. 170-1
29. Trotsky, **My Life**, p. 529

Chapter 8: THE GENERAL STRIKE IN BRITAIN

1. **Workers Weekly**, 18 September 1925
2. R. Page Arnot, **The General Strike**, London 1926, p. 66
3. See T. Cliff and D. Gluckstein, **The Labour Party, a Marxist History**, London 1988, Chapter 5
4. **International Trade Union Unity**, London 1925, p. 18
5. **Trotsky's Writings on Britain**, Vol. 2, London 1974, pp. 4, 6, 9
6. Ibid., p. 140
7. Ibid., p. 142
8. Ibid., p. 36-7
9. Ibid., pp. 51-2
10. Ibid., p. 46
11. Ibid., p. 39
12. Ibid., p. 92
13. Ibid., pp. 85-7
14. Ibid., p. 105
15. Ibid., pp. 93-4
16. Ibid., p. 248
17. Ibid., p. 57.
18. Ibid., p. 128
19. Ibid., p. 153
20. Ibid., p. 248
21. Ibid., p. 245
22. Ibid., p. 141
23. Ibid., pp. 138-9
24. Trotsky, **Challenge (1926-27)**, p. 196
25. **Trotsky's Writings on Britain**, Vol. 2, p. 140
26. Ibid., p. 138
27. Page Arnot, p.34, quoted in T. Cliff and D. Gluckstein, **Marxism and the Trade Union Struggle. The General Strike of 1926**, London 1986, p. 129
28. Ibid., p.35, Cliff and Gluckstein, op cit., p. 129
29. Quoted in G.M. Young, **Stanley Baldwin**, London 1951, p. 99; Cliff and Gluckstein, op cit., p. 130
30. A. Bullock, **Ernest Bevin**, London 1960, Vol. 1, pp. 289-90 in Cliff and Gluckstein, op cit., p.170
31. **Sunday Worker**, 23 May 1926, Cliff and Gluckstein, op cit., pp. 246-7
32. **Sunday Worker**, 13 June 1926, Cliff and Gluckstein, op cit., pp. 258-9

33. Ibid.
34. **Trotsky's Writings on Britain**, Vol. 2, pp. 144-6
35. G. Hardy, **Those Stormy Years**, London 1956, p. 188
36. **Workers Weekly**, 21 May 1926
37. **Workers Weekly**, 13 May 1926
38. **Report, Theses and Resolutions of the Eighth Congress of the Communist Party of Great Britain.** Battersea, 16-17 October 1926, p. 12; Cliff and Gluckstein, **Marxism and the Trade Unions**, pp. 278-9
39. Degras, Vol. 2, p. 262
40. Stalin, **Works**, Vol. 8, pp. 193-4
41. **Trotsky's Writings on Britain**, Vol 2. p. 227
42. Degras, Vol. 2, p.314
43. **Trotsky's Writings on Britain**, Vol. 2, pp. 118-9
44. Cliff and Gluckstein, **Marxism and the Trade Unions**, p. 155

Chapter 9: THE CHINESE REVOLUTION

1. Serge, p. 216
2. C. Brandt, B. Schwartz and J.K. Fairbank, **A Documentary History of Chinese Communism**, London, 1952, p. 52
3. **Protokoll des Vierten Kongresses der Kommunistischen Internationale**, Hamburg 1923, p. 632
4. Degras, Vol. 2, pp. 5-6
5. Brandt et al, p. 70
6. C. Brandt, **Stalin's Failure in China, 1924-1927**, Cambridge Mass., 1958, pp. 32-33
7. Brandt et al, p. 75
8. Ibid., p. 71
9. Ibid., pp. 68-9
10. **International Press Correspondence**, 7 January 1926, H. R. Isaacs, **The Tragedy of the Chinese Revolution**, London 1938, p. 94
11. Ibid., p. 138
12. **Piatnadtsaiia konferentsiia VKP(b)**, pp. 27-9
13. Stalin, **Works**, Vol. 8, pp. 387-9, 385, 390
14. **Leon Trotsky on China**, New York 1976, pp. 160-1
15. Trotsky, **The Third International After Lenin**, p. 178
16. **Leon Trotsky on China**, pp. 207-8
17. Trotsky, **The Third International After Lenin**, pp. 172-174
18. **Leon Trotsky on China**, p. 403
19. Lenin, **Works**, Vol. 13, p. 111
20. Lenin, **Works**, Vol. 8, p. 27

21. Lenin, **Works**, Vol. 9, p. 314, Cliff, **Lenin**, Vol. 1, London 1986 pp. 205-6
22. Lenin, **Works**, Vol 27, pp. 305-6
23. C.M. Wilbur and J. L. How, eds., **Documents on Communism, Nationalism, and Soviet Advisers in China, 1918-1927**, New York 1956, p. 251
24. Ibid., pp. 252-3
25. Ibid., pp. 259-60
26. Ibid., p. 264
27. Ibid.
28. Isaacs, pp. 107-8
29. Ibid., pp. 119-20
30. Wilbur and How, pp. 297-8
31. Isaacs, pp. 110-11
32. Ibid., p. 117
33. Ibid., p. 118
34. Ibid., p. 126
35. Ibid., p. 128
36. Trotsky, **The Stalin School of Falsification**, p. 173
37. Degras, Vol. 2, p. 337
38. Ibid., pp. 345-6
39. Isaacs, p. 148
40. Ibid., pp. 151, 157
41. Ibid., p. 157
42. Trotsky, **Problems of the Chinese Revolution**, Ann Arbor 1967, p. 357
43. Isaacs, p. 191
44. **Leon Trotsky on China**, pp. 225-6
45. Ibid., p. 134
46. **Biulleten Oppozitsii**, July 1932, pp. 21-22
47. Isaacs, p. 202
48. Ibid., pp. 203, 208
49. Ibid., p. 215
50. 'The Questions of the Chinese Revoltuion: Theses of Comrade Stalin for Propagandists, Approved by the CC of the CPSU', **International Press Correspondence**, 28 April 1927, emphasis added. **Leon Trotsky on China**, pp. 64-5
51. Degras, Vol. 2, pp. 384-7
52. Ibid., p. 388
53. Ibid., p. 389
54. **Leon Trotsky on China**, pp. 223, 234-5
55. Isaacs, p. 279
56. Ibid.
57. Degras, Vol. 2, p. 391
58. **Pravda**, 25 July 1927
59. **Leon Trotsky on China**, pp. 410-11

60. Isaacs, p. 360
61. Ibid., p. 366
62. Ibid., pp. 370-1
63. **Leon Trotsky on China**, p. 460
64. Ibid., p. 221
65. **Protokoll des Vierten Kongresses der Kommunistische Internationale**, p. 632
66. **T. 933, Arkhiv Trotskogo**, Moscow 1990, Vol. 2, pp. 192-3
67. Trotsky, **Challenge (1923-25)**, p. 305
68. Trotsky, **Challenge (1926-27)**, p. 45
69. Ibid., p. 176
70. Ibid., p. 193
71. **Leon Trotsky Speaks**, p. 201
72. **Leon Trotsky on China**, pp. 265, 269
73. Ibid., p. 348
74. Ibid., pp. 490-1
75. Ibid., p. 107
76. Ibid., pp. 182-3
77. Ibid., pp. 183-4
78. Ibid., pp. 199, 202-3
79. Ibid., pp. 228, 232
80. Ibid., pp. 122, 124
81. G. Zinoviev, 'Theses on the Chinese Revolution', in Trotsky, **Problems of the Chinese Revolution**, p. 307ff
82. **T934, Arkhiv Trotskogo**, Vol. 2, p. 194
83. See Peng Shu-tse, 'Introduction' to **Leon Trotsky on China**
84. **Leon Trotsky on China**, pp. 249-50
85. Ibid., pp. 262-3
86. Ibid., pp. 490-1
87. Ibid., p. 493
88. Trotsky, **My Life**, p. 530

Chapter 10: THE PENULTIMATE EPISODE OF THE UNITED OPPOSITION

1. Trotsky, **Challenge (1926-27)**, p. 298
2. **T. 944, Arkhiv Trotskogo**, Vol. 2, p. 248
3. **T. 3059, Arkhiv Trotskogo**, Vol. 3, p. 43
4. **T. 958. Arkhiv Trotskogo**, Vol. 3, p.127
5. Trotsky, **Challenge (1926-27)**, pp. 226-239
6. **Leon Trotsky on China**, pp. 221-2
7. Ibid., pp. 225-6, 228
8. Trotsky, **My Life**, p. 530

9. Stalin, **Sochineniia**, Vol. 9, pp. 311-12
10. **Pravda**, 3 August 1927
11. **T. 966, 3075, Arkhiv Trotskogo**, Vol. 3, p. 212
12. Trotsky, **The Stalin School of Falsification**, pp. 126-48
13. E.H. Carr, **Foundations of a Planned Economy**, Vol. 1, p. 740
14. M. Reiman, **The Birth of Stalinism**, London 1987, p. 38
15. Trotsky, **Challenge (1926-27)**, pp. 245-6, 248
16. **T. 965. Arkhiv Trotskogo**, Vol. 3, p. 219
17. Trotsky, **Challenge (1926-27)**, p. 253
18. 'The War Danger-The Defence Policy and the Opposition', in Trotsky, **The Stalin School of Falsification**, pp. 162-77
19. Stalin, **Works**, Vol. 10, pp. 90-96
20. **KPSS v rez**. Vol. 2, pp. 267-74
21. See Zinoviev, 'Draft Speech', **T. 995. Arkiv Trotskogo**, Vol. 4, pp. 71-3
22. **T. 997. Arkhiv Trotskogo**, Vol. 4, pp. 80-1
23. Serge, p. 222
24. Trotsky, 'An Appeal to Party Members', **New International**, November 1934
25. Cliff, **Trotsky**, Vol. 2, pp. 239-44
26. See ibid., pp. 269-72
27. Trotsky, **Challenge (1926-27)**, pp. 326, 329
28. Ibid., pp. 327-9
29. Ibid., pp. 331-2
30. Ibid., p. 337
31. **KPSS v rez.** Vol. 2, p. 620
32. Trotsky, **Challenge (1926-27)**, p. 331
33. Ibid., p. 330
34. V.M. Smirnov, 'Under Lenin's Flag', **T. 963, 964, Arkhiv Trotskogo**, Vol. 3, p. 150
35. Trotsky, **Challenge (1926-27)**, pp. 311-3
36. Ibid., pp 313-5
37. Ibid., p. 316
38. Ibid., p. 317
39. Ibid., pp. 318-20
40. Ibid., p. 344
41. Ibid., pp. 351, 358
42. Ibid., pp. 351-2, 354
43. Ibid., p. 392
44. Trotsky, **The Third International After Lenin**, p. 128
45. **Direktivi KPSS i Sovetskogo Pravitelstva po khoziaistvennym Voprosem**, Moscow 1957, Vol. 1, pp. 590-96
46. E. A. Preobrazhensky, **The New Economics**, London 1965, p. 88
47. Ibid., p. 89
48. Ibid., p. 240
49. Ibid., pp. 250-1

50. Ibid., pp. 122-3
51. Ibid., p. 137
52. **T. 2984, Arkhiv Trotskogo**, Vol. 1, p. 225
53. Marx, **Selected Writings**, ed. D. McLellan, Oxford 1978, pp. 170-1
54. Quoted by A. Nove in his 'Introduction' to Preobrazhensky, **The New Economics**, p. xv

Chapter 11: THE UNITED OPPOSITION IS SMASHED

1. Serge, p. 223
2. Trotsky, **Challenge (1926-27)**, p. 416
3. **The New International**, November 1934, p. 124
4. Stalin, **Works**, Vol. 10, p. 179-80
5. Reiman, p. 32
6. Stalin, **Works**, Vol. 10, p. 196
7. **KPSS v rez.**, Vol. 2, p. 311
8. Trotsky, **My Life**, pp. 531-2
9. Ibid., pp. 532-3
10. Serge, p. 219
11. Trotsky, **My Life**, pp. 533
12. Ibid., p. 534
13. Serge, pp. 226-7
14. Trotsky, **My Life**, p. 534
15. **Izvestiia Tsentralnogo Komiteta**, 15 November 1927
16. Trotsky, **My Life**, p. 537
17. Ibid.
18. Reiman, pp. 19-20
19. Ibid., p. 22
20. Ibid., p. 24
21. Ibid., p. 27-8
22. Serge and Sedova, p. 137
23. Stalin, **Works**, Vol. 11, pp. 288-9
24. Stalin, **Works**, Vol. 10, pp. 344-5
25. **T.3100, 3161, Arkhiv Trotskogo**, Vol. 4, p. 223
26. **T.1010, Arkhiv Trotskogo**, Vol 4, p. 99
27. Trotsky, **Challenge (1926-27)**, p. 45
28. M. Fainsod, **Smolensk under Soviet Rule**, Cambridge 1958, p. 48
29. **T.1006, Arkhiv Trotskogo**, Vol. 4, p. 188
30. Trotsky, **Stalin**, pp. 399-400
31. Trotsky, **The Stalin School of Falsification**, p. xi
32. **Pravda**, 12 August 1927; Carr, **The Foundations of Planned Economy**, Vol. 2, p. 35
33. **Pravda** and **Izvestiia**, 27 October 1927; Carr, **The Foundations of Planned Economy**, Vol. 2, p. 42

34. Serge, p. 232
35. **T.3105. Arkhiv Trotskogo**, Vol. 4, pp. 267-8
36. Stalin, **Works**, Vol. 10, pp. 273-4
37. Trotsky, **Challenge (1925-26)**, pp. 481-3
38. Stalin, **Works**, Vol. 10, p. 378
39. **Piatnadtsatii sezd VKP(b)**, pp. 251-2
40. **T.1061. Arkhiv Trotskogo**, Vol. 4, pp. 275-6
41. **KPSS v rez.**, Vol. 2, p. 371
42. Trotsky, **Challenge (1926-27)**, p. 505
43. Popov, Vol. 2, p.327
44. Trotsky, **Challenge (1928-29)**, p. 94
45. Ibid., p. 340
46. Ibid., p. 298
47. Ibid., p. 153
48. Ibid., p. 114
49. Serge and Sedova, pp. 156-8
50. Ibid.
51. Carr, **Foundations of a Planned Economy**, Vol. 2, p. 56-7
52. Trotsky, **Stalin**, p. 405
53. Ibid., p. 404

Index

Other publications from Bookmarks

Previous volumes in this series.

1: Towards October
1879-1917

This volume shows how Trotsky learned from the revolution of 1905 and developed the theory of permanent revolution, giving him the grasp of the revolutionary process that he needed to organise the insurrection of October 1917. 320 pages.

2: Sword of the Revolution
1917-1923

Soviet power has been won, now the revolution must be defended and spread. How Trotsky built the Red Army and, with Lenin, the Communist International. 320 pages.

£6.95 / $11.95 each

The Lessons of October / *Leon Trotsky*

A key document in which Trotsky analyses the causes of the defeat of the German revolution and throws light on the growing Stalinist bureaucracy in Russia. 84 pages. £1.95 / $3.95

Literature and Revolution / *Leon Trotsky.*

The classic work on the relationship between art, culture and society. With a new introduction by Lindsey German. Published by Redwords, distributed by Bookmarks. 284 pages. £7.95

Marxism and the Trade Union struggle. The General Strike of 1926 / *Tony Cliff and Donny Gluckstein*

The Nine Days of May provided one of the greatest ever opportunities for the British working class movement. This book looks at how and why the opportunity was squandered. 320 pages. £6.95 / $11.95

State Capitalism in Russia / *Tony Cliff*

The classic analysis of Russia under Stalin, when a new state capitalist ruling class rose to power on the ashes of the revolution, now republished with a postscript covering the years between Stalin and Gorbachev. 377 pages. £5.95 / $9.00

Lenin: Building the Party 1893-1914 / *Tony Cliff*

The first volume of Tony Cliff's political biography of Lenin, showing his battle to turn Marxist ideas into practical daily action through the medium of the Bolshevik Party. 398 pages. £7.95 / $12.50

Lenin: All power to the Soviets 1914-1917 / *Tony Cliff*

This second volume shows the crucial interaction between the working class, the party and Lenin, which led to the climax of insurrection in October 1917. 424 pages. £7.95 / $12.50

Lenin: Revolution Besieged 1917-1923 / *Tony Cliff*

This final volume covers Lenin's struggle after 1917 to defend fragile workers' power against attack from without and bureaucracy from within. 496 pages. £8.95 / $16.50

Rosa Luxemburg / *Tony Cliff*

A political biography of the most original contributor to Marxism after Marx himself, who was murdered during the German revolution of 1919. 96 pages. £2.50 / $4.75

Russia: From workers' state to state capitalism
/ *Peter Binns, Tony Cliff and Chris Harman*

In 1917 the hopes of millions were placed on the revolution in Russia—but what went wrong? This book offers some hard answers to tough questions. 112 pages. £2.50 / $4.75

The Lost Revolution: Germany 1918-1923 / *Chris Harman*

Revolutions that are defeated are soon forgotten—yet the defeat of the great working class upheavals that shook Germany after the First World War was a key link in the rise to power of both Hitler and Stalin. 336 pages. £5.95 / $11.00

The Comintern / *Duncan Hallas*

The Communist International, born of 1917, aimed to spread workers' power throughout the world. This book traces it from the vital contributions of the early years to its degeneration into a tool of Stalin's foreign policy. 184 pages. £4.95 / $7.95

Lenin's Moscow / *Alfred Rosmer*

An account of the 'centre of world revolution', when Moscow was capital city of the first workers' revolution and headquarters of the Communist International—of which Rosmer was a leading member. 288 pages. £4.95 / $9.95

The Western Soviets / *Donny Gluckstein*

In 1915-20 the workers' councils of Italy, Germany, Britain and Russia proposed an alternative mass democracy to the parliamentary channels that had failed in 1914 and have failed the workers since. This book shows what they offered. 280 pages. £6.95 / $11.00

Women and perestroika / *Chanie Rosenberg*

This study of the lives of women in Russia—under the Tsar, the 1917 revolution, Stalin and Gorbachev—uses their changing conditions as a touchstone by which to judge the effects of perestroika on the lives of workers, women and men alike. 128 pages. £3.95 / $7.50

Festival of the Oppressed / *Colin Barker*

The trade union Solidarity was the largest working-class movement for half a century—and shook the Eastern bloc to its foundations. This book tells the story of its rise and analyses the causes of its setback in 1981. 272 pages. £4.95 / $8.50

Class struggles in Eastern Europe 1945-83 / *Chris Harman*

Gorbachev and his reformers want to change Russia from above—but will he unleash change from below? This book looks at Hungary 1956, Czechoslovakia 1968 and Poland 1980, and reveals some of the potential for upheavals to come. 382 pages. £7.95 / $13.50

The English People and the English Revolution / *Brian Manning*

The highly praised classic, back in print again, with a new introduction refuting the revisionist accounts which have proliferated since the book's original publication. £12.95

The Road to Tiananmen Square / *Charlie Hore*

Mass action in 1989 nearly tore down the Chinese regime. This book studies the nature and evolution of the modern Chinese state, and the pattern of struggles against it. 160 pages. £4.95 / $9.50

All available from good bookshops, or by post from Bookmarks (add 10 per cent to cover postage—minimum 35p or $1).

BOOKMARKS

265 Seven Sisters Road, London N4 2DE, England.
PO Box 16085, Chicago, IL 60616, USA.
GPO Box 1473N, Melbourne 3001, Australia.